DATE DUE

OCT 1 0 2018			
			PRINTED IN U.S.A.

The Montessori Method

The Montessori Method

The Origins of an
Educational Innovation:
Including an Abridged and
Annotated Edition of
Maria Montessori's
The Montessori Method

Maria Montessori, edited by Gerald Lee Gutek

ROWMAN & LITTLEFIELD PUBLISHERS, INC.
Lanham • Boulder • New York • Toronto • Oxford

ROWMAN & LITTLEFIELD PUBLISHERS, INC.

Published in the United States of America
by Rowman & Littlefield Publishers, Inc.
A wholly owned subsidary of The Rowman & Littlefield Publishing Group, Inc.
4501 Forbes Boulevard, Suite 200, Lanham, MD 20706
www.rowmanlittlefield.com

P.O. Box 317, Oxford OX2 9RU, UK

British Library Cataloguing in Publication Information Available

Library of Congress Cataloging-in-Publication Data

Montessori, Maria, 1870–1952.
 [Metodo della pedagogia scientifica. English]
 The Montessori method : the origins of an educational innovation,
including an abridged and annotated edition of Maria Montessori's The
Montessori method / Maria Montessori ; edited by Gerald Lee Gutek.
     p.   cm.
 Includes bibliographical references and index.
 ISBN 0-7425-1911-2 (cloth : alk. paper)—ISBN 0-7425-1912-0 (pbk. :
alk. paper)
 1. Montessori method of education. 2. Education,
Preschool—Philosophy. 3. Montessori, Maria, 1870–1952. 4. Women
educators—Italy—Biography. I. Gutek, Gerald Lee. II. Title.

 LB775.M76M6713 2004
 372.139'2—dc22

                                                              2004000420

Printed in the United States of America

♾TM   The paper used in this publication meets the minimum requirements of American
National Standard for Information Sciences—Permanence of Paper for Printed Library
Materials, ANSI/NISO Z39.48-1992.

For my grandchildren, Abigail Lee and Luke Kenneth Swiatek,
and their parents, Laura Lee and Andrew Swiatek.

Contents

Editor's Note

Maria Montessori and the Montessori Method: The Origins of an Educational Innovation creates the context in which Maria Montessori developed her philosophy of early childhood education. It examines how a determined young woman overcame the obstacles that blocked the educational and career opportunities in Italy during the late Victorian age. Following Montessori, who was the first woman to earn a medical degree from the University of Rome, the biographical introduction takes her story to the establishment of the first Montessori school, the *Casa dei Bambini* in the slums of Rome. It then analyzes the sources and influences that shaped the creation of the Montessori philosophy of education. Special attention is given to *The Montessori Method* as the book that introduced this educational innovation to an American audience.

This book is divided into several sections. It begins with a biography of Maria Montessori and an introductory commentary on the Montessori Method of Education. Part I contains an abridged and annotated edition of Maria Montessori's *Montessori Method* (1912). Part II contains related documents.

The biography of Montessori (1870–1952) discusses her family, education, career in medicine and education, establishment of the first Montessori school, *Casa dei Bambini* in Rome, the development of her philosophy and method of education, her lecture tour in the United States in 1913, and subsequent events in her life. In examining Montessori's development of her educational method, it treats the influence of her medical education, especially the importance given to clinical observation and the use of science. The influence of Itard and Seguin, two French physicians and educators, who developed methods for educating children with physical and mental handicaps is discussed. An important section of the biography deals with the first attempt to introduce the Montessori method of the United States in 1913, especially the efforts of the publicist and journalist, S. S. McClure and Anne E. George, the first American trained by Montessori. The essay follows Montessori from the time of the American lecture tour, to her work in Europe and Asia.

The commentary on the Montessori method analyzes how her medical education exercised an influence on her work in education. It then analyzes her concept of the child, children's sensitive developmental periods, the education of the senses, practical skills, and the child's explosion into reading and writing. The Montessori curriculum and didactic materials are discussed. The section concludes with Montessori's ideas on moral development and education.

Part I is an annotated and abridged edition of Maria Montessori's, *The Montessori Method.* This English language translation by Anne E. George is highly important in the Montessori literature because it served as the first major introduction to her method in the United States. When read as a background to her first lecture tour of the United States, it provides a clear and detailed discussion of the Montessori method. The book became a best-selling nonfiction work in the year of its publication. The editor provides a series of explanatory notes to persons and trends mentioned by Montessori.

Part II provides two related documents: (1) Anne E. George's notes that were used in the translation of Montessori's lectures into English during the 1913 speaking tour arranged by the American publisher S. S. McClure; (2) selected critical excerpts from William H. Kilpatrick's *The Montessori System Examined* (1914). George, trained as a directress by Montessori, was a leading proponent of the method in the United States. She established the first American Montessori school at Tarrytown, New York. Kilpatrick, a professor of education at Columbia University's Teachers College, was a disciple of John Dewey's Pragmatist philosophy. A leading progressive educator, Kilpatrick was highly critical of the Montessori method.

NOTE

Page number references (indicating deletion) in editor's notes refer to Montessori's original (1912).

Introduction: A Biography of Montessori and an Analysis of the Montessori Method

BIOGRAPHY

Today, Maria Montessori enjoys global acclaim as one of the world's great educators. Her life story is a remarkable one—one in which a dedicated woman used her scientific training, her experience, and her insights to develop a method of education that challenged conventional patterns of education. The conventions she challenged were not only educational ones: she had to surmount the obstacles that limited the freedom of women to enter into new careers.

Maria Montessori was born on August 31, 1870, in Chiaravalle, a hill town overlooking the Adriatic Sea, in Italy's Ancona province. She was the only child of Alessandro Montessori, a business manager in the state-run tobacco monopoly; and Renilde Stoppani, the well-educated daughter of a highly respected family.[1]

Maria Montessori was born only ten years after Italy's unification, under the House of Savoy. As a result of the "Risorgimento," led by Camillo Cavour, a liberal statesman, and Giuseppe Garibaldi, a fiery patriot, the small states and principalities on the Italian peninsula were finally united as one country in 1871. Giuseppe Garibaldi's red-shirted volunteer army, the Carbonari, had toppled the old bourbon kingdom of the "Two Sicilies," and the armies of Piedmont-Sardinia had brought Victor Emmanuel to Italy's throne as a constitutional monarch.

The new Italy was a product of the forces of nationalism and liberalism. Nationalists, such as Garibaldi, wanted Italy to take its place in the political sun. Liberals such as Cavour wanted to move Italy forward as a modern industrialized nation. Strong remnants of conservatism and traditionalism, however, resisted Italy's modernization. Serious opposition came from the pope, who, smarting from the annexation of the Papal States to Italy and regarding himself as the "prisoner of the Vatican," refused to recognize the new political reality. Maria Montessori's uncle, Antonio Stoppani, a noted naturalist and Roman Catholic priest, called for reconciliation between church and state. Maria's father, Alessandro, while remaining a committed Catholic, took a position in the new state's civil service.

Although Italy's emergence as a sovereign nation was recent, Italian culture reached back to the antiquity of ancient Rome. The new nation in which Montessori was born, in 1870, remained still very much the old, traditional, and conservative Italy. Although industrialization was slowly changing the class structure, social and gender roles were inherited across time and generations. *La famiglia*, the family, was the primary focus of most Italians' identification, loyalty, and commitment. A person's education and career remained largely determined by family background and social status. The children of peasants were destined to take their parents' place on Italy's farms and landed estates. Middle-class males were likely to oversee estates, manage businesses, or engage in commerce. Children of the landed aristocracy would continue to enjoy the benefits of inherited wealth that made them a leisure class.

If family and class determined the status and careers of Italian males, women's roles were even more fixed by custom and tradition. While membership in a particular class was a conditioning factor, women were expected to become the central sustaining force in their families as wives and mothers. With their roles so determined, higher and professional education were not usually accessible to women. Society allowed and economic necessity required women of the lower socioeconomic classes to work as agricultural, domestic, or factory laborers. Daughters of the lower-middle class might become elementary school teachers or nurses. Young women of the aristocracy might attend finishing schools or convent schools to learn art, music, and literature. Challenging Italy's nineteenth-century gender conventions, Maria Montessori would enter a technical secondary school to study engineering and, later, the University of Rome's medical school to become Italy's first degreed female physician.

Alessandro Montessori's position in the Italian civil service provided his family with economic security. The Montessori family was comfortably situated in the European bourgeoisie, the middle class. Signor Montessori, a decorated veteran of the war for Italian unification in 1848, retained his military bearing throughout his life. Despite the social and economic transformation that was taking place in the new Italy, he epitomized the attitudes and values of Victorian middle-class respectability. His strong-willed daughter was to challenge many of these traditional expectations about the proper role to be played by a young woman.

Renilde, Alessandro's wife, was a niece of Father Antonio Stoppani, a scholar-priest, known for his work as a natural scientist and geologist. Though a traditionally educated middle-class woman, Renilde was more willing to break with tradition than her husband. At certain crucial times, she supported her daughter's challenges to convention. At first, Alessandro would balk at supporting his daughter and wife, but eventually he acquiesced.

In 1875, Alessandro was assigned to a position in Rome, and the Montessori family moved to the Eternal City, and Italy's capital. Here, in one of the most important centers of Western civilization, Maria, the family's only child, enrolled in the state elementary school located on the Via di San Nicolo da Tolentino. Maria's education in the local primary school followed the traditional approach that learning comes from the teacher's transmission of information to children, through textbooks and recitations. The key instructional routines involved memorization of textbooks, the recitation, and dictation. In Italian schools, the children often used a single textbook that combined in one volume all the subjects taught—reading, writing, arithmetic, history, and geography. The recitation method required children to stand at attention when questioned by the teacher and provide accurately memorized responses from the textbook. Italian schools in particular featured dictation, in which students would copy word-for-word statements made by the teacher. Each letter of the alphabet had to be placed squarely in a small box marked on a copybook. While providing basic literary and mathematical skills, traditional schools discouraged and often punished children's spontaneity and creativity. In this view, the teacher held center stage in the classroom, and the student was a passive receptacle of information, which was to be stored in the mind and recalled for examinations and possible use in the future. Later educators such as Paulo Freire would call this storage-and-retrieval approach to learning the "banking" method of education in which information was deposited and stored for later use.[2] When she created her method of education, Montessori turned this view upside down. The individual child would become the focus, the center of education; and the teacher, a director, who unobtrusively guided the child's own self-learning.

The Italian educational system in the late nineteenth century followed the continental European pattern of being heavily class determined. The Cassati Law of 1859 provided for the establishment of national primary (or elementary) schools. Compulsory education laws were not rigorously enforced, however. Italy, especially the southern regions, had a high percentage of illiterates.[3] At the secondary level, the schools followed the continental European model and were specialized into the highly academic college-preparatory schools, the *liceos*, and into a range of technical and vocational schools, specializing in engineering, art, agriculture, and commerce. Only a very small number were admitted to university studies. As a member of the middle class, Montessori had the opportunity to complete elementary school. Her determination to pursue a technical secondary education and medical school, however, departed radically from the educational expectations at the time, which would have sent her to a finishing school, generally operated by a religious order of nuns, or to a normal school to prepare as an elementary school teacher.

Maria's parents carefully monitored their daughter's education. Her father, who recognized his daughter's academic abilities, encouraged her study of mathematics. Although her father sometimes resisted Maria's unconventional career decisions, her mother generally supported Maria's decisions. At age twelve, Maria displayed her characteristic independence by declaring her intention of entering a technical secondary school.

In 1883, thirteen-year-old Maria Montessori enrolled in the Regia Scuola Technica Michelangelo Buonarroti, a state technical school. As a student in the Scuola Technica, Maria pursued a seven-year curriculum, approved by the national ministry, that included Italian literature, French, mathematics such as algebra and geometry, sciences such as chemistry and physics, history, and geography. Instruction followed the conventional method of attending lectures, memorizing textbooks, and responding to the instructors' questions with structured recitations. Montessori graduated from the technical school in the spring of 1886 with high marks in her subjects and with a final cumulative grade of 137 out of a possible 150.[4]

Upon completing her studies at the Scuola Technica, Maria next entered the Regio Instituto Technico Leonardo da Vinci, in which from 1886 to 1890 she studied subjects related to engineering. In 1890, in an important career decision, she decided to leave her engineering studies to study medicine. Her application to the University of Rome's School of Medicine was at first rejected by the all-male faculty. The highly determined young woman persisted, and the faculty agreed to admit her to the University of Rome in the fall of 1890 as a student of physics, mathematics, and natural sciences. She passed the examinations for the *diploma di licenza* in 1892, earning a final grade of eight out of a possible ten points. She was now academically eligible to begin the actual study of medicine, anatomy, pathology, and clinical work. Montessori was the first woman to be admitted to the medical school.[5]

Since medical studies, like the medical profession, were completely male dominated, Montessori encountered regulations and practices that discriminated against women. Her male colleagues shunned and tried to isolate her. She could not enter a classroom until all the male students were seated. Since dissection of a naked cadaver was regarded as improper for a woman, she could only use the anatomy laboratory in the evenings, when male students were absent. Determined to surmount these obstacles, Montessori distinguished herself, winning scholarships in surgery, pathology, and medicine.[6]

During her last two years of medical school, Montessori studied pediatrics at the Children's Pediatric Hospital, an experience that moved her toward what would be her lifelong calling. She also served as an adjunct, or assistant, doctor at the women's hospital of San Salvator al Laterano and at the Ospedale Santo Spirito for men, in Sassia. In 1896, Maria Montessori achieved another distinction. She was the first woman in Italy to be awarded the degree of Doctor of Medicine. The twenty-six-year-old physician accepted a position at the university's San Giovanni Hospital, and she also began private practice.

Montessori's achievements in education and medicine had made her a woman of distinction in turn-of-the-century Italy. Although her contributions to the women's movement have been overshadowed by her achievements in education, Montessori was influential in the European women's movement. She was a member of the Italian delegation to the International Women's Congress, in Berlin, in September 1896. When tensions between socialist and bourgeois women threatened to disrupt the congress, Montessori, urging compromise, argued that the rights of all women, not class and political differences, should be the focus of the women's movement. In several addresses to the congress, she called for the improvement of Italian women's social and economic status. She urged women to take a leading role in educational reform and to work as literacy volunteers among the poor. She also sponsored a resolution demanding equal pay for equal work.[7]

In February 1899, Montessori was on a lecture tour, speaking on the "new woman." In many respects, she herself was the model for this new woman. According to Montessori, the women of the twentieth century would be the "new women," in transition from the old order to the new. She was optimistic about the liberating powers of science and technology that she predicted would free the new women from the gender-designated drudgery of domestic work. Science and technology would free them to genuinely fulfill themselves as persons. The process of liberation, she advised, would require women to educate their children according to the new pedagogy based on the scientific study of children's needs.

In developing her case for the new woman, Montessori attacked the stereotypes used to support the theory of female inferiority. She condemned scholars who, failing to use scientific research, relied on unsubstantiated clichés about women's alleged inferiority. Montessori challenged the French historian Jules Michelet (1798–1874), who argued that women were naturally weak and required tutelage and training from the more powerful

and intelligent males.[8] She discounted the argument of the radical syndical-
ist theorist Pierre Joseph Proudhon (1809–1865), who, in his critique of the
capitalist economy, argued that capitalism relegated a woman to either being a housewife or a prostitute.[9] It should be noted that Proudhon was not
arguing that women were limited to these unenviable situations by their nature; rather, the system of private property placed them in subordinate positions. Montessori challenged the Italian criminologist and physician Cesare Lombroso (1835–1909), who was regarded as an expert on criminal
anthropology. Montessori stated that there was no scientific support to sub-
stantiate Lombroso's definition of a woman as an incomplete organism in a
state of arrested development.[10] She firmly rejected the opinion of one of
her former teachers at the University of Rome, the noted anthropologist
Giuseppe Sergi, who predicted that women's social equality would destroy
the family and erode the stability of society.[11]

Calling on them to become scholars and scientists, Montessori urged
women to overturn the pseudoscientific antiwoman rationales that justified
keeping women in second-class status. The triumph of feminism, she predicted, would come, not by polemical counter propaganda, but by social and
technological inevitability. Science would provide empirical evidence of
women's independence, and equality and technology would reduce the work
of the housewife and leave more of her energy and time free. According to
Montessori:

> Eventually, the woman of the future will have equal rights as well as equal du-
> ties. She will have a new self-awareness and will find her true strength in an
> emancipated maternity. Family life as we know it may change, but it is absurd
> to think that feminism will destroy maternal feelings. The new woman will
> marry and have children out of choice, not because matrimony and maternity are
> imposed on her, and she will exercise control over the health and well being of
> the next generation and inaugurate a reign of peace, because when she can speak
> knowledgeably in the name of her children and in behalf of her own rights man
> will have to listen to her.[12]

Taking her own advice seriously, Montessori became the scientist that she
urged other women to become. Wanting to be more than a medical practitioner,
she set out to discover the cause and cure of human illnesses, especially those
of the mind. She joined the University of Rome's Clinica Psichiatrica as a voluntary assistant to research her thesis "A Clinical Contribution to the Study of
Delusions of Persecution." She pursued an in-depth study of the literature on
mental illnesses and psychological disorders.[13] Her research, too, was moving
her closer to a lifelong commitment to early childhood education.

Itard and Seguin

Montessori's research on mental retardation and other psychological disorders in children led her to the work of Jean-Marc Gaspard Itard (1774–1838) and Edouard Seguin, (1812–1880) two French physicians and psychologists. Montessori's study of Itard and Seguin had a highly significant formative influence on the development of her educational method.

Itard, a specialist in Otiatria, worked with deaf and hearing-impaired children. He pioneered in transferring the method of clinical observation practiced by physicians of their patients to the educator's observation of children. His most famous case was his well-publicized treatment of the "wild boy of Aveyron," a feral youth, apparently abandoned or lost as child, who had been found living in the forests with animals. The boy, about age twelve, was without language and practical skills. Itard undertook to educate the boy, training him in practical life skills and in speech. While he had some limited gains in educating the boy, Itard's experiment did not have promising results. The boy, a difficult pupil with limited abilities, resisted many of Itard's efforts.[14]

Itard's experiment with the "wild boy" and his work with mentally-impaired children led him to theorize that human beings went through specific, definite, and necessary stages of human growth. Itard was not the first educational theorist to emphasize the importance of stages of human development. The Roman rhetorician Quintilian (ca. AD 35–100), the Czech theologian and educator John Amos Comenius (1592–1670), and the French philospher Jean-Jacques Rousseau (1712–1778) had all recognized the crucial importance of developmental stages in education. Unlike these earlier educators who based their ideas about development on introspection or reflection, Itard came to his ideas through empirical observation of actual children. According to Itard, children experienced their stages of development by engaging in activities that were appropriate to the particular period and for which they were physiologically and psychologically ready. However, abnormal children, especially those who were severely impaired physically or mentally, tended to miss the full potential of the development stage and were left with deficits that impaired their further growth.[15] He concluded that children needed to experience the activities appropriate to their stage of development at the right time or else suffer the consequence of continual and cumulative impairment.[16]

Itard's work touched on several important themes: nature and natural education and the degree to which human intelligence is hereditary or learned. A contrast can be made between Rousseau's fictional "noble savage," Emile, who, isolated from society, learns primarily though direct sensory interactions. While Rousseau's Emile grows into a benevolent natural man, Itard's work with the real wild boy was quite different. Unlike Emile's laissez-faire and permissive tutor, Itard sought to find specific ways to train the child. In dealing with intelligence, Itard found that intelligence, while a given, developed by having the appropriate experiences at the right time of development.

Montessori was deeply impressed by Itard's work. A physician like Itard, Montessori was trained in clinical observation. Readily accepting Itard's ideas on empirical observation, she called his efforts practically "the first attempts at experimental psychology."[17]

Seguin, a physician, who had studied medicine with Itard, worked with mentally impaired children and applied his methods at the Hospice de Bicetre, a training school for children taken from the insane asylums of Paris.[18] Seguin believed that institutions for handicapped children should become centers of training and education and that both medical and pedagogical knowledge should be used to treat the handicapping condition. He increasingly emphasized the physiological measurement and observation of the child as a means to diagnosis, treatment, and education. Seguin devised a series of didactic apparatus and materials to train the senses and improve the physical skills of children with mental handicaps. In his work with these children, Seguin developed several techniques that would be adopted by Montessori, such as basing instruction on developmental stages using didactic training materials and training children to perform practical skills so that they could achieve some degree of independence.[19] Seguin's pioneering efforts in special education were a catalyst that stimulated Montessori to delve more deeply into education. From the work of Itard and Seguin, Montessori developed two principles: first, that mental deficiency required a special kind of education and not only medical treatment; second, that this special kind of education was enhanced by the use of didactic materials and apparatus. However, in the education of mentally deficient children and, indeed, all children, the teacher's activities were spiritual in that it was necessary to act on the spirit of the child, which was a "sort of secret key."[20]

Education of Children with Mental Handicaps

In September 1898, Montessori addressed the Pedagogical Congress in Turin on the subject of the education of mentally retarded children. At that time, mental retardation was not categorically defined but included a range of children, including those who were physiologically impaired as well as those who were referred to as "laggards," delinquent, and emotionally disturbed children. Condemning the prevailing practice of confining mentally impaired children to insane asylums with adults, she urged that they be admitted to educational institutions. Arguing that mental retardation was primarily a pedagogical problem, rather than a medical one, she recommended that these problem children be gathered together in special educational environments. This separation, she argued, would free the teacher of regular classes from having to cope with serious cases of disability. Further, children in the special classes would receive the necessary individual attention, and they could therefore proceed at their own pace without having to move with the larger group. In addition, these special classes were to have the services of a psychiatrist and pediatrician—specialists who could determine each child's individual needs and prepare an individualized learning prescription for each child.[21]

In light of today's mainstreaming of children with handicaps into the least restrictive classroom environment, Montessori's call for special classes needs to be considered in the context of 1890s. At that time, in Italy, mentally retarded children were often identified as "idiots" and confined with adults in insane asylums with no special care. Children who were called "laggards" (or delinquents), who were disruptive and chronically truant from schools, were usually expelled and either roamed the streets or were exploited as child laborers. In the context of the times, Montessori was suggesting a reform. If we take her recommendation out of its context, she might be criticized (by modern standards) as suggesting the social and educational isolation of children with special needs. When considered in terms of historical sequence, the creation of special classes might be judged to be a necessary first step for today's mainstreaming. In any event, her recommendation that a teacher, pediatrician, and psychiatrist diagnose children with special needs anticipated what today is called the multidisciplinary staffing. In this staffing, a team of experts provides a comprehensive assessment of an individual child's learning difficulties and how they might be remedied.

In 1900, the Scuola Magistrale Ortofrenica, the Orthophrenic School, opened with Montessori and Dr. Giuseppe Montesano as codirectors. By training hearing-impaired and mentally deficient children, the school provided an educational environment in which teachers could be prepared to work with children who had these handicapping conditions. Montessori directed the Orthophrenic School for two years, from 1900 to 1901.

Based on her own medical education, which was based on extensive work with mentally deficient children and on her reading of Itard and Seguin, Montessori concluded that the methods used in training children with mental deficiencies could be applied to normal children, especially those of a young age. Seeing a parallel between the two, she wrote, "During the period of early infancy when the child who has not the force to develop and he who is not yet developed are in some ways alike."[22] Specifically, the parallelism was evident in children's motor coordination and their sensory and language development. Methods that aid in the training of children with mental deficiencies could be applied, with great success, to the education of normal children.

At the Orthophrenic School, Maria and Giuseppe developed an intimate relationship. Montessori became pregnant and bore Giuseppe's son, a boy, whom they named Mario. The date of Mario Montessori's birth is not firmly established. He claims his birth date on March 31, 1898, but Kramer, a Montessori biographer, indicates it was more likely in 1901. Shortly after his birth, Mario was sent to live with a wet nurse in the country. Montesano's family, especially his mother, opposed a marriage. Montesano made it a condition of his legally recognizing the child that the birth be kept secret except for family members. Montessori, who seemed to have her way on so many other decisions, apparently acquiesced. Shortly afterward, Montesano married another woman, and Montessori left the Orthophrenic School. Montessori's child was raised by others and at seven went to a boarding school near Florence.[23] When Mario was fifteen, after the death of Montessori's mother, Mario came to live with his mother. He was first publicly presented as Montessori's nephew and then as her adopted son.[24] Over time, Mario Montessori would become his mother's closest associate in publicizing and implementing the Montessori method and in founding and administrating the Association Montessori Internationale.

Situating Montessori in Educational Theory

Montessori's study of children's mental illnesses motivated her to study education as a more general field. She decided that she needed to pursue more advanced studies in the foundations of education. She returned to the University of Rome, where she studied psychology, anthropology, educational history and philosophy, and pedagogical principles.

The world of educational theory Montessori entered at the beginning of the twentieth century was itself undergoing fundamental revision. While textbooks and recitations still dominated instruction in schools, educational pioneers such as Rousseau, Pestalozzi, and Froebel had provided new insights into children's nature and children's education. The French philospher Rousseau, in his classic work *Emile*, expounded a theory of natural education in which children were liberated from oppressive social conventions.[25] Despite Rousseau's emphasis on children's freedom, Montessori found much to question in Rousseau's ideas, especially his romantic view that children learn best by following their instincts and impulses in an unstructured natural environment. The Swiss educator Johann Heinrich Pestalozzi (1774–1827) had developed a theory of education that urged that schools be reformed into homelike places where children felt emotionally secure and in which they learned by using their senses in specially designed object lessons.[26] Pestalozzi's emphasis on learning through sensation and through work with objects was an antecedent of Montessori's emphasis on sensory training. Of the three educators, Montessori was most often compared to and contrasted with the German educator Friedrich Froebel (1782–1852), the founder of the kindergarten.[27] Like Montessori, Froebel had developed the idea that early childhood education should take place in a specially created environment, the kindergarten, or the "child's garden." According to Froebel, an adherent of idealist philosophy, children were endowed with inner spiritual powers that unfolded in an educational environment that encouraged learning through self-activity and the use of specially designed materials, such as (what he termed) "gifts and occupations."

As she became more knowledgeable about these important educational theories, Montessori recognized their value but also found them scientifically inadequate. Through promoting children's dignity and freedom, she found that Rousseau, Pestalozzi, and Froebel had relied on a philosophical, rather than a scientific, view of children. From introspecting on their childhood experiences, they had deduced what it is like to be a child and had generalized these views to embrace all childhood. Rousseau's wild romanticism had ignored the child's need for a structured learning environment. Pestalozzi's emphasis on using objects as the basis for learning, while on the right track, was too formal, routine, and mechanical. Froebel's kindergarten was so steeped in philosophical idealism that it was not grounded in modern science and psychology. Though recognizing the contributions of her predecessors, Montessori would remedy their deficiencies by turning to the actual observation of children, in clinical fashion, for her ideas on educational method.

At the same time that Montessori had determined to create a scientifically based pedagogy in Italy, educators elsewhere in the world were developing new insights into education. In the United States, progressive educators were developing new methods of education. At the Cook County Normal School in Chicago, Colonel Francis Parker (1837–1902) stressed learning through experience by means of nature studies, field trips, and activities.[28] John Dewey (1859–1952), an experimentalist philosopher, was using his Laboratory School, at the University of Chicago, as a center to test his theory of learning through experience, activities, and problem solving.[29] During much of Montessori's life, Dewey was the dominant theorist in American education; however, his idea of how science should be applied to education was significantly different from that of Montessori. While Dewey's philosophy was based on relativism, Montessori emphasized universals. William Heard Kilpatrick (1871–1965), a leading progressive, would become an early and severe critic of Montessori.[30] Kilpatrick would implement Dewey's pragmatic philosophy into his highly popular project method. Kilpatrick would fault Montessori on being out-of-date and inadequate in the areas of the child's socialization and creativity. These progressive educators—Parker, Dewey, Kilpatrick—who would become dominant figures in American educational theory, were taking a different path in early childhood education than that of Montessori. The progressives came to stress the school as a socially oriented embryonic society in which children learned by using the scientific method in a permissive environment. Enthusiastically calling for democracy in education, the progressives denied the role of absolute principles and urged freedom and activity. Montessori's approach to education, with its emphasis on learning in a structured environment with didactic materials would differ from that of the American progressives.

Still, yet another highly significant way of looking at childhood was emerging in Europe. In Vienna, Sigmund Freud (1856–1939), in his development of psychoanalytic psychology, was coming to recognize the role that the irrational played in human growth and development.[31] Childhood, Freud was finding, was more than spontaneous freedom and imitative play, as Rousseau, Pestalozzi, and Froebel had suggested. It was more than the opportunity to become democratic participants in an open-ended society, as Dewey, Kilpatrick, and the American progressives were urging. Freud's ideas were beginning to reshape the conception of children's nature. For him, early childhood was a time of sexual feelings and societal repressions that shaped the human being's psyche and had consequences for the adult personality. The "Oedipus complex" was a theory Freud developed regarding infant sexuality, in which the child desired to possess the parent of the opposite sex. Freud believed that children go through a sequence of psychosexual developmental stages. If the child was overgratified or repressed during any particular stage, the personality would become fixated at that stage. The way in which needs were satisfied or blocked had consequences for the person's self-esteem and personal, social, and sexual relationships. Lingering unresolved issues and conflicts, originating during the stages of development, may cause problems of psychological balance and adjustment throughout a person's life. Psychoanalytical therapy was a means of identifying the conflict, lodged in the subconscious, and bringing it to consciousness. In this way, the person could recognize the issue, examine it, and resolve it.

There were some parallels in the paths that Freud and Montessori took in their careers. Like Montessori, Freud was a medical doctor who, studying mental illnesses specialized in neurology, then moved on to psychology. Both Montessori and Freud had arrived at a theory of child development. Like Montessori, Freud lectured in the United States. Freud and Montessori were aware of each other's views on early childhood. Though Montessori and Freud both advocated children's freedom, their theories of development were quite different. Montessori rejected Freud's ideas on infant sexuality and the long-term significance of emotional conflict on later development.[32]

Between 1904 and 1908, Montessori began to establish her own place in the field of education. She lectured at the University of Rome's Pedagogical School, on the application of anthropology and biology to education. Montessori's movement into the field of physiological anthropology was part of a general development that was taking place at the time in science and social science in Italy. Cesare Lombroso and Giuseppe Sergi had developed the field of physical anthropology in Italy. Montessori was familiar with Lombroso's research on criminal anthropology, which involved taking the measurements of criminals, especially the size and shape of the head and face, and trying to generalize to some conclusion of the criminal type. She was most influenced by Sergi, who founded the Institute of Experimental Psychology at the University of Rome and with whom she had studied. Physical anthropology focuses on the scientific study of the human being as a physiological organism; it uses empirical means to measure, record, and quantify the anatomical and morphological variations in humans. Its sub-field, anthropometry, measures human physical characteristics with a variety of instruments.

Montessori extended the field of physiological anthropology to education.[33] She especially emphasized the importance of taking exact physical measurements of children's height, weight, head, pelvis, and limbs, as well as noting any types of malformations. These measurements were to be systematically recorded as an individualized empirical record, a biographical chart that was to be maintained for each child. She organized her lectures around the themes of the scientific approach to pedagogy; the correct techniques of clinically observing both abnormal and normal children; the scientific techniques of collecting and interpreting data; and how this anthropological information could be used in generalizing educational strategies.[34]

A popular lecturer, Montessori developed a following among the students because of her highly motivated and energetic presentations. Because she could draw from a variety of disciplines, ranging from medicine to anthropology and psychology, she gave her students a multidisciplinary breadth of knowledge that was unusual at the time. She published her lectures as *L'Antropolgia Pedagogica (Pedagogical Anthropology)*, a book that combined insights from pediatric medicine, child psychology, and cultural anthropology and applied them to children's development and education.[35] What was beginning to emerge at this stage in Montessori's development as an educational theorist was a holistic conception of education that drew from a number of academic disciplines. She showed her tendency to take a holistic and multidisciplinary approach to education by drawing materials from her background in medicine, psychology, and (her latest interest) anthropology.

The Casa dei Bambini

An important opportunity in Montessori's career came in 1907, when Edoardo Talamo asked her to establish a school in a slum area in Rome. At the time, Talamo was director general of the Istituto Romano di Beni Stabili (the Good Building Association), a philanthropic society established to improve housing conditions of the poor. The association was acquiring and remodeling run-down, overcrowed, and unsanitary city tenements. It was engaged in the rehabilitation of housing in the San Lorenzo quarter, a poverty-affected area of Rome. Talamo's invitation to Montessori was an attempt to resolve a very practical problem. When parents who lived in the remodeled housing development went to work, their children, under school-age, were left alone and unsupervised. The association decided to establish the school as a kind of day-care center for these children. Montessori, however, now had the opportunity to create a school that could serve as a laboratory to test her ideas. Under much more favorable circumstances, John Dewey, too, was testing his educational ideas at the University of Chicago Laboratory School. In the cases of both educators, these experiments in education would establish their names as leading educators.

Montessori opened her first school, the Casa dei Bambini, or Children's House, in a large tenement at Via dei Marsi 58, in Rome's poverty-ridden San Lorenzo district, on January 6, 1907. Her first pupils were fifty children, from ages three to seven, whose families resided in the tenement.

The San Lorenzo district, a depressed slum area, was similar to those found in the growing big cities of Europe and America. Like Montessori, Jane Addams, the pioneering American social worker, had established a settlement house for the poor, Hull House, on Chicago's west side. The Casa dei Bambini and Hull House were but two of the efforts to ameliorate the distress of the poor through philanthropic and educational means.

In post-Risorgimento Italy, internal migration brought large streaming tides of former peasants to cities such as Milan and Rome, in search of employment. In these cities, tenement districts arose to house the industrial underclass. This underclass was ill prepared for life in an urban setting. Montessori called the squalid conditions—the crime and vice—she encountered in the San Lorenzo district a dim "world of shadows."[36]

Anticipating by nearly one hundred years such contemporary approaches to urban education as the American "Operation Head Start," Montessori realized the crucial importance that the education of a child's early years held for later success. In the case of poverty-affected children, it was important that they experience the kind of education that might lift them from the cycle of deprivation. She considered the school to be the initial microcosmic attempt at a larger effort to bring about social reform through educational means. Montessori's broad understanding of the nature of social change and its relationships to education positioned her among the leading social reformers of the early twentieth century.

In founding the Casa dei Bambini, Montessori was guided by sociological and educational aims that she had developed during the various stages of her career. Located within the tenement, where the children's families' lived, the school was to act as an vital organic connection between education and society, represented by the family. Not only was her method a means to educate children more humanely and effectively, but it was intended to aid in the social regeneration of San Lorenzo's impoverished residents. Like Jane Addams, Montessori believed that in modern society, aid could no longer be in the form of alms' giving to the poor, as in the older medieval view of charity. In the past, charity was given by well-intentioned individuals to aid the victims of poverty and disease.

In the modern era, with its rapid industrialization and urbanization, Montessori believed that to bring about social reform the concept of private charity needed to be rethought and enlarged into a more comprehensive and more focused effort. Unless larger, more concerted, and planned efforts were made to reduce the sectors of poverty such as San Lorenzo, Montessori feared that modern society would face a great divide, a large chasm separating the rich and the poor. If the trend continued, the poor would be isolated in poverty-ridden ghettoes, which Montessori called "islands of the poor."[37] In the modern era, the concepts of charity needed to be reconstructed to not only provide immediate relief to the poor but to remediate the conditions that caused social and economic distress. Individual charity needed to be socialized by creating established agencies to prevent illness, improve diet and hygiene, educate children and adults, and reform society. These social agencies, Montessori argued, would improve the quality of life, be more efficient than unorganized individual efforts, stimulate economic productivity, and make individuals independent of the dole.[38]

Educationally, the Children's House was designed to be a school-home, an educational agency in close proximity to the children's family homes. Indeed, it was actually in the building where the children lived. Montessori stated, "We have placed the school within the house . . . as the property of the collectivity." The school would contribute to the socialization of the family and household, which in turn would connect the household to the larger community.[39]

The actual physical proximity of the children's home to the school had a socioeconomic dimension related to Montessori's model of the twentieth century's "new woman." The Casa dei Bambini was located in a working-class area where the majority of mothers toiled in Italy's developing industries.

However, Montessori reasoned that not only would working-class women be employed outside of the home but also more women of all socioeconomic classes would join the workforce in the future. Industrialization and technological innovation was the driving force in bringing about this change in women's work. Schools, as educational institutions, needed to recognize this technologically generated change and provide for the children of working mothers. Schools, such as the Casa dei Bambini, would make it possible for mothers to safely leave their children and "proceed with a feeling of great relief and freedom to their own work." Despite the change in working patterns and locations, Montessori advised that mothers would nevertheless continue to have the greatest responsibilities for the physical and moral care of their own children. The Casa dei Bambini would assist them to meet these maternal responsibilities while finding work and recreation outside of the home.[40]

Montessori then had several motives in mind when establishing the Casa dei Bambini, the prototype of all later Montessori schools: first, the social and economic motives of social reform, especially the improvement of the condition of the working class; second, the motive that the school was a means of aiding working mothers who would contribute to the general movement for women's equality and rights. However, the Casa dei Bambini was primarily a place for children's education; it was not a design to create a social utopia, nor was it merely a center for children's day care for working mothers. As the new school for the new age, it offered education based on the principles of scientific pedagogy.

One of Montessori's overarching pedagogical principles was that children's learning was best accomplished in a structured and orderly environment. She insisted that children attending her school and their parents follow some explicit regulations. No matter how poor they were, children were expected to come to school with clean bodies and clothing. They were to wear a clean smock or apron. Believing schools were most effective when closely related to the children's families and homes, parents were expected to be interested in and support their children's education and to attend frequent conferences, termed "parent–directress" conferences (to be explained in the following).

Like John Dewey at the University of Chicago Laboratory School, Montessori made sure that the school's physical arrangements, the tables, chairs, and apparatus, were suited to children's needs rather than adult preferences. She did not want the classroom and its furniture to limit the children's freedom of movement, as it did in traditional schools. Tables and chairs were sized according to children's heights and weights. Washstands were positioned to be accessible for younger children. Classrooms were lined with low cupboards where children could easily reach didactic materials and be responsible for returning them to their proper place. The Montessori school was designed to cultivate children's sensory sensitivity and manual dexterity, to allow them a degree of choice within a structured environment, to build a climate of order, and to cultivate independence and self-assurance in performing skills.

Montessori's conception of the role of the teacher varied from that of the traditional school. While teachers in conventional elementary schools occupied the center of the educational stage as the focal point for the children's attention, Montessori renamed her teacher a "directress" who was to guide children as they taught themselves to learn. The directress, an educator properly trained in the Montessori method, was to guide children in their own self-development.[41] Trained in the clinical observation of children and scientific pedagogy, the directress needed to be sensitive to children's readiness and stages of development. She was to establish the prepared environment, with its appropriate apparatus and materials, and cooperate in the children's own self-education.

The curriculum of the Casa dei Bambini was based on Montessori's principle that children experience crucial times in their development, called "sensitive periods." During these sensitive periods, the children were in a high state of readiness for particular kinds of learning activities, such as sensory training and language learning, as well as exercising motor skills and acquiring social adaptation. To aid the children's development during these sensitive periods, the children were provided with self-correcting didactic materials and apparatus that they selected themselves. Montessori skillfully surmounted the problem of motivating learners that teachers faced in group-learning situations in traditional schools. Since the children selected their own activities and materials, they were self-motivated. Since the materials were self-correcting, each child working at his or her own pace required little teacher intervention. The use of self-correcting educational materials was based on Montessori's belief that children would acquire self-discipline and self-reliance by becoming aware of their own mistakes and repeating a particular task until they had mastered it.

Based on her theory of sensitive periods, Montessori, through observation and experimentation, designed a curriculum that sought to develop children's competencies in three areas: practical life skills, motor and sensory training, and more formal literary and computational skills and subjects. This curriculum was not all in place when Montessori opened the Casa dei Bambini, but its various pieces came together to form a complete method of education.

First Group: Exercises of Practical Life

Montessori designed the practical exercises so that children could use them to develop the skills needed in everyday life, such as serving food, washing one's hands and face, tying a shoelace, or buttoning a shirt or blouse. The aim of the exercises was to move children from being dependent on adults to performing the exercises independently. The practical skills were generic in that once a child had mastered a particular skill, such as tying, lacing, or buttoning, the skill could be transferred to the many occurrences when it was needed in daily life. Designed to exercise and develop motor, muscular, and coordination skills, the successful performance of everyday skills gave children a sense of independence and a self-confidence that they could do things without adult assistance. The everyday life activities included washing and dressing oneself, setting tables and serving meals, housekeeping, gardening, gymnastic activities, and rhythmic movements. Using frame pieces of cloth with buttons, laces, and hooks, the children practiced fastening, buttoning, zipping, lacing, and tying skills that they could transfer to the buttoning and hooking of their own clothing and the tying of their own shoes. The school also utilized ordinary household objects—washbasins, dishes, silverware, and gardening tools. Washstands and tables were proportioned to the children's sizes so that they could easily reach them. Cabinets to store materials were accessible so that children could reach them and then return materials to their proper location.

Second Group: Sensory Training

Montessori designed the materials and activities for sensory education to develop the children's ability to perceive distinctions in color and hue and in sound and tone, and the curriculum included the skills needed to manipulate various kinds of objects. The sensory exercises were designed to cultivate three kinds of skills: discernment of color and hue, sensitivity to smell and sound, and making comparisons and contrasts. Montessori developed an order to using the materials. They began with a series of solid insets—wooden cylinders of different sizes, to be inserted in holes of the same size in a wooden block. Then, with ten pink wooden cubes of graduated size, the child built a tower, then knocked it down and rebuilt it. In addition, there were ten brown wooden prisms and ten red rods with which the child built a broad and long stair. There were geometric solids (pyramids, spheres, cones), little boards with rough and smooth surfaces and others of different weights and colors, and pieces of fabric of different textures. There were wooden plane insets, a little cabinet of drawers, each containing framed geometrical figures—blue triangles, circles, squares of different sizes—to be taken out and replaced correctly in their frames. There were cards with paper geometrical shapes pasted on them, a series of cylindrical boxes filled with different materials that produced different sounds when shaken; sixty-three little tables in nine different shades, from light to dark and of seven different colors. A series of musical tone bells was used with a wooden board that had musical staff lines and a set of wooden disks to represent the notes. The tone bells were used to develop the child's ability to discriminate between various tones. Sensory boxes included those filled with spices with distinctive odors. As the child worked with the didactic materials, he or she learned to recognize, group, and compare similar objects and contrast them from dissimilar ones.

Third Group: Language Development

In her work at the Casa dei Bambini, Montessori faced the common problem that besets all primary school teachers—how to teach reading and writing. Montessori opposed the commonly held idea that reading and writing needed to be imposed on children. Convinced of the power of what she termed "auto-education," she believed that when children were ready to read and write, they would do what was needed to develop these skills. Through trial and error, she developed materials that were conducive for readiness for reading, writing, and arithmetic. These materials included sandpaper letters, boxes of color-cardboard letters and numbers, and counting rods—square-sided sticks of different lengths and different colors representing different numbers—as well as strings of different lengths with various numbers of beads of different colors.[42]

Montessori's claim that children of four and five years "burst spontaneously into writing" attracted considerable attention from her proponents and some skepticism from critics. Montessori saw writing and reading as being developed in close relationship. To create readiness for them, she devised letters cut out of cardboard and covered with sandpaper. As the children touched and traced these letters, the directress would voice the sound of the letter. While the children were being prepared to write the letter by the movements needed to trace its shape, they fixed the letter in their minds and came to recognize the sound it represented. Children discovered reading when they understood that the sounds of the letters that they were tracing, and then writing, formed words. When the children knew all of the vowels and some of the consonants, they were ready to form simple words. Using the vowels, the directress would show the children how to compose three-letter words and pronounce them clearly. In the next step, the children would write the words dictated by the directress. After enough practice, the children were able to compose words without assistance. In teaching arithmetic, counting was taught by arranging objects according to their number and by measuring them using a series of colored rods of varying lengths.

Children learned about the natural environment by planting and cultivating gardens, which Montessori believed established the intellectual connection about the sprouting of seeds and the growing of plants within the larger world of nature. The keeping of small animals in the school introduced children to the beginnings of zoology and provided a way to develop a sense of responsibility in caring for them.

Through her work at the Casa dei Bambini, Montessori tested many of the ideas and principles that she had developed earlier from her work with mentally impaired children; her reading of Itard and Seguin; her clinical observation of children; and her background in medicine, psychology, and anthropology. She implemented the principle of a child's freedom in the arrangement of materials and in the structure of the prepared environment. According to her principle of auto-education, a child's freedom made it possible for children to select their own learning activities. Montessori's ability to match the child's readiness to the materials and activities was one of her most significant methodological achievements. Readiness, in turn, was based on children's developmental periods, especially the sensitive period when they were ready to learn and needed to learn. Although children have a great capacity for acquiring and incorporating knowledge, the exercises for acquiring this knowledge needed to be appropriate to their particular stage of development. Determining what kind of content and activities were appropriate to children's readiness to learn remains one of the great pedagogical problems. Montessori turned to the children themselves to solve the problem of matching their needs and readiness with the materials and situations available to them by creating the prepared environment in which they were free to choose from a number of materials. Drawing from Itard's and Seguin's work with mentally impaired children, Montessori developed didactic materials designed to exercise children's motor and sensory skills, and she stocked the prepared environment with them. When children reached a sensitive readiness to try to master the skills, they themselves matched their readiness with the material. Her experience at the Case dei Bambini united her theory with her practice.

Montessori's success at the Casa dei Bambini led to the establishment of several additional schools in Rome—a second in the San Lorenzo district, two in a middle-class area of the city, and one at the villa of the British ambassador to Italy. In 1911, she left the original Casa dei Bambini to establish her work more widely. Montessori gained the support of the Societa Umanitaria, the Humanitarian Society of Italy, which publicized and provided financial support for her method. With the society's support, a Montessori school was established in Milan, Italy's leading industrial city. Montessori's method went through a process similar to that experienced by other educational innovations, such as Pestalozzi's object method and the American Head Start. These educational approaches were initially designed to educate socially and economically disadvantaged children. As the new methods attained a reputation for having results, they were then quickly appropriated by the middle and upper classes. The same kind of adoption and adaptation occurred with Montessori's method.

Montessori Gains Educational Recognition

By 1910, Montessori had earned recognition as a significant innovative educator in her native Italy, where she presided over a demonstration school and a training institute for directresses. Her growing reputation attracted attention in educational circles in other European nations and in North America, especially in the United States. At this point, she faced the problem of how to disseminate and institutionalize her method. Educational innovators often attract enthusiastic and well-intentioned, but untrained or ill-disciplined, disciples. When they are removed from the innovator and the center of innovation, they often distort it. Montessori now had to make some key decisions about how her innovative method should be maintained and disseminated. Essentially, she determined that she would keep control firmly in her own hands. She would control the training of Montessori educators, to prevent any deviation from her method as she had conceived it. She would control production and distribution of Montessori materials and apparatus. Her decision would have important consequences for the Montessori method.

To reach larger audiences, Montessori used two established means of diffusing her method: public speaking and publication. As a university professor, Montessori became an adept lecturer, and she used public speaking to her advantage. Her American tour in 1913 is an example of her use of the public podium to introduce her method to a wider audience. Again, as a university professor, Montessori was also skilled in using publications to disseminate her ideas to both professional educators and the public. She wrote about her work at the Casa dei Bambini in *The Method of Scientific Pedagogy Applied to Infant Education in the Children's Houses*, in 1910. *Scientific Pedagogy*, retitled *The Montessori Method* (1912), was published in eleven languages. *The Montessori Method* was followed by *Dr. Montessori's Own Handbook* (1914), which she wrote as a kind of official guide to the method that would distinguish it from others who were writing about Montessori education. Her two-volume work, *The Advanced Montessori Method*, appeared in 1918 and 1919.[43] In the world of educational theory and practice, however, publications are subject to critical review, especially in higher education. Montessori, however, was more concerned with disseminating her method as she had conceived of it rather than engaging in the larger educational discourse and debate.

Along with public speaking and publication, the Montessori method was diffused to a worldwide audience by means of the educational visitation. Educators and other interested individuals came to Rome from other countries, including the United States, to attend her lectures, interview her, and observe her method and schools. Among the Americans were the child psychologists Arnold and Beatrice Gesell, the publisher Samuel S. McClure, and such professors of education as Howard Warren of Princeton, Arthur Norton of Harvard, Lightner Witmer of the University of Pennsylvania, and William Heard Kilpatrick of Columbia University's Teachers College.[44] Some of these visitors were intent on becoming disciples who would introduce the Montessori method to their own countries; others were educational journalists who were researching articles and books about the Italian educator. Still others, such as Kilpatrick, would become severe critics.

In terms of perpetuating an innovation, it is necessary that it have continuity across time so that it has a life that extends beyond that of its originator. To perpetuate her method and to ensure that it was being introduced without distortion, Montessori turned to teacher preparation. She established a training school to prepare Montessori directresses. An American disciple who journeyed to Italy ecstatically praised Montessori as a "magical personality that makes her words seem winged messengers of light and the mighty fever of enthusiasm is amazing to the beholder."[45]

Montessori trainees were generally young women, often talented in art and music but drawn to education. In the early twentieth century, elementary teaching was highly feminized, and the propensity of Montessori education to attract women to its ranks was to be expected since Montessori schools were early childhood schools, generally taught by women. Montessori's relationship to her trainees was that of the mother-leader. Her students were her disciples. Demanding loyalty and commitment, she expected those whom she prepared as directresses to maintain the method in its pure form, as she had designed it. This kind of relationship was not satisfactory to some of the trainees, especially those who wanted to put their own personal stamp on it. Montessori regarded experimentation with her method to be a disloyal kind of revisionism. Because of this attitude, there was a coterie of loyal Montessorians but also those regarded as schismatics, who deviated from the system. It is an interesting incongruity that Montessori, who wanted children to become independent and who wanted women in general to become independent, did not accept independence from her educational associates.

A characteristic of Montessori's approach to teacher education was that the method should be learned and used without deviation from her original pattern. While this guaranteed methodological consistency, it created some serious obstacles to its dissemination. First, the number of directresses would be small since Montessori so rigorously controlled their training. Further, there were questions about the need to reformulate the method to increase its applicability in different national and cultural settings.

Montessori Comes to the United States

Montessori and her method aroused international interest. The United States, where over one hundred Montessori schools were operating in 1913, seemed particularly receptive to the Italian educator. American enthusiasts formed a national organization, the Montessori Educational Association, to promote her method. Many of her American advocates were individuals who generally supported progressive causes. The association, with Mrs. Alexander Graham Bell as president, included such prominent individuals on its board of directors as Margaret Wilson, the daughter of President Woodrow Wilson; Philander P. Claxton, the U.S. commissioner of education; Samuel S. McClure, publisher of the widely read *McClure's Magazine*; and Dorothy Canfield Fisher, a well-known writer on education and cultural subjects.[46]

Dorothy Canfield Fisher (1879–1958) provides an example of some Americans who were attracted to the Montessori method and who promoted it in the United States.[47] Fisher was a well-known author who supported progressive causes. Like Montessori, she urged modern women to pursue careers while maintaining their familial roles as wives and mothers. Although not a professional educator, Fisher wrote on educational topics for the general reader. She visited Montessori's school at the Franciscan Convent, on the Via Giusti in Rome, in 1911. Upon her return, she began to publicize and promote the Montessori method. Her book *A Montessori Mother* was published in 1912. Enthusiastically endorsing the Montessori method, Canfield wrote,

> The teacher, under this system is the scientific, observing supervisor of this mental "playground" where the children acquire intellectual vigor, independence, and initiative as spontaneously, joyfully, and tirelessly as they acquire physical independence and vigor as a by-product of physical play.[48]

Along with Fisher, one of Montessori's leading American disciples was Anne E. George, who had been a teacher at Chicago's Latin School. After visiting Montessori's school in Rome in the summer of 1909, George wrote,

> Dr. Montessori took me to her schools, showing me in detail how she gave her lessons. The impression made by those mornings has stayed with me and has been my guide in all my work since. Dr. Montessori's simplicity was a revelation. Whenever we entered a class-room, I distinctly felt that a new and sweeter spirit pervaded the place, and that the children were, in an indescribable way, set free. Yet there was order in everything. With a straightforwardness often stripped entirely of words, Maria Montessori taught, or to use her own word, "directed," her children. She treated the children not as automatons, but as individual human beings. She never forced her personality or her will upon them, and made none of the efforts to attract and interest, which I had often made use of.[49]

George was so impressed with Montessori and her method that she returned to Rome in 1910 and enrolled in an eight-month training program. She was the first American to be trained in the method by Montessori herself. Returning to the United States, George conducted the first Montessori school in the country, which had been established in Tarrytown, New York, by Frank A. Vanderlip. Claiming that the Montessori method required no adaptation for American children since it was applicable to children universally, George sought to implement the method "precisely" as Montessori had developed it.[50] However, she did note some differences between the American children and the Italian. The American children in the Tarrytown school were predominately middle class while the Italian children she had observed were working class. After learning how to use the didactic materials correctly, the American children tended to experiment and find new ways to use them. Further, the American children, more used to seeing writing used in their homes, were not as enthusiastic as the Italian children were about learning to write.

George defended the Montessori method against the charge that it failed to develop children's imagination (a charge frequently made against it by kindergarten educators). She wrote,

The Italian educator, it is said, makes the mistake of bringing the children too closely to the earth, as distinguished from other methods which encourage imagination and deal in fairies and knights and imaginative games. Dr. Montessori makes the children see the world as it really is. To her a block is a block, not a castle; the hands and fingers are anatomical structures, not pigeons; the children learn real geometrical forms by their right names—triangles, squares, circles, ovals—and not as symbolic abstractions.[51]

In 1913, George placed her assistant, Miss Bagnell, in charge of the Tarrytown Montessori school and then established a Montessori school of her own, the "Children's House," in Washington, D.C. She sought to make this school an accurate reproduction of Montessori's schools in Rome so that the method would be a "pure application of Dr. Montessori's principles."[52] George was so recognized in the American Montessori movement that she did the English-language translation for *The Montessori Method* published by the New York company of Frederick A. Stokes in 1912. She would also translate Montessori's lectures when the Italian educator made her first visit to the United States, in 1913.

Montessori's leading promoter in the United States was Samuel S. McClure, the publisher and editor. McClure, an enthusiastic and opportunistic promoter of the Montessorian method, saw himself as the leader of the movement in the United States. He hoped not only to make a contribution to American education by his promotion of Montessorianism but also to make a financial profit by publicizing Montessori and sharing in the sale of Montessori publications and apparatus.

McClure's Magazine ran a series of laudatory articles on Montessori and her method; for a time, the magazine featured a monthly section entitled the Montessori Department. Touting Montessori as an "educational wonder worker," McClure proclaimed that the development of the Montessori method marked "an epoch in the history of education and a turning point in the lives of all who take part in it."[53] Ellen Yale Stevens, principal of the Brooklyn Heights Seminary, praised McClure's efforts in bringing Montessori to an American audience:

> For the first time, I believe, in the history of educational thought, a new movement has come to the front through the medium of a popular magazine instead of by means of a scientific treatise by a specialist in education, which would naturally have limited appeal. The result of this is that the interest of the whole country has been aroused, not only in the work of Dr. Montessori in Italy, but in the present state of education in this country.[54]

In November 1913, McClure was in Rome to arrange Montessori's projected speaking tour in the United States. The ambitious publicist sought exclusive rights to market Montessori's method and materials in the United States. He wrote to his wife about some motion pictures of Montessori classes that he planned to use in his own lectures, calling them "sublime and wonderful material." McClure found Montessori's book *The Montessori Method* to be "really extraordinarily eloquent & luminous."[55] While in Italy, McClure developed the plan for the lectures Montessori would deliver in the United States. First, he would describe the history and spirit of the Montessori system and his own visit to the Casa dei Bambini. Second, he would show and comment on the motion pictures of the school. Third, McClure would then introduce Montessori, who would speak for thirty minutes in Italian. This would be followed by Ann George's translation of Montessori's lecture.[56] The format was changed during Montessori's American lecture tour. Montessori was welcomed by a leading local educator, such as John Dewey in New York or Ella Flagg Young in Chicago, and then introduced by McClure; she would deliver her lecture in Italian and Anne E. George would translate her remarks. The presentation concluded with the showing of the motion pictures of children engaged in activities at Montessori's school in Rome. When preparing his plan, McClure apparently was also looking ahead to a later lecture tour that he would make to promote the sale of Montessori apparatus.

With boundless enthusiasm, McClure developed an ambitious plan to bring Montessori to the American public. His plan included a joint lecture tour with Montessori, establishing Montessori schools, creating a teacher education institute, and founding a company to manufacture and market her didactic materials.[57] He believed that he had successfully negotiated with Montessori and had gained the right to control her lecture and the films. Throughout his dealing with Montessori, however, there were tensions and serious misunderstandings. Montessori, determined to control the method and materials she had designed, distrusted McClure. McClure, in turn, found her a difficult and obstinate person to work with.[58]

The American Montessori Association sponsored a nationwide lecture series by Montessori in December 1913. As indicated, McClure had arranged the tour. Montessori arrived in the United States on December 3 and began her tour with an inaugural address in Washington, D.C., which was followed by lectures in New York, Philadelphia, Boston, Chicago, and San Francisco. John Dewey, the pragmatist philosopher, was chairperson of her first lecture, in New York City. Ella Flagg Young, superintendent of Chicago Public Schools, and Jane Addams of Hull House, gave official welcomes at the two Chicago lectures. Since Montessori did not speak English, her lectures were delivered in Italian and then translated into English by Anne E. George. George's translations accentuated the following points: Montessori's emphasis on the child's liberty, both externally (as the freedom of movement) and internally (as the freedom of the spirit); the child's own aim to grow to independence and maturity; the child's need to explore the environment, to feel and touch things, and to organize his or her own movements; how didactic materials were used to develop sensory skills and the skills of practical life; the spontaneous development of reading and writing; a sense of discipline that comes from work—that is, staying on a task until it is mastered.[59]

Montessori's lectures attracted large audiences and received wide and favorable newspaper coverage. They were regarded as highly successful and as a prelude to a concerted Montessorian presence in American education. Montessori departed for Italy on December 24. Henry Suzzallo, professor of philosophy of education, Teachers College, Columbia University, recognized the impact that Montessori had made. He wrote,

> Among a considerable number of laymen and a smaller number of teachers, the interest amounts to enthusiasm. The doctrines of the Italian educator are so warmly espoused by some that schools modeled on the plan of the Casa dei Bambini have been established in various parts of the country, where they rival and challenge the existing kindergartens and primary schools. To many of its adherents this movement constitutes an educational revolution that in time will completely change the education of children.[60]

Though recognizing the great enthusiasm generated by Montessori, Suzzallo was suspicious about some of the pedagogical features of the Montessori method. He urged American educators to stand back from the wave of enthusiasm and to take a critical and skeptical view. He advised them to avoid being swept up by enthusiastic propaganda and to examine the Montessori method detail by detail.[61]

When Montessori returned to Italy, tensions were further aggravated between her and McClure and their agreement began to unravel. McClure had expected to make a considerable financial profit from his promotion of Montessori schools and materials. Montessori had grown increasingly suspicious of McClure's motives. When McClure's brother Robert met with Montessori in Rome (on behalf of McClure), he found that she wanted to end her relationship with the publisher. Montessori strongly denied that she had authorized McClure to market her materials, and she strongly objected to McClure's entrepreneurial attempts to ride the coattails of her prominence. Only she would control her training courses, publications, and materials. Further, she affirmed that she would only establish schools in the United States if they were under her control. McClure's proposed lectures on the Montessori method were to be his own project and not done in association with her.[62]

Montessori had initially agreed to cooperate with McClure without the advice of legal counsel. She now decided to formally repudiate her agreement with him. She engaged a New York law firm, Briesen and Knauth, to investigate who actually controlled the Montessori films. The motion pictures were of Montessori's schools in Italy and showed children using the didactic materials and performing the sensory and practical life exercises. The possession of the films sparked the threat of litigation between Montessori and McClure. Briesen and Knauth requested McClure to produce a copy of the written agreement relating to the films.[63] McClure was distressed, as his relations with Montessori deteriorated to the breaking point. He had placed great hope in using his sponsorship of the Montessori method to advance what he regarded to be one of the great educational achievements of modern times. In addition to promoting an important educational method, McClure had also seen himself reaping considerable financial profits from manufacturing and selling Montessori apparatus. McClure's wife, Harriet, who had been continually appraised by her husband of his expectations for the Montessori method in the United States, watched the deteriorating relationship between the pedagogue and the publicist. She advised her husband to disengage himself from Montessori, saying, "How can you renew relations with her? There is no peace for you in connection with her."[64] McClure's relationships to Montessori continued to flounder, and eventually it reached a final impasse. She sent him a cablegram on April 15, 1914, clearly warning him: DO NOT DO ANYTHING WITHOUT REGULAR CONTRACTS FORBID PUBLICATION LAST YEARS LECTURES.[65] At last, McClure understood that his relationship with Montessori had reached an unhappy conclusion. He formally renounced the power of attorney that he had executed with Montessori in 1911 and ended his efforts to promote Montessori in the United States.

Montessori's relationship with McClure provides a fascinating sidelight on what appeared to be a successful lecture tour. The two strong personalities were in frequent conflict. McClure, a publicist, had decided that he would capitalize on Montessori's method and become its leading proponent in the United States. Montessori, in turn, was further convinced that only she would control the method that she had developed.

In April 1915, Montessori came to the United States for a second visit, now under the auspices of the National Education Association (NEA). She was accompanied by her son, Mario Montessori, and she remained in the United States until 1917. Her lectures and demonstration classes were timed to coincide with the meetings of the NEA and the International Kindergarten Union. Montessori addressed both groups and set up a model Montessori class in the Palace of Education at the Panama-Pacific International Exposition in San Francisco. The demonstration school at the exposition attracted scores of visitors, who observed the children through glass walls.[66] She also gave a course for teachers in San Francisco, from August through November, giving four lectures a week and supervising students who observed the demonstration class. She also gave lectures and classes in Los Angeles and San Diego. During part of the time, Helen Parkhust, a professor at the State Teachers College in Wisconsin, accompanied her. Montessori was plagued with financial problems during her stay in California. She returned to Italy at the end of November upon receiving word of her father's death. She made several personal visits to the United States after that—her last one in 1918. By the end of her second visit to the United States, national attention on Montessori and her method was fading. However, she still attracted audiences to hear her promotion of her new book, *Dr. Montessori's Own Handbook*, and to see her demonstrations and exhibits of didactic materials.[67]

Montessori's lecture tours and the growing number of Montessori schools established between 1910 and 1920 constitute the first wave of Montessorianism in the United States. This initial wave of enthusiasm, however, failed to firmly establish the Montessori philosophy and method in the United States. Although Montessori was given a generally receptive response from her American audiences and although she enjoyed complimentary comments in newspapers and magazines, several American educators began to criticize her method and its applicability to American children.

Montessori's critics in America generally came from two camps: Froebelian kindergarten advocates and progressive educators. By the time of Montessori's visit to the United States in 1913, the kindergarten was a firmly established part of many American public school systems. The kindergarten itself was no longer an experimental institution but was now part of the educational establishment. Kindergarten teachers met in annual conventions, and Froebel's writings had been translated into English and published in the United States. Since the kindergarten and the Montessori method were intended for essentially the same age group, comparisons and contrasts were often made between the two methods. In introducing an article on the Montessori method and the Froebelian kindergarten, the editor of McClure's Magazine wrote, "Since the beginning of the Montessori movement in this country, the kindergarten method and the Montessori method have been issues in a great controversy which has stirred the whole educational world. The two methods have been constantly compared and contrasted, and each one has been criticized from the point of the other."[68]

Both Froebel and Montessori believed that children possessed an interior spiritual force that stimulated their self-activity. They also believed in the importance of a prepared educational environment. For Froebel, this was the kindergarten, the "child's garden"; for Montessori, it was the prepared environment of the Casa dei Bambini. Montessori made some distinctions between her method and the Froebelian kindergarten. Learning, which she called auto-education, was not to be wasted in chaotic activity for the sake of movement. It was a force to be used in conjunction with the child's stages of development—to further motor, intellectual, and social growth and to cultivate well-being in a prepared environment.

Montessori concluded that some of Froebel's "gifts and occupations"—the materials and activities used in kindergartens—were not compatible with children's readiness. For example, she believed that the Froebelian exercises of weaving and sewing on cardboard were ill adapted to the physiological development of the children's eyes and their ability to coordinate eye and hand movements. She did, however, retain clay modeling, which she found to be the most rational of Froebel's exercises.[69]

More generally, Montessori believed that there were important differences between her didactic materials and Froebel's gifts. Froebel's gifts were objects in their finished form that were given to the children, such as the sphere represented by the ball. The ideal underlying the Froebelian gifts was that the concrete object would stimulate the recall of the concept, such as sphericity, that was latently present in the child's mind.[70] Further, the sphere, according to Froebel's idealist philosophy, had a powerful symbolic significance in that the circle united all people into a great chain of humanity and that the earth itself was a sphere. Montessori rejected much of the Froebelian symbolism as being based on unscientific metaphysics. She further claimed that her didactic materials were self-correcting whereas the kindergarten teacher had to intervene with the Froebelian objects to make sure the children were using them correctly. In using the Montessori materials, the apparatus itself corrected the child, who would repeat the task until it was mastered.[71]

During the effort to introduce and publicize the Montessori method, several of Montessori's American proponents argued that the two methods could complement, rather than supplement, each other. In his introduction to *The Montessori Method*, Henry W. Holmes, professor of education at Harvard University, predicted that the early childhood education of the future would combine both Froebelian and Montessorian elements.[72]

Generally lauding the Montessori method, Holmes devoted much of his introduction to comparing and contrasting the Montessori and Froebel methods. Holmes noted that the kindergarten teacher relies heavily on group work while the Montessori directress stresses individual work. Montessori's sensory training is much more specific than that of Froebel's kindergarten approach. Although both methods feature free body activity and rhythmic exercises, the kindergarten uses imaginative group games while the Montessori method stresses specific individual exercises to develop physical skills and functions. While the kindergarten's group games are highly imaginative and symbolic, the Montessori school's activities are directed to performing the work of real life.[73] Holmes concluded,

> Compared with the kindergarten, then, the Montessori system presents these main points of interest: it carries out far more radically the principles of unrestricted liberty; its materials are intended for the direct and formal training of the senses; it includes apparatus designed to aid in the purely physical development of the children; its social training is carried out mainly by means of present and actual social activities; and it affords direct preparation for the school arts.[74]

Ellen Yates Stevens, principal of the Brooklyn Heights Seminary, undertook a comparative investigation of the kindergarten method and the Montessori method. Specifically, she used the following questions to guide her research: Has the Montessori method successfully "broken down the wall between the kindergarten and primary classes"? Is the Montessori approach to early child education "better than that of Froebel, and if so why"?[75] To answer these questions, Stevens went to Italy, where she interviewed Montessori and spent seven weeks visiting Montessori schools and comparing them to Italian kindergartens that used the Froebelian method. The results of her research were then published in *McClure's Magazine*.

Stevens gave the Montessori method her unreserved approval. Calling Montessori "a genius," Steven acclaimed *The Montessori Method* as "one of the most impressive and illuminating books I have ever read." In comparison with Froebelian kindergarten, she found the Montessori method to be "more direct," avoiding Froebel's symbolism. The Montessori material was "more practical." Most important, Montessori had solved the problem of matching children's readiness with appropriate learning materials and activities, by individualizing their work. Stevens noted Montessori's highly significant achievement, stating that the children's "individual development was possible to a much greater degree" because the Montessori method provides for "the varying rates of progress always found among children of the same age."[76]

Believing that the Montessori method should be applied to American children, Stevens noted some differences between Italian and American children that needed to be recognized in adapting the method in the United States. Compared to the Italian child, the American child was "less responsive to sense impressions" and "less docile" but had "more imagination," "more power of invention," and a "greater fund of nervous energy." She commented that

> our children love the mysterious, the unreal, the myth, the fairy story; and this need should be provided for by the story, the song, and the game. I expect our children to be freer with the material—to take some of the steps more quickly and omit others altogether.[77]

Like Professor Holmes, Stevens looked forward to a combination of selected elements of the Froebelian kindergarten with the Montessori method. She proposed that the American kindergarten and primary grades be reconstructed according to Montessori's philosophy and method, "using her materials, but keeping the kindergarten's morning circle and the story, many of the songs and games, and some of the occupations, especially the clay."[78]

While there was some fusion of Froebelianism and Montessorianism, the two methods remained distinct. Rather than being absorbed or changed by Montessori, the American kindergarten slowly reconstructed the Froebelian method, making it less symbolic and more informal. This change in kindergarten practices was more influenced by child-centered progressivism rather than Montessori's method. Elizabeth Harrison, a well-known authority on kindergarten education, gave the generalized kindergartner response to the Montessori method. Despite some positive features, Harrison said that it overemphasized individual work to the detriment of group work and that it failed to cultivate children's imaginative, dramatic, and poetic activities.[79]

In addition to the reservations made by traditional kindergarten educators about the Montessori method, an important group of opponents included some university professors of education, many of whom were progressives associated with John Dewey's instrumentalist philosophy. The progressive educators were gaining prominence in the United States and were beginning to dominate teacher education programs in colleges and universities. For a time, Montessori's method had been considered to be compatible with and perhaps a European variation of progressive education. Some leading progressive educators were now determined to show that Montessorianism was not a genuine progressive method of education. In a strong attack, Walter Halsey, a professor at the University of Omaha, labeled the Montessori method as a mere "fad promoted and advertised by a shrewd commercial spirit" that was being enthusiastically accepted by the "novelty loving American public."[80]

A serious and highly critical attack came from William Heard Kilpatrick, a prominent professor at Columbia University's Teachers College. A disciple of Dewey's pragmatic instrumentalist philosophy, Kilpatrick sought to devise ways to implement Dewey's concepts of social intelligence and problem solving into the school curriculum. Kilpatrick's efforts led him to develop the group-centered, activity-based project method, which became a highly popular method of instruction in American schools in the 1920s and 1930s.[81]

Before writing his critique of Montessori's method, Kilpatrick had gone to Rome to visit Montessori schools and to interview Montessori. He then turned to a detailed analysis of Montessori's *The Montessori Method*. Representing the instrumentalist–progressive response to Montessori, Kilpatrick's critical book *The Montessori System Examined*, published in 1914, called the Montessori method a mid-nineteenth-century piece that was "fifty years behind" modern educational thought.[82]

Kilpatrick, operating from an experimentalist–progressive frame of reference, wrote a detailed analysis of the Montessori method. While commending Montessori's interest in science and in the application of science to education, Kilpatrick found many of her generalizations to be unscientific claims that were based on limited observations and on a very restricted knowledge of recent developments in educational psychology.[83] Further, Kilpatrick claimed that Montessori, in the tradition of Rousseau, Pestalozzi, and Froebel, believed that children's development was an unfolding of latently present interior potentialities. Her view of inner development caused her to neglect the importance, emphasized by Dewey and the experimentalists, of education as a series of transactions between the child and the environment that resulted in intelligent adaptations to changing circumstances.[84] Kilpatrick, referring to Dewey, challenged Montessori on not providing or encouraging the group work that is needed for social intelligence and that arises from children's own needs for joint action to deal with a situation or to solve a problem.[85]

Kilpatrick was indeed critical of the didactic apparatus and materials that were prominently featured aspects of the Montessori method. While approving of Montessori's emphasis on the child's freedom to perform a self-selected task, he found that Montessori's didactic apparatus and materials presented "a limited series of exactly distinct and very precise activities, formal in character and very remote from social interests and connections. So narrow and limited a range of activity cannot go far in satisfying the normal child."[86] The consequence, according to Kilpatrick, was that the Montessori schools did not provide adequately for stimulating children's imagination and creativity. Neither did Kilpatrick find much to praise about the exercises of practical life. He found the claims of children's practical abilities and skills in Montessori schools to be exaggerated. Rather than being generic activities, Kilpatrick, in true progressive fashion, argued that the practical life activities should reflect the conditions and situations in local communities in which the school was located.[87]

Proceeding to deflate Montessori as an educational innovator, Kilpatrick put her outside the current research in educational psychology. Based on his interview with her, Kilpatrick concluded that Montessori accepted the largely discarded doctrine of formal discipline. Her approach to sensory education rested on a belief that the mind's powers could be specifically trained.[88]

Kilpatrick's stinging critique had a significant negative impact on the entry of the Montessori method into the teacher preparation programs in colleges and universities. Although a number of teachers, journalists, and lay people were receptive to Montessori, she made only a slight impact on the educational establishment—the public schools and the colleges of education—in early-twentieth-century America. Educational administrators were more concerned with designing facilities and schedules for large urban systems. John Dewey, William H. Kilpatrick, and other progressives were dominating the educational scene.

The first entry of Montessori education in the United States was marked by some short-term successes, but it also revealed serious weaknesses that would jeopardize its long-term success. Montessori's name and method had reached an American audience. She enjoyed the support of some prominent and influential persons; however, they were mainly journalists and public figures, people not well positioned in the educational and academic communities.

Montessori's scientific pedagogy failed to make a significant impact on educational psychology, as it was conceived of in departments and schools of education in the United States from 1910 to 1930. The functional, behavioral, and psychoanalytic schools of psychology, then dominant, overshadowed Montessori's ideas on educational psychology.[89] According to J. M. Hunt, Montessori's recommended pedagogical treatment for mental retardation was "out of step" with J. McKeen Cattell's doctrine of fixed intelligence and with Edward L. Thorndike's stimulus-response theory.[90] Montessori's contention that intellectual development could be deliberately stimulated in early childhood life and her emphasis on the transfer of training were not generally accepted by the academic psychologists of the period. Further, her view of the scientific importance of clinical observation was not regarded to be as creditable as verification of a hypothesis in a controlled laboratory setting. W. F. Connell, a historian of education, concluded that Montessori did "not experiment" in the true scientific sense. She failed to select "appropriate samples of children" and "control the variables" in her experiments. Further, Connell judged her educational conclusions to be based on anecdotes rather than on carefully "controlled experimentation." Critically, he assessed her work as a "curious mixture of perceptive and liberal ideas with traditional and mystical nonsense."[91]

As with most educational movements, however, there was a struggle to control the Montessori method. There was Montessori, who was determined that the movement was to be controlled by her alone. There was the journalist S. S. McClure, who sought to exploit it as a means of reviving his sagging magazine and personal finances. Further, like any movement, there were rival factions jockeying for control in the Montessori Education Association (MEA).[92] When Montessori left the United States in 1915, she authorized the establishment of the National Montessori Promotion Fund, with herself as president and with Helen Parkhurst (1887–1973) as its chief on-site administrator. The Montessori Education Association, under Mrs. Alexander Graham Bell, continued to function. Tensions developed between the fund and the association, which seemed to have a dual but unclear role in promoting the method. In 1916, the association voted to dissolve. Finally, there were tensions between Parkhurst and Montessori. Parkhurst left the fund and abandoned Montessorianism to develop her own version of child-centered progressivism, the Dalton plan. Montessori, who did not take kindly to revisionists, regarded Parkhurst as a betrayer.[93]

The entry of the United States into World War I caused a shift in interest from European educational ideas to ways to mobilize the country for victory against the kaiser. By 1917, the first wave of enthusiasm for Montessorianism was ebbing severely. The Montessori method did not make significant inroads into colleges of education at leading universities, and it did not enter into the mainstream of American teacher education at the very time when education was being firmly established as a field in American universities. Neither did it enter in any significant way into public schools in the United States. The Montessori school would be located at the periphery of the public educational system, but it would later come to occupy a major sector of the private part of that periphery. It would not be until the 1950s that a second and much more substantial wave of Montessorianism occurred in the United States. This second American Montessori movement would lead to the establishment of hundreds of Montessori schools throughout the United States.

Montessori Education as a Worldwide Movement

In the United Kingdom, Montessorianism fared better than it did in the United States. As in the case of Americans, a number of British teachers journeyed to Rome to be trained as directresses by Montessori. A British Montessori Society was established in 1912 to promote the method. In 1919, Montessori made an extended trip to the United Kingdom, where she supervised a training course, lectured, and attended numerous receptions and meetings in her honor. English-language translations of Montessori's books attracted a wide readership. By the 1920s, a large number of Montessori schools and classes were functioning in the United Kingdom.

As in the United States, a number of critics appeared after the initial enthusiasm had waned. While some British educators remained committed to Montessori education, others attacked the method as being culturally and aesthetically deficient. Additionally, Montessori insisted that only she could train Montessori teachers, and she aimed to keep personal control of the movement. However, the Montessori method persisted as a force in British early childhood education, especially in the private sector of schooling.

On the European continent, the Montessori method registered more substantial gains than in the United Kingdom and the United States. Municipal officials in Barcelona, Spain, supported by the Catalon regional government, invited Montessori to come to Spain in 1916 to lecture and establish schools. The Escola Montessori, with infant and primary departments for three- to ten-year-olds; and the Seminari Laboratori de Pedagogia, an institute for teaching, research, and training in the Montessori method were established and supported by the Catalan government.[94] Additionally, there were two public Montessori schools, one established by the regional government and one by the municipal authorities. Spain was Montessori's principal base of operations from 1916 to 1927. In 1924, the authoritarian government of Primo de Rivera, seeking to suppress the Catalonian movement for autonomy, closed the model Montessori school in Barcelona. When the second republic was established, in 1932, the new government sponsored a Montessori international training course in Barcelona. When the Spanish civil war broke out in 1936, Montessori, generally a nonpolitical person, left Spain.

In 1917, during her first visit to the Netherlands, Montessori presented a lecture to the Pedagogical Society of Amsterdam. The establishment of the Netherlands Montessori Society followed her visit. In 1920, she gave a series of lectures at the University of Amsterdam. Later on, she would make the Netherlands the center for Montessori education and establish the headquarters of the Association Montessori Internationale in Amsterdam.

In 1922, Benito Mussolini and his Fascists marched on Rome and established a Fascist regime in Italy. Mussolini's intense Italian nationalism drew the support of some leading Italian intellectuals, such as the idealist philosopher Giovanni Gentile (1875–1944).[95] In Gentile's interpretation of idealism, the overarching idea of the nation-state embraced and surmounted all the individuals within it. His emphasis on the paramount role of the nation-state attracted him to Mussolini's Fascist ideology, which glorified and exalted the total state as the sum of all human loyalties. In 1923, Mussolini appointed Gentile minister of education. As president of the Supreme Council of Public Education from 1926 to 1928, he influenced the direction of education in Fascist Italy. Gentile's emphasis on children's self-education, or auto-education, caused him to look favorably on the Montessori method. Gentile, along with Queen Margherita, was interested in promoting the Montessori method in Italy.

Through the auspices of Gentile, Mussolini and Montessori met in 1924, and the duce expressed an interest and commitment in establishing Montessori schools. It is assumed that Mussolini was interested in a method that he believed instilled discipline and order and in which children learned to read and write at age four. He also wanted to use Montessori's name and her associations and societies in other countries to popularize his Fascist ideology. Montessori, in turn, was receptive to receiving official support for her educational ideas. In 1926, Montessori was officially recognized by the Tessera Fascista, the Fascist women's organization, and was made an honorary member of the party.[96] The Ministry of Education officially appointed Montessori to conduct a six-month training course for Italian teachers in Milan. Mussolini accepted the honorary presidency of the course and authorized a subsidy for its support. In March 1927, Montessori and Mussolini met again in a private audience. There was more cooperation between Montessori and the Fascist government. The government advised the mayor of Rome to establish a Montessori training school. The government also supported a monthly publication, *L'Idea Montessori*. By 1929, the Italian government was sponsoring several Montessori enterprises, such as a training college in Rome (the Regia Scuola Magistrale di Metodo Montessori), a Montessori training course in Milan, and seventy infant and elementary classes in schools throughout Italy.[97]

The years 1929–1930 marked the high point of Montessori's educational work in Italy with the support of Mussolini's Fascist state. There was a six-month international training course in Rome in 1930 under the auspices of the Opera Montessori. Mussolini accepted the presidency of the fifteenth International Theoretical and Practical Training Course on Child Education, with Gentile as acting president. Mussolini intended to use the international Montessori course to showcase modern Italian culture and education.[98] However, Mussolini, like McClure, had not counted on meeting the firm resolve of Maria Montessori and her determination to control her own method of education and keep it as she had designed it.

In 1929, Montessori and her son, Mario, established the Association Montessori Internationale (AMI) to control and supervise Montessori activities, including training programs, throughout the world. Montessori sought to unite all the Montessori movements throughout the world in a single international organization. At first the AMI met in a concurrent conference with the New Education Fellowship, an organization of progressive and innovative educators. After 1933, it met as a completely independent organization in the annual Montessori Congresses. Montessori was appointed lifetime president of the AMI, which was headquartered in Berlin until 1935 and then in Amsterdam. The AMI controlled rights to the publication of Montessori's books and the manufacture and sale of the materials and training course fees. Mario became her agent, protector, and representative. Both she and Mario insisted that there be no deviation from the approved pedagogical line that Montessori had instituted.[99]

Mussolini, whose slogan was "Everything in the State, nothing against the State, nothing outside the State" and who was growing steadily more totalitarian, was crushing opposition and coercing those suspected of dissent. He was determined to instill the Fascist ideology throughout Italy, including its schools and youth organizations.[100] Bent on instilling Fascism in Italy's children and youth, he established a number of Fascist children's and youth organizations. The Balilla was established for boys from eight to fourteen, and the Avanguardisti, for youth from fourteen to eighteen. Girls were enlisted in the Piccole Italiane. Dressed in uniforms, like the national Fascist militia, the children drilled and paraded through the streets of Italy's cities and villages. The Fascist regime was also tightening its control of Italy's schools, with all teachers required to take a loyalty oath.[101]

Cooperation between Mussolini's Fascist government and Montessori was always uneasy. Mussolini wanted to make political capital out of Montessori. Montessori, however, did not accept the Fascist ideology and viewed her role to be that of an international educator rather than a promoter of Italian nationalism. In fact, she believed that the child's nature and stages of development were universal and not determined by national, racial, or ethnic origins. In 1934, the Italian government, seeking to capture publicity, wanted to name Montessori as Italy's children's ambassador. Montessori refused to accept the appointment unless the Italian government recognized her as the sole authority of the AMI. The Fascist government responded to Montessori's intransigence by closing the Montessori schools and suppressing the movement.[102] Maria Montessori left Italy as an exile.

Montessori's brief involvement in Italy with Mussolini's Fascist regime shows her reluctance to become enmeshed in politics. Although she was an

economically and socially concerned educator who made connections between education and society, she was not politically attuned to, nor actively
involved in politics, as were Jane Addams and John Dewey. Montessori did
have some influential politically connected supporters throughout her career,
but she placed her method of education above politics and above nationality.

In discussing Montessori and politics, her own leadership style can be examined as internal and external to her educational movement. Her view of internal politics seems to be that of leader and disciple. She was the leader, always in firm in control of the Montessori method and movement. For
example, only she could train and officially certify approved Montessori directresses. Only she could approve the manufacture of official didactic materials. Those who joined her cause had to accept her style of leadership and the
supervision that came with it. For her, leading an educational movement did
not mean being a negotiator involved with transactions among her followers.

In terms of external politics, she accepted official government financial support for her training centers and schools but would not accept government control or interference. While she took official government support, she would not
lend her name, nor her method, to political party politics or ideologies. In
Barcelona, she was supported by the municipal government and the Catalon regional government but stayed aloof from the politics of regional autonomy and
separatism. In the Vienna of the 1920s, socialists operated the leading Montessori school, but Montessori did not espouse socialism. In Italy, she accepted
Fascist support, met with Mussolini, and received official recognition from the
regime; but she did not accept Fascist ideology, and she rejected political control. While Jane Addams served on the Chicago Board of Education and organized her ward politically and while John Dewey was closely identified with
progressivism and liberalism, Montessori was not directly involved in partisan
political activities. The Montessori movement and method were not tied to a
particular ideological or political persuasion. When she did get involved in political conflict, as in Italy in 1934, it was when she believed political authorities
such as the Italian Fascists were interfering in the application of her method.
She believed her method transcended and was above politics.

Believing that she had developed a truly global method of education,
Montessori was an international presence who traveled the world to promote
her method of education. She conducted training classes and addressed conferences in Italy, the United States, the Netherlands, Spain, France, the United
Kingdom, Ireland, India, and other countries. Living through two world wars,
she argued that the true way to peace would come as children were educated
in the ways of peace.

For Montessori, children have a nature that is universal, as are the periods
of human development. Although cultural contexts have some conditioning

significance, what Montessori claimed was that her discovery of the nature of childhood and her method of early childhood education are universal, not culturally relative or culturally determined. Individuals go through the same process of development everywhere, regardless of place or clime. Thus, the Montessori method is transnational and transcultural. Its application may be conditioned by the cultural context, but it is not dependent on it nor is it determined by it. Although different cultural settings might require slight adaptation, Montessori believed her method could function in any culture because of the universality of human and child nature. She stated,

> There is no sense in talking about differences of procedure for Indian babies, Chinese babies, or European babies; nor for those belonging to different social classes. We can speak of one method; that which follows the natural unfolding of man. All babies have the same psychological needs, and follow the same sequence of events, in attaining to human stature. Every one of us has to pass through the same phases of growth.[103]

In 1936, Montessori, accompanied by her son, Mario, moved her educational activities in the Netherlands, making Amsterdam the headquarters of the Association Montessori Internationale. It was from this location that she continued her worldwide activities, addressing Montessori congresses and conferences, lecturing, and conducting training classes.

In October 1939, Montessori, at age sixty-nine, traveled to India to conduct a training school sponsored by the Theosophical Society at Adyar, in Madras. When Italy, a member of the Axis, invaded France and entered World War II in 1940 on the side of the Germans, Italian nationals in Great Britain and its colonies were interned. Montessori, an Italian national, was not actually interned by the British authorities in India but was confined to the compound of the Theosophical Society. The British easily decided that Montessori posed no security threat, and they released her to carry on her educational activities in India.[104] She was in India during the war years, and as a result many of her books were published by Indian publishers.

When World War II ended, Montessori returned to Europe, arriving on July 30, 1946, in Amsterdam, at the AMI headquarters. She continued to give training courses. In 1947, she returned to Italy, at the invitation of the government, to reestablish the Opera Montessori and help reopen Montessori schools.

In July 1947, Mario, divorced from his first wife, married Ada Pierson, who had cared for his children in the Netherlands during World War II while he was with his mother in India. The aging Montessori delegated many of the administrative responsibilities of the international society to Mario, who was her trusted confidant and aide. Maria Montessori died on May 6, 1952, in

Noorwijk aan Zee, a small village near The Hague, and was buried in the local Catholic cemetery.

Revival of Montessori Education in the United States

In 1925, there were one thousand Montessori schools in the United States. After this peak period, Montessorianism in the United States experienced a sharp decline, and only a few schools continued to operate. Then, in the mid-1950s, the Montessori method enjoyed a significant revival in the United States. Throughout the world, there was a growing interest in early childhood education. In the United States, working parents explored various kinds of play schools, day care, and early childhood agencies. Parents who were seeking a more academically oriented early-childhood school rediscovered Montessori's method as a viable alternative to what was available in many public school kindergartens or progressive private schools. Indeed, by the mid-1950s, progressive education, which had eclipsed the first attempt to introduce the Montessori method in 1914 to 1918, was on the defensive and declining. A major leader in launching the American Montessori revival was Nancy McCormick Rambusch, founder of the Whitby School, in Greenwich, Connecticut. Although deeply committed to Montessori's philosophy of early childhood education, Rambusch believed that the method needed to be modernized to incorporate new developments in education. Those who wanted a more up-to-date Americanized version of Montessorianism organized the American Montessori Society in 1960. By the end of the 1950s, over two hundred Montessori schools and several large training schools were functioning.[105] The AMI, headed by Mario Montessori, was critical of the American version of the method, on the grounds that it had departed from the founder's original ideas and philosophy.

In the second wave of Montessori education in the United States, the demand for Montessori schools exceeded the supply of trained Montessori directresses. As a result, schools and teacher preparation programs proliferated without any one set of accreditation standards. While some schools held closely to Montessori's original method, others were more flexible about making adaptations. The two organizations that provide recognition to Montessori schools are the Association Montessori Internationale (AMI) and the American Montessori Society (AMS). In the 1960s, the Montessori method gained a further impetus during President Lyndon Johnson's "Great Society" initiative in the "war against poverty." Part of the antipoverty legislation was directed toward providing compensatory education programs for poverty-affected children. Some "Operation Head Start" programs, designed to provide early learning experiences for socially and culturally disadvantaged children, adopted the Montessori approach. This use of the Montessori method was a return to its original purpose at the first Casa dei Bambini, in Rome's San Lorenzo district.

As of 2003, approximately six thousand Montessori schools are operating in the United States. Most of these schools are nonpublic institutions that primarily enroll children between the ages of two and six. The majority of schools offer early childhood and primary programs. A few schools offer programs for intermediate and upper-grade pupils. There has been a recent but still limited movement of the Montessori method into the public school sector, with some five hundred Montessori magnet schools, or divisions, operating.[106] The recent trend to charter schools has aided interested groups of parents and teachers to establish Montessori schools in public school districts.

Conclusion

Maria Montessori made a significant contribution to educational theory and practice, especially to early childhood education. In particular, she called attention to the formative significance of the early years of childhood on later development. She was a significant voice in the period from 1910 to 1920, when such ideas were generally ignored or rejected. She anticipated and led what is now the current movement to provide more and earlier educational opportunities for children. Seeking to provide early childhood with a scientific, rather than a speculative philosophical foundation, Montessori's work provided new insights and stimulated research into children's nature, their stages of development, and the educative role of the environment; furthermore, it stimulated the growing worldwide interest in early childhood education. Among Maria Montessori's enduring contributions to education are, first, the clear recognition of the significance of early stimulation on later learning, especially its implications for socially and economically disadvantaged children; second, the concept of sensitive periods, or phases of development, when certain activities and materials are appropriate to learning specific motor and cognitive skills; third, the recognition that learning is complex and multifaceted and involves a variety of experiences; and fourth, the recognition that the school must be part of the community and must involve parents, if instruction is to be most effective.

Much of this preceding introduction of the Montessori method to the United States focused on her biography and the first wave of Montessorianism in America, from 1910 to 1920. Today, the implementation of Montessori education in the United States, witnessed by the hundreds of well-attended Montessori schools functioning throughout the country, provide definite evidence of its success. However, the initial efforts to introduce Montessorianism had a short period of optimistic success, but then floundered. The shortfall of the first attempt can be explained by several factors. First, the origins of Montessori's method came from her work in medicine and the treatment of mentally deficient children, rather than from the leading developments in educational psychology, Freudian psychoanalysis, or the progressive education associated with John Dewey. The roots of her theory were not those that dominated mainstream twentieth-century education. Kindergarten advocates took other paths, instead of Montessori's, to modify the doctrines of Friedrich Froebel. Child-centered progressives, such as her critic William H. Kilpatrick, relied heavily on Dewey's experimentalism and faulted the Montessori method as inadequate in the group-based projects that developed children's socialization, creativity, and problem-solving skills. Second, Montessori herself carefully guarded and protected her method, insisting that only she could properly prepare teachers. She rebuffed those who sought to create a more flexible pattern of the Montessori method. Montessori was convinced that her ideas would be distorted unless they were practiced exactly as she had developed them. The price paid for this doctrinal purity was the association of a certain doctrinaire rigidity with Montessori.[107] As a result, the Montessori method had only a slight impact on public schooling and a limited influence on professional teacher education in the United States. However, in the private sector of education, the second wave of Montessorianism, after 1950, has been a resounding success. Montessori may have lost the first battle in introducing the method to the United States, but has since won the war.

As a person, Montessori occupies a place in educational biography that is somewhat like that of Jane Addams. Maria Montessori, like Addams, was a woman who wanted to shape her own destiny and life. Both lived at a time when women's careers were largely other determined, either by custom and tradition or the prescriptions of a male-defined society. Maria Montessori determined early in her life that she would be a self, rather than an other-determined person. As a student of medicine and as a world-famous educator, she broke new pathways not only for herself but for other women as well.

THE MONTESSORI METHOD

Maria Montessori's *The Montessori Method* was a highly significant book in bringing her educational philosophy and method to a worldwide audience. It moved the Montessori method out of its local context, Italy, and made it a force on the worldwide educational scene. Its English translation stimulated the founding of a national Montessori organization and the establishment of Montessori schools in the United States. It was a key element in Montessori's American lecture tours.

A blending of autobiography, educational philosophy, and teaching methods, Montessori's book was her story. She told of how she had arrived at her theory, how it was implemented in the first Casa dei Bambini, and how her method could be implemented. In addition to its educational significance, Montessori's book was also a commentary on the social and economic changes that were affecting women, children, and families in the early twentieth century.

The Montessori Method can be examined in terms of, first, Montessori's early career as a medical physician, educational theorist, and practitioner; second, the method as educational theory and practice; and, third, its larger historical and contemporary significance.

Montessori as Physician and Educator

Montessori's education in medicine at the University of Rome introduced her to the scientific method and to the importance of clinical observation of patients. These elements would become highly important in her development of the Montessori method. Montessori's grounding in the scientific method caused her to begin her work in education from a base in fields directly related to medicine, such as physiology, anatomy, and pathology. She would later broaden her scientific repertoire to include social sciences, such as psychology and anthropology. It is important to note that Montessori sought to create a scientific pedagogy, a method of education based on science.

In seeking to develop "scientific pedagogy," Montessori devised her method and operated from what she regarded to be the scientific method. It is necessary, however, to analyze the definition of science. Montessori construed science to be a method of discovering truths about education; once these truths had been discovered, they were to be perfected. Science, for her, was not a critical, relativistic method of inquiry, but rather provided a means of finding the truth.

Montessori advised educators that empirically generated scientific findings were a means to an end—an interpretive means—rather than the end itself. Educators were to use science as a mode of investigation and interpretation but were not to become limited by scientific or empirical literalness. For example, she commented that children's measurements were used to design desks to correct curvature of the spine. However, this literalness had the consequence of confining children to scientifically designed but rigid and unmovable desks, which limited their freedom to move.[108]

Drawing upon physical anthropology, Montessori regarded the human being as a biological organism who could be studied quantitatively and scientifically. She was especially interested in applying anthropometry, a subfield of physical anthropology, which stressed the measurement of human physical characteristics through a variety of apparatus and the detailed recording of these observations. Montessori applied physical anthropology and anthropometry to her work with children. Children were to be periodically measured and weighed, with attention paid to the size and shape of head, face, pelvis, limbs, and any malformations. These findings were carefully recorded in an individualized record, a "biographical chart," to be jointly maintained by the teacher, a pediatrician, and a psychologist; and to be shared with parents. Scientific pedagogy, she advised, required the methodical study of children, informed by pedagogical anthropology and experimental psychology. She advised teachers to "make the anthropological study of the pupil precede his education."[109] However, she warned that the experimental study of children is not the same as their education; it is rather a guide to their education.[110]

Closely allied to her use of the scientific method, as she conceived of it, Montessori used clinical observation. In her medical training, she had learned clinically to observe patients to diagnose illnesses, prescribe treatment, and document recovery. As she turned to educational research, Montessori applied the tool of clinically observing children to find out when and how they learned. In her discussion of education, Montessori's medical training and use of clinical observation were clearly evident. Before discussing sensory education related to sound, for example, she first discussed the anatomy and physiology of the ear. Only then would she turn to educating the sense of hearing.

Montessori's first observations were with mentally impaired children, then labeled as mental defectives. When she had success in training these children to achieve some degree of independence, Montessori then turned her observation to normal children. She concluded that the materials used to train mentally impaired children could be used to educate normal children. More accurately stated, these materials could be used by the children who were actually educating themselves.

From her integration of science and clinical observation, Montessori moved to still larger and broader generalizations about early childhood education and education in general. Montessori saw herself as a pioneer in a new field, "scientific pedagogy," which, like medicine and education, was freeing itself from speculative metaphysical philosophy and becoming a scientific discipline.[111] In early childhood and elementary education, in particular, she had to find sources that were different from the largely philosophically based theories of those regarded as the great European educators—Comenius, Rousseau, Pestalozzi, Froebel, and Herbart.

Montessori's emphasis on clinical observation led her to one of her most important educational principles: the freedom of children to act to achieve their own growth and development. If clinical observation was to be a source of valid findings about children's behavior, it needed to be free from unnecessary adult constraints so children could act on their own needs and inter-ests.[112] For Montessori, clinical observation and early childhood education were to be guided by one necessary principle: "the liberty of the pupils in their spontaneous manifestations."[113]

Although she emphasized children's liberty, Montessori did not construe the child's freedom to be a romanticized Rousseauean absent of all controls. It did not mean "doing your own thing." For Montessori, the child's liberty meant the freedom to act within a structured environment. Not an end in it-self, a child's freedom was rather a means in child study, which in turn in-formed the educator about children's behavioral and learning processes. So informed, the educator could use the insights gained to construct a prepared learning environment that provided materials, opportunities, and occasions for children to interact with the environment in an educative way. While Montessori was creating more pedagogical avenues for children to travel through, it needs to be stated that whoever controls the environment in which learning occurs places some limits on that freedom.

The Method as Educational Theory and Practice

As indicated in the previous section, Montessori's method of education was based on her conception of science, on her observations of children, and on her extensive research in anthropology, psychology, and pedagogy. From re-search and experience, she arrived at a series of "discoveries," or assump-tions, about children's growth, development, and education. To examine her method, we begin with Montessori's concept of the nature of the child as a learner.

Nature of the Child as a Learner

Though regarding her method as "scientific pedagogy," Montessori's concept of child nature was spiritual, indeed almost metaphysical. She claimed each child, at birth, possesses a psychic power, an inner self-teacher that stimulates learning. Children innately possess the interior power to absorb and assimilate many ele-ments of a complex culture without direct instruction.[114] Despite reaching into the spiritual to describe her concept of children's nature, Montessori sought to move away from abstract philosophical generalizations to the use of the scien-tific method to discover the patterns of children's development. By so doing, she could structure an educative environment and a set of instructional processes that fully accentuated the patterns of human growth and development.

For Montessori, the educative process embraced two key and necessary el-ements: the individual child and the environment. The primary element is the individual child's physiological and mental constitution, which gives her or him the power to act. As a real biological entity, the living child has a body, a physiological structure that grows and develops; however, each child also has a spiritual soul, a psychic form that manifests itself. The environment, the secondary element, provides the necessary milieu in which the human being develops. While the environment the child inhabits can modify development, it can never create a human being's primary physical and mental constitution. The child's education requires an environment in which he or she can develop the powers given by nature. Education then is a process of collaboration with the child's nature and stages of development.[115]

Through their interaction and involvement with the environment, children adapt to objects and situations encountered in the environment. Children's physiological and psychic powers move them to free activity in exploring the environment. These interactions and the information that they bring with them are then incorporated into the child's developing self, experience, and conceptual network.[116] It is imperative that children be free to act on their environment. Their free activity discloses the cues of child development to the educator, leading to the discoveries that make it possible to design a method of instruction.[117]

Unlike conventional educators who believed that children needed to have their interests shaped for them, Montessori contended that children naturally possessed a strong propensity and capacity for mental concentration. The key to exercising this self-activity came, however, from sources internal rather than external to the child. If they were truly interested in their activity, children would concentrate their attention and energy on it. They would stay with and continue to act on it until they had mastered the task.

Like her educational predecessors Rousseau, Pestalozzi, and Froebel, Montessori rejected the concept that children were innately disorderly and needed to have their willfulness curbed through strong external discipline. She firmly rejected the notion that children had to be prodded to learn by rewards and punishments. Montessori found that, rather than being disorderly, children actually desired order and strongly preferred to be in a structured environment. Montessori believed that, rather than diminish freedom, structure actually enhanced the child's freedom. In a structured learning environment, the ideas of place and space and expectations were clearly known by the children. Furniture and other items in their school space were made for them and accommodated to their size, rather than be imposed on them. If didactic apparatus and materials were in an accessible place, a child would make certain that their placement remained accessible by replacing them in their proper space in an orderly fashion.

Further, children were eager to master new skills. On their own initiative, they would keep at the task and continue to repeat it until they had mastered it. Children realized that the mastery of practical skills, such as tying a shoelace, buttoning a jacket, and putting on gloves and overshoes, without the help of an adult gave them freedom and independence. Montessori concluded that children did not have to be forced to learn and, if permitted to choose between work and play, would often choose the former. In such a learning climate, artificial rewards and punishments were not only unneeded but could distort the learning experience.

Montessori shared with Froebel a conviction that, while learning, children were unfolding, or externalizing, their true personality and humanness. However, the child's early years were of such crucial importance in setting the proper course for later learning that they should not be left to chance. As Froebel created his kindergarten, Montessori devised her school, a prepared environment for children's early learning, growth, and development.

At first glance, there appears to be a similarity between (a) the American progressives' emphasis on the freedom of the child and their basing education on the children's interests and needs and (b) Montessori's concept of the liberty of the child and respect for the spontaneity of children's actions. It may have been this appeared similarity that attracted some progressives to Montessori during the first wave of Montessorianism in the United States. However, the progressive view of the child, especially that of Dewey and the experimentalists, was quite different. Montessori defined children's nature as a combination of physiological and psychic powers and development. Her environment is a carefully prepared one in which the child is free to act within a structured setting. Montessori's structured environment is quite different from the progressive's open-ended environment. Dewey commented that the Montessori techniques "are so anxious to get at intellectual distinctions" that they ignore the "crude handling of familiar material" and that they introduce children to "material that expresses the intellectual distinctions" made by adults. He preferred the "trial and error" learning that results from the child's interaction with the material at hand.[118]

The Educational Process

Montessori defined education as a dynamic process in which children develop according to the "inner dictates" of their life, by their "voluntary work" when placed in an environment prepared to give them freedom of self-expression.[119] Children, she claimed, are naturally and energetically striving to achieve functional independence. An innate drive, which Montessori called a "divine urge," stimulates the child to self-activity to perform actions that promote growth, which leads to further development and greater independence.[120] For children, independence means being free to do the things that make them free of adult interference. For the child, it simply means being able to "do it all by myself." Montessori realized that appropriate adult intervention is needed at certain times but should decrease steadily as children learn how to do things for themselves. Independence, based on the freedom to be self-active, is the foundation for the values of perseverance at a task, persistence in doing something until it is done correctly, and satisfaction at a job well done—all desirable qualities in the independent adult with a sense of high self-esteem.

Montessori's philosophy of education requires a reformulation of the definition of a school. She defined a school as a prepared environment in which children are able to develop freely, at their own pace, unimpeded in the spontaneous unfolding of their natural capacities. The school's prepared environment enabled children, through the manipulation of a graded series of self-correcting didactic materials, to exercise and develop their senses and thinking and to reach greater independence.[121] Montessori stated, "The school must permit the free, natural manifestations of the child if in the school scientific pedagogy is to be born."[122]

Using her principles of "the liberty of the pupils in their spontaneous manifestations" and "liberty in activity," Montessori redesigned the classroom environment. She replaced the conventional classroom's rows of immovable standardized desks with lightweight, child-sized tables and chairs that the children could move about. Her classroom featured a series of accessible cupboards for the storage of materials that children could easily access. In her prepared educational environment, discipline (or classroom management) was redefined to no longer mean keeping children seated at their desks. It meant that the classroom's very structure and the directress's management style empowered pupils to control their own behavior. Montessori stated, "A room in which all the children move about usefully, intelligently, and voluntarily, without committing any rough or rude act, would seem to be a classroom very well disciplined indeed."[123]

Montessori's admonition that true learning comes from children's liberty to choose their work and to complete it also required a reformulation of what it meant to be a teacher. In conventional classrooms, teachers, usually at center stage, often struggle to motivate and engage a group of children who are at different levels of readiness and ability. They are forced to use various motivational devices to entice or coerce children to act as a group. Montessori believed that these various teacher-generated strategies to gain the attention and to engage a group of children often had the unintended effect of confusing and distracting them in ways that blunted the child's self-activity to learn.

The Montessori directress's role is to guide the children's learning without interfering with it. The directress's first requirement is to re-create the prepared environment so that the children have the appropriate setting in which to learn. While not imposing tasks or activities on the children, the directress clearly follows the ground rules based on Montessori's principles that govern the school. The directress is a diagnostician of each child's educational profile. She notes the child's physical development, previous learning, and readiness for new learning experiences; and she is aware of each child's special interests and needs. She is to ensure that the learning environment contains the materials and opportunities that excite children's desire to learn and become independent. She then guides, but does not push, each child to the appropriate activity, material, or apparatus.

In dealing with motivation, the educational psychologist J. M. Hunt credited Montessori with solving the "problem of the match." According to this problem, if the circumstances the child encounters are attractive and interesting yet sufficiently challenging to bring about accommodative changes that constitute learning, they must be matched to those "standards" the child has already developed in his or her experience. Montessori solved the problem by encouraging the individual child to follow his or her interests by working with a variety of graded didactic materials at his or her own pace. Since the child was free to select the material upon which to work, the child could follow personal interests and proceed from one level of complexity to a higher level one.[124]

In solving the "problem of the match," Montessori minimized "collective," or group, lessons, known as simultaneous instruction of a class or pupils at a single lesson. For Montessori, an overreliance on group instruction made the teacher act as a drill sergeant in that by her commands she tried to get all the children to all follow her orders as a unit. Montessori, in contrast, focused on the individual child, who by independent activities worked on her or his own task.

Stages of Development

Montessori's method rested on her principle that a child's education should grow out of and coincide with the child's own stages of development. She was convinced that children progressed through a series of developmental stages, each of which required an appropriate and specifically designed kind of learning.

For Montessori, each stage of human development was a psychic "rebirth," with one phase on the developmental sequence dramatically flowing into the next. She identified three major developmental periods: first, from birth to age six (the stage of the "absorbent mind"); second, from age six to twelve; third, from age twelve to eighteen. Montessori's first stage, the period of the "absorbent mind," was further subdivided into two subphases, from birth to age three and from age three to six. During the first stage, children, through environmental explorations, absorbed information, constructed their concepts about reality, began to use language, and entered into the larger world of their group's culture. During the second period, roughly coinciding with childhood, from age six to twelve, the skills and powers that had surfaced and were being developed in the first period were further exercised, reinforced, polished, and expanded. The third period, from age twelve to eighteen, coinciding with adolescence, was a time of great physical change, with the person's striving to reach full maturity. The third period was subdivided into two subphases, ages twelve to fifteen and fifteen to eighteen.[125] During the third period, the adolescent sought to understand social and economic roles and to find her or his place in society.

Although she developed an educational regimen for each of the three major developmental planes, her book *The Montessori Method* focused on the "sensitive periods," which were included in the period of the "absorbent mind." Montessori's use of the term "absorbent" reflected her belief that children in this stage were engaged primarily in absorbing sensory impressions and information from their environment. The impulse for this absorption was driven by the child's interior impulse to acquire this knowledge for self-development and for eventual independence. Since the content of the knowledge so absorbed depended heavily upon the learning possibilities found in the child's environment, it was very important to prepare or to structure the environment so that it contained the greatest possibilities for appropriate exploration and absorption. As they explored the environment, the information that children absorbed was clustered in the mind, around points of sensitivity. These points of sensitivity dealt with powers such as judging distances, making comparison, and developing language. These points of sensitivity stimulated children to identify a task, a particular kind of work, and to perform a certain series of actions with a sufficient duration to lead to its mastery. Thus, a connection was made between the sensitive point in the mind and the action being performed.[126]

The period of the "absorbent mind" was divided into an early phase, from age one to three, when the child's mind functions unconsciously and learning results from interacting with and responding to environmental stimuli. During this key period, children begin to construct their own personality and intelligence through their environmental explorations and the sensations they experience during these encounters. The children begin to acquire the language and culture into which they are born. During the later phase, from age three to six, the child is more conscious of and directive of his or her environmental explorations. Montessori characterized this second phase of the "absorbent mind" as a time of "constructive perfectionment," during which the child, through his or her own self-activity, deals consciously and deliberately with the environment. Montessori's use of the term "constructive" may sound similar to the current constructionist approach to curriculum in which children construct, or create, their own knowledge and their own concept of reality through interaction with the environment. For Montessori, however, children's interactions were not random activities but were the work necessary for independence.[127]

During the second phase of the "absorbent mind," from age three to six, the child needs to find the tasks or activities that stimulates her or his interest and needs to learn how to correctly perform the action to do it. The "perfectionment" aspect comes from the desire and need to do and accomplish tasks—the child's work—with a sense of precision. Children are especially attracted to manipulative tasks, with how to do things, which satisfies their need to coordinate and control their movements.

The child, involved in a piece of work, will repeat the same series of movements over and over until it is mastered. This repetition, Montessori asserted, was the means of establishing in his or her nervous system a new system of control that related mind and body, bringing about muscle coordination with the mental goal of completing the task. The repetitions fix the power of knowing that something is being done correctly, which in turn leads to the empowerment that leads to independent performance.

The period of the "absorbent mind," especially its second phase, from age three to six, is highly significant for later development and education. The repertoire of skills and the world that the child constructs lay the foundation for future learning. Indeed, the child's ways of moving and doing will become fixed for the rest of her or his life.[128]

The period of the "absorbent mind" is not only crucial for motor, skill, and cognitive development but also for establishing patterns for socialization and acculturation. Montessori believed that children, during early childhood, absorb the distinctive linguistic and cultural patterns of their cultural group. As they absorb their group's language by hearing it spoken, they simultaneously absorb its values, customs, morals, and religion. Language acquisition involves absorbing a pattern of speech. A pattern is a stable and precise framework in which the various pieces of language and culture are ordered into a whole. The patterns of language and the culture it conveys become part of the child's being. These cultural patterns, according to Montessori, represent the summarized part, the collective memory that is repeated in the habitual life—the traditions and customs—of a particular people. As an individual grows and matures, he or she will continue to develop and to make cultural and social adaptations and revisions to the patterns acquired in early childhood. However, any changes will take place in the network of cultural patterns already absorbed during early childhood.[129]

Progressive educators such as Kilpatrick, who followed John Dewey's experimentalist philosophy of education, criticized the Montessori method as lacking sufficient opportunities for children's socialization. While Dewey emphasized the child's participation and interaction with the group as giving rise to social intelligence, Montessori's view of socialization focused more on absorbing the existing culture and creating mental patterns based on that absorption. For both Dewey and Montessori, socialization came as a result of children's interaction with their environment, which contained a network of sociocultural relationships. The difference was that Dewey saw the child creating his or her own social relationships as a result of human association, or group-centered experience. For Montessori, the child's interaction with environment conveyed an existing cultural pattern to the child that might be altered in the future.

The Montessori Curriculum

The curriculum that Montessori emphasized in *The Montessori Method* was that during the period of the absorbent mind, the first six years of life. Her curriculum design was shaped by several sources: her view of scientific pedagogy, the influence of Itard and Seguin, her work with mentally defective children, and her application of her ideas to the general education of normal children. Montessori believed that the curriculum should be based on a true science of education, which involved information from the medical sciences and anthropology and the clinical observation of children. Her research into the education of children with special needs—physical, mental, and psychological—led her to the work of the French physicians Itard and Seguin. She adapted and reformulated their ideas, especially the materials developed by Seguin, to the education of children with special needs. The highly significant ideal that caused her to generalize her ideas into general education was that the materials used to train children with handicaps could be applied to normal children. Most important, however, normal children could use these materials in their own self-motivated and self-directed "auto-education." For the normal child, the didactic material controls every error, and the child works to correct his or her errors until the task is done correctly.

During the various stages of her work that led to the publication of *The Montessori Method*, Montessori devised her basic curriculum. As discussed, to be used appropriately and effectively, the curriculum needed to be situated in a prepared structured environment. The children, within this environment, were to be free to explore it and select the materials upon which they would work. Within the prepared environment, the materials and activities of the curriculum were those that related to practical life skills; sensory education; language and mathematics; and more general physical, social, and cultural development.

Practical Life Skills

An important aim of the Montessori philosophy is that children are to have the freedom they need for their own self-development. To be free means that one has the power, the skill, to do what is necessary to live. For children, this freedom meant that they would gain the knowledge and skill, based on their particular readiness and stage of development, to perform the tasks of practical life. The practical life skills include a range of activities designed to develop the child's independence and self-reliance. The activities include those tasks that are part of living as a member of a family in a home (setting the table, serving food, doing dishes, cleaning up after a meal); those required for personal cleanliness and hygiene (washing the face and hands, brushing teeth); and those needed to dress oneself (buttoning smocks and lacing and tying shoes). Special didactic apparatus—lacing and tying frames—gave children an opportunity to practice a particular skill. Included in the practical life skills were muscular exercises related to physiological development, such as motor coordination, walking, and respiratory skills. By repetitive trials, they learned to stay with a particular skill until they had mastered it. Through the practical life activities, the children develop muscular coordination and learn to persevere in mastering a task.

Sensory Skills

The sensory materials and activities are designed to develop the child's sensory acuity and ability. By using specially designed apparatus and materials, children learn to order, classify, and compare sensory impressions by touching, seeing, smelling, tasting, listening, and feeling the physical properties of the objects in the environment. Sensory skills include those related to sound and the ability to distinguish between tones; those related to sight and the ability to recognize and distinguish color, hue, and shading; and those related to touch and the ability to feel texture, softness, hardness, cold, and warmth. Again specialized didactic apparatus and materials were used, such as cylinders, tone bells, stacking blocks, materials of various colors, and so on. Montessori's sensory education activities had three projected outcomes: first, improve children's sensory abilities by exercising their powers of discrimination; second, improve children's general sensory functions; third, develop children's readiness to perform more complicated activities.[130]

Language Skills

Montessori believed that language, as an instrument of human collective thought, was the human power that transformed the raw environment into civilization. While all humans possessed the general power to absorb and acquire language, a particular language was the key element in defining and making a particular human group distinct. As with other elements in the environment, children absorb language.[131]

Language development, which Montessori distinguished from language teaching, is a spontaneous creation of the child. Regardless of the particular language used in the child's culture, language development follows the same patterns for all children. All children pass through a period in which they can only pronounce syllables, then whole words, and then they begin to use syntax and grammar.[132] Language learning came from work with sounds and letters. Letters were cut out and mounted on sandpaper outlines that the children could trace and pronounce phonetically. The children composed words by using the letters of a movable alphabet. Montessori claimed that children burst spontaneously into writing and reading.

Arithmetic was taught by the manipulation of geometrically shaped objects, by using rods of various lengths and by organizing quantities of objects in counting boxes. As in learning the letters, children traced sandpaper-covered numbers.

Physical, Social, and Cultural Skills

More general physical, social, and cultural skills were acquired through individualized physical activities, through shared responsibilities in carrying for plants and animals, and through the creating of a generalized respect for one's own work and for the work of others. Again, children themselves developed an awareness of the larger world in which they lived. As they give order to the sensory information that they have absorbed, they grow increasingly aware that they need more knowledge about the larger world in which they live.

Value Formation and Character Education

Although she recognized that discussions of moral education generated controversy, Montessori believed that an almost universal consensus existed on what constitutes good character. Her assumption rested on her commitment to universal values. Deep within human nature, she stated, there was power, a tendency that moved people to seek the higher spiritual values. This power, intrinsically lodged in human nature, motivated people to search for spiritual improvement.[133] Montessori's belief in universal values most likely was a product of her Catholic upbringing. Her views on the universality of human nature and values sharply contrasted those of Dewey, Kilpatrick, and other progressive educators who argued that value formation was culturally relative and conditioned by the time, place, and circumstances of human life.

Turning to moral education, Montessori found that most prescriptions about character formation were made for and by adults without a genuine consideration of the child's nature and development. Genuine moral education follows a natural sequence, she argued, and it is attuned to the child's stages of development. Just as she ties motor and cognitive skill development to the stages of development, Montessori used the same format to examine character education. Eliding character formation to the major periods of development, Montessori identified three significant phases:

1. From birth to six years, the period of the absorbent mind, when the small child has no sense of right and wrong and lives outside of adults' moral prescriptions.
2. From six to twelve years, when children begin to be conscious of right and wrong in terms of their own and other's actions; a sense of moral consciousness is being formed, which leads to group and social values.
3. From twelve to eighteen, when the adolescent develops a love of country and a sense of national identity.

When a child successfully and appropriately experiences each period, the moral and social foundation is established for the one following it. The more fully that the needs of one period are met, the greater the success of the next.[134]

As she formulated her method at the Casa dei Bambini, Montessori was most involved in the moral education of young children, those of the first period, from birth to age six. During this period, the children's character formation, like their cognitive and skill development, requires the freedom to engage with the environment. The moral sense develops according to the successes experienced in surmounting obstacles and mastering challenges that occur in this interaction. During this crucial period, children undergo experiences that shape their personalities and their character. If they have been injured, if they have experienced cruelty and violence, or if they have faced obstacles beyond their readiness to deal with them, negative personality deviations may result. If they meet with challenges appropriate to their development and have the freedom provided by the structured learning environment, they are likely to develop positive self-esteem and a healthy personality.[135]

Again, Montessori, drawing from her medical background, emphasized the importance of clinical observation to detect deviations in the child's development, which could be corrected by education. Key events and influences on the child are to be noted, recorded, and traced back to when they occurred. There are constitutionally strong children who resist and overcome the obstacles they meet, and there are weaker children who fall victim to unfavorable conditions. As with skill and other kinds of learning, Montessori reiterated the importance of the prepared educational environment in repairing earlier psychological and emotional damage. The prepared environment is especially curative in that it encourages the child to act spontaneously and freely, to select the task, and to build self-esteem by meeting and mastering the challenges found in the safe learning setting.

Unlike the prepared environment of the Montessori school, Montessori found that conventional schools, which group children into classes for simultaneous instruction, typically organize students into three categories: first, those whose defects clearly require remediation; second, those who appear to be good, obedient, and docile and are identified as exemplary pupils but are really passive rather than active learners; third, those thought to be superior and gifted. Conventional teachers typically consider the passive child, who causes "no trouble," to be the most desirable type of student. While they claim to enjoy working with gifted children, they often find them to be too challenging.

Montessori argues against this conventional classification, which is based on organizing instruction on gross categories of children rather than on individual learners. In contrast, the Montessori method is attuned to the education of the individual child, who, while in a group setting, independently pursues his or her own work. Rather than confining children in categories ranging from those who need remediation to those who are gifted, she argued that there is really only one type of child—the child who is free to explore the environment and spontaneously choose and engage in activities that lead to independence.

Moral education, like cognitive and skill learning, relates to the general topic of discipline, or the teacher's style of classroom management. In conventional classrooms, teachers continually strive to motivate students to keep them interested in the lessons being presented. Failing to motivate them, teachers often turn to using rewards and punishments, or even to more coercive methods—sometimes threatening or actually inflicting physical or psychological punishment.

Montessori, in contrast, argued that true discipline is self-discipline. Since children in the prepared Montessori environment are free to follow their interests in choosing their work, they are self-motivated. It is within the context of the learner's freedom of activity that genuine self-discipline occurs. The child's liberty is limited only when it interferes with the collective interest and freedom of other children. Rewards and punishments are unnecessary. Rather than being teacher managed, the children in the Montessori school are self-managed and self-disciplined. Children, working in freedom and being absorbed in completing and mastering self-selected tasks, create their own self-discipline.[136] It is this self-discipline and self-control that leads to positive character development.

Montessori viewed self-discipline as a path that leads to continuing and ongoing character formation. On the path to discipline, the child has a "mental grasp" of the idea that begins the repetition—the successive actions—needed to accomplish the task. When children master a challenge by performing the needed repeated activities, they are training their own positive willpower; they are harnessing their own powers of moral development. Real discipline, she stated, comes through activity directed to spontaneous work in which the child, through his or her own efforts (often repetitive ones), accomplishes his task.

Discipline, according to Montessori, related to the child's own selfhood, as a person in the process of self-formation, and to the child's social relationships and responsibilities. Her principle of "collective order" explained her concept of the evolving ethical relationship of the individual to others. The concept of "collective order" implied that the child was developing a sensitivity to achieving a balance between the behaviors and activities appropriate for individual expression and those needed for group order and social life. She used the metaphor of musicians in an orchestra to illustrate the relationship between individual freedom of performance and collective order. The musicians need to be individually competent in playing their instruments, but they also need to act as an orchestra, a collective association, in following the voiceless commands of the conductor.[137]

Working to master external challenges stimulates the child's sense of accomplishment and independence. The first dawning of real discipline comes through work—activity directed to spontaneous work, which leads to self-discipline. To be effectively disciplined, the child must be able to differentiate between good and evil. The teacher's challenge is to ensure that the child does not confuse good with immobility, and evil with activity.

Montessori distinguished her concept of children's freedom from that of overly permissive educators who consider children's freedom to be an end rather than a means. The overly permissive educators are often disciples of the wildly romantic Rousseau, or they are neo-Freudians who believe children should be free from repressions. They are also child-centered progressives who continue to battle against the restrictions they themselves felt in their own Victorian childhoods. The overly permissive educator believes that children should be totally liberated from repressive regulations and that there should be no corrections nor submission to authority. Romantic permissiveness, unguided by scientific pedagogy, often causes a chaotic release of childish impulses that are no longer controlled as they once were by adults. For Montessori, this kind of permissiveness to "let the child do as he likes," when no powers of control have been developed, violates the true idea of freedom.[138]

Genuine freedom is a consequence of development, aided by education, as children actively construct their own personalities through their own self-active sustained work. The key to moral development comes from "concentration" on a piece of work. Concentration requires children to use objects for the purposes for which they were designed. In so doing, the child develops the sense that thought (the idea in mind) is related to action and that actions have consequences. Not only does this performance lead to the motor coordination of physical movements, but it simultaneously motivates the child to stay with a task and to meet and surmount a challenge. Concentration stimulates the development of the value of perseverance, using repetition to carry through, to complete the task that was begun.[139] As Montessori stated, "The essential thing is for the task to arouse such an interest that it engages the child's whole personality." Children, whose moral sensitivity is developing normally, demonstrate spontaneous discipline, continuous and happy work, and social sentiments of help and sympathy for others.[140]

An interesting difference can be noted in (a) Montessori's view of the correct use of an object and an activity related to it and (b) Dewey's experimentalism and Kilpatrick's progressivism. Montessori's operational premise was that an object possessed an antecedent structure that defined it and its proper use. Correct concentration, the key to developing the moral character, meant that the child was to perform an activity on the object correctly. The Montessori didactic materials were designed to be self-correcting. If the child did not perform an exercise correctly, he or she would fail in the task. Only as the child used the material correctly would the task be accomplished, with success in doing something right as its own reward. For Dewey and Kilpatrick and other experimentalist progressives, objects were instrumentally open to a variety of uses; their definition came from their practical use, rather than from their intrinsic nature. For the progressive educators, children exercised their creativity by designing innovative ways of using objects. For Kilpatrick, Montessori's concepts of concentration on an object and using it in a predetermined way were actually obstacles to the child's creativity. In contrast, Montessori believed children will focus first on an object involved in an activity and then on the knowledge derived from exploring and using it. The child becomes absorbed in seeing how a thing is made and learning how it works or functions. According to Montessori:

To know, to love and to serve is the trinomial of all religions, but the child is the true maker of our spirituality. He teaches us the plan of nature for giving form to our conduct and character, a plan fully traced out in all its details of age and work, with its need for freedom and intense activity in accordance with the laws of life. What matters is not physics, or botany, or works of the hand, but the will, and the components of the human spirit which construct themselves by work. The child is the spiritual builder of mankind, and obstacles to his free development are the stones in the wall by which the soul of man has become imprisoned.[141]

NOTES

1. Rita Kramer, *Maria Montessori: A Biography*, 22–24.
2. Freire, *Pedagogy of Freedom*, 32–33.
3. Justman, *The Italian People and Their Schools,* 24.
4. Kramer, *Maria Montessori: A Biography*, 33.
5. Kramer, *Maria Montessori: A Biography,* 34–35.
6. Gitter, *The Montessori Way,* 7.
7. Kramer, *Maria Montessori: A Biography,* 55.
8. Jules Michelet (1798–1874) was a noted French historian and writer who headed the historical section of the national archives and was professor of history at the College de France. His major work was the multivolume *Histoire de France* (1833–1867).
9. Pierre Joseph Proudhon (1809–1865) was a radical socialist theorist who developed the political ideology of syndicalism. He attacked private property, particularly capitalism, claiming that it was a system that exploited the working classes. He believed that humankind could make sufficient ethical progress so that government would wither away. His most important work is *The Philosophy of Poverty* (1846).
10. Cesare Lombroso (1835–1909), a leading Italian criminologist and physician who pioneered in the field of criminal anthropology, was professor of criminal anthropology at the University of Turin. He sought to develop a scientific approach to studying criminology using empirical data, such as skull measurements and facial structures. Although Montessori disagreed with Lombroso's view of women, she was influenced by his contributions to the scientific study of anthropology. Lombroso's most important work was *L'uomo delinquente* (1896–1897).
11. Giuseppe Sergi was a professor of anthropology at the University of Rome, where he established the influential Institute of Experimental Psychology. Sergi's development of physical anthropology, especially his emphasis on the laboratory method of science, influenced Montessori.
12. Kramer, *Maria Montessori: A Biography,* 79–81.
13. Kramer, *Maria Montessori: A Biography,* 48.
14. Two accounts of Itard's experiment with the wild boy of Aveyron were published: *De l'education d'un homme sauvage ou des premiers developpements physiques et moraux du jeune sauvage de l'Aveuron* (1801) and *Rapport sur les*

nouveaux developpements et l'etat actuel du sauvage de l'Aveyron (1807). For an English version, see Itard, *The Wild Boy of Aveyron.*

15. Itard's major work was the two-volume *Traite des maladies de l'oreille et de l'audition* (1821).

16. Seldin, "Montessori," 1676.

17. Maria Montessori, *The Montessori Method*, 33–34.

18. Seguin's major work was *Traitement Moral, Hygiene et Education des Idiots,* which was published in France in 1846. After his immigration to the United States, it was republished in English in 1886 as *Idiocy and Its Treatment by the Physiological Method.*

19. Kathrina Myers, "Seguin's Principles of Education," 538–41.

20. Maria Montessori, *The Montessori Method*, 37.

21. Kramer, *Maria Montessori: A Biography,* 73–76.

22. Maria Montessori, *The Montessori Method*, 44.

23. Kramer, *Maria Montessori: A Biography,* 92–93.

24. Kramer, *Maria Montessori: A Biography,* 185.

25. For Rousseau's theory of natural education, see Rousseau, *Emile, or On Education;* for a biography, see Cranston, *The Noble Savage.*

26. For Pestalozzi's philosophy of education, see Pestalozzi, *How Gertrude Teaches Her Children*; for a discussion of Pestalozzi's philosophy of education, see Gutek, *Pestalozzi and Education.*

27. For Froebel's educational philosophy, see Froebel, *The Education of Man*; for a biography, see Downs, *Friedrich Froebel.* Froebel's educational materials, the gifts and occupations, are discussed in Brosterman, *Inventing Kindergarten.*

28. For Parker's philosophy of education, see Parker, *Talks on Pedagogics;* for a biography, see Campbell, *Colonel Francis W. Parker.*

29. For Dewey's philosophy of education, see Dewey, *Democracy and Education.* For the Laboratory School, see Tanner, *Dewey's Laboratory School.*

30. For a biography of Kilpatrick, see Tenebaum, *William Heard Kilpatrick.*

31. For Freud's psychoanalytic theory, see Freud, *An Outline of Psychoanalysis.* For a biography of Freud, see Gay, *Freud: A Life for Our Time.*

32. Kramer, *Maria Montessori: A Biography,* 320–21.

33. Kramer, *Maria Montessori: A Biography,* 68–69.

34. Kramer, *Maria Montessori: A Biography,* 96–97.

35. Montessori, *Pedagogical Anthropology.*

36. Maria Montessori, *The Montessori Method*, 51.

37. Maria Montessori, *The Montessori Method*, 55.

38. Kramer, *Maria Montessori: A Biography,* 82–83.

39. Maria Montessori, *The Montessori Method*, 63.

40. Maria Montessori, *The Montessori Method*, 60–61.

41. Ward, *The Montessori Method and the American School,* 31.

42. Kramer, *Maria Montessori: A Biography,* 209–10.

43. Montessori, *The Advanced Montessori Method.*

44. Kramer, *Maria Montessori: A Biography,* 154.

45. French, "The Working of the Montessori Method," 423.

46. Standing, *Maria Montessori: Her Life and Work,* 62–66.

47. See her *Montessori for Parents* and *The Montessori Manual.* For Fisher's biography, see Washington, *Dorothy Canfield Fisher: A Biography.*

48. Fisher, *A Montessori Mother,* 21.

49. George, "The First Montessori School in America," 178.

50. George, "The First Montessori School in America," 178.

51. George, "The First Montessori School in America," 187.

52. Stevens, "The Montessori Movement in America," 222.

53. The Montessori Department, *McClure's Magazine* 41 (June 1913): 184.

54. Stevens, "The Montessori Method and the American Kindergarten," 77.

55. S. S. McClure to his wife, Hattie McClure, letter, November 10, 1913. McClure Manuscripts. Manuscript Collections. Lilly Library, Indiana University, Bloomington, Indiana.

56. S. S. McClure to his wife, Hattie McClure, letter, November 12, 1913. McClure Manuscripts. Manuscript Collections. Lilly Library, Indiana University, Bloomington, Indiana.

57. Kramer, *Maria Montessori: A Biography,* 182.

58. S. S. McClure to his wife, Hattie McClure, letter, 1913 (day and month not indicated). McClure Manuscripts. Manuscript Collections. Lilly Library, Indiana University, Bloomington, Indiana.

59. Anne E. George, "Interpretation of Dr. Montessori's Lecture," typescript. Lecture given at the Academy of Music, Brooklyn, New York, December 11, 1913. McClure Manuscripts. Manuscript Collections. Lilly Library, Indiana University, Bloomington, Indiana.

60. Suzzallo, "Editor's Introduction," vii.

61. Suzzallo, "Editor's Introduction," viii–ix.

62. R. B. McClure to S. S. McClure, letter, April 8, 1914. McClure Manuscripts. Manuscript Collections. Lilly Library, Indiana University, Bloomington, Indiana.

63. Briesen and Knauth to S. S. McClure, letter, April 9, 1914. McClure Manuscripts. Manuscript Collections. Lilly Library, Indiana University, Bloomington, Indiana.

64. Harriet McClure to S. S. McClure, letter, April 14, 1914. McClure Manuscripts. Manuscript Collections. Lilly Library, Indiana University, Bloomington, Indiana.

65. Maria Montessori to S. S. McClure, cablegram, April 15, 1914. McClure Manuscripts. Manuscript Collections. Lilly Library, Indiana University, Bloomington, Indiana.

66. Kramer, *Maria Montessori: A Biography,* 212–16.

67. Montessori, *Dr. Montessori's Own Handbook.*

68. Stevens, "The Montessori Method and the American Kindergarten," 77.

69. Montessori, *The Montessori Method,* 162.

70. Brosterman, *Inventing Kindergarten,* 40–88.

71. Montessori, *The Montessori Method,* 171.

72. Holmes, "Introduction," xx.

73. Holmes, "Introduction," xxi–xxiii.

74. Holmes, "Introduction," xxv.
75. Stevens, "The Montessori Method and the American Kindergarten," 78.
76. Stevens, "The Montessori Method and the American Kindergarten," 80.
77. Stevens, "The Montessori Method and the American Kindergarten," 81.
78. Stevens, "The Montessori Method and the American Kindergarten," 81.
79. Harrison, "The Montessori Method and the Kindergarten."
80. Halsey, "A Valuation of the Montessori Experiments," 63.
81. Kilpatrick, "The Project Method," 319–35.
82. Kilpatrick, *The Montessori System Examined.*
83. Kilpatrick, *The Montessori System Examined*, 8–9.
84. Kilpatrick, *The Montessori System Examined,* 9–10.
85. Kilpatrick, *The Montessori System Examined*, 20.
86. Kilpatrick, *The Montessori System Examined*, 27.
87. Kilpatrick, *The Montessori System Examined*, 40–41.
88. Kilpatrick, *The Montessori System Examined*, 48–49.
89. Hunt, "Introduction," xiv.
90. Hunt, "Introduction," xv–xvii.
91. Connell, *A History of Education in the Twentieth Century World,* 133–34.
92. Kramer, *Maria Montessori: A Biography,* 222–23.
93. Kramer, *Maria Montessori: A Biography,* 225–26.
94. Kramer, *Maria Montessori: A Biography,* 249.
95. Giovanni Gentile (1875–1944) was a noted Italian philosopher and educator who was a proponent of idealism in philosophy and education. He was professor of the history of philosophy at the University of Rome, and he supported Mussolini's Fascist regime, serving as its first minister of education. His books include *The Theory of Mind as Pure Art* (1916); *The Reform of Education*, trans. G. Bigongiari (London: Benn, 1923); and *Genesis and Structure of Society* (1943). For an interpretation of Gentile's idealism, see H. S. Harris, *The Social Philosophy of Giovanni Gentile* (Urbana, Ill.: University of Illinois Press, 1960).
96. Kramer, *Maria Montessori: A Biography,* 300.
97. Kramer, *Maria Montessori: A Biography,* 302–4.
98. Kramer, *Maria Montessori: A Biography,* 311–12.
99. Kramer, *Maria Montessori: A Biography,* 317.
100. Mussolini, *Fascism,* 40.
101. Connell, *A History of Education in the Twentieth Century World,* 250–54.
102. Kramer, *Maria Montessori: A Biography,* 326–27.
103. Montessori, *The Absorbent Mind*, 75.
104. Kramer, *Maria Montessori: A Biography,* 343–44.
105. Ahlfeld, "The Montessori Revival," 75–80.
106. Seldin, "Montessori," 1697.
107. Kramer, *Maria Montessori: A Biography,* 224–25.
108. Montessori, *The Montessori Method,* 19–29.
109. Kramer, *Maria Montessori: A Biography,* 68, 96–99.

110. Montessori, *The Montessori Method,* 9–10.

111. Montessori, *The Montessori Method,* 72.

112. Montessori, *The Montessori Method,* 28.

113. Montessori, *The Montessori Method,* 80.

114. Montessori, *The Absorbent Mind,* 7.

115. Montessori, *The Absorbent Mind,* 89.

116. Montessori, *The Absorbent Mind,* 102.

117. Montessori, *The Absorbent Mind,* 104–5.

118. Dewey, *Democracy and Education,* 153–54.

119. Montessori, *The Discovery of the Child,* ix, in Kramer, *Maria Montessori: A Biography,* 305.

120. Montessori, *The Absorbent Mind,* 83.

121. Kramer, *Maria Montessori: A Biography,* 373.

122. Montessori, *The Montessori Method,* 15.

123. Montessori, *The Montessori Method,* 93.

124. Hunt, "Introduction," xxviii–xxix.

125. Montessori, *The Absorbent Mind,* 19–20.

126. Montessori, *The Absorbent Mind,* 51.

127. Montessori, *The Absorbent Mind,* 167.

128. Kramer, *Maria Montessori: A Biography,* 180–81.

129. Montessori, *The Absorbent Mind,* 189.

130. Connell, *A History of Education in the Twentieth Century World,* 135.

131. Montessori, *The Absorbent Mind,* 108–10.

132. Montessori, *The Absorbent Mind,* 110–11.

133. Montessori, *The Absorbent Mind,* 209.

134. Montessori, *The Absorbent Mind,* 194–95.

135. Montessori, *The Absorbent Mind,* 195.

136. Montessori, *The Absorbent Mind,* 202.

137. Montessori, *The Montessori Method,* 117.

138. Montessori, *The Absorbent Mind,* 205.

139. Montessori, *The Absorbent Mind,* 217.

140. Montessori, *The Absorbent Mind,* 206–7.

141. Montessori, *The Absorbent Mind,* 220–21.

MONTESSORI WEBSITES

Association Montessori Internationale: www.montessori-ami.org.htm. The international organization established by Maria Montessori and Mario Montessori.

International Montessori Society: http://turst.edn.com/ims.htm. Founded in 1979, to support the worldwide application of Montessori principles.

American Montessori Society: www.amshq.org.html.

BIBLIOGRAPHY

Ahlfeld, Kathy. "The Montessori Revival: How Far Will It Go?" *Nation's Schools* 85 (January 1970): 75–80.

Brosterman, Norman. *Inventing Kindergarten.* New York: Harry N. Abrams, 1997.

Campbell, Jack K. *Colonel Francis W. Parker: The Children's Crusader.* New York: Teachers College Press, 1967.

Connell, W. F. *A History of Education in the Twentieth Century World.* New York: Teachers College Press, 1980.

Cranston, Maurice. *The Noble Savage: Jean-Jacques Rousseau 1754–1762.* Chicago: University of Chicago Press, 1991.

Dewey, John. *Democracy and Education: An Introduction to the Philosophy of Education.* New York: Macmillan, 1916.

Downs, Robert B. *Friedrich Froebel.* Boston: Twayne Publishers, 1978.

Fisher, Dorothy Canfield. *A Montessori Mother.* New York: Henry Holt, 1912.

——. *Montessori for Parents.* Cambridge: Robert Bentley, 1965.

——. *The Montessori Manual.* Cambridge: Robert Bentley, 1964.

Freire, Paulo. *Pedagogy of Freedom: Ethics, Democracy, and Civic Courage.* Lanham, Md.: Rowman & Littlefield, 1998.

French, Ruth M. "The Working of the Montessori Method." *Journal of Education* 77 (October 1913): 423.

Freud, Sigmund. *An Outline of Psychoanalysis.* Translated by James Strachey. New York: W.W. Norton, 1949.

Froebel, Friedrich. *The Education of Man.* Translated by W. H. Hailman. New York: D. Appleton, 1896.

Gay, Peter. *Freud: A Life for Our Time.* New York: W.W. Norton, 1988.

George, Anne E. "The First Montessori School in America." *McClure's Magazine* 39 (June 1912): 177–87.

——. "Rhythm Work in the Children's House at Washington." *McClure's Magazine* 41 (May 1913): 182–86.

Gitter, Lena L. *The Montessori Way.* Seattle, Wash.: Special Child Publications, 1970.

——. *Montessori's Legacy to Children.* Johnstown: Farew, 1970.

Gutek, Gerald L. "Maria Montessori: Contributions to Educational Psychology." In *Educational Psychology: A Century of Contributions,* ed. Barry J. Zimmerman and Dale H. Schunk. New York: Lawrence Erlbaum, 2003: 171–186.

——. *Pestalozzi and Education.* Prospect Heights, Ill.: Waveland Press, 1999.

Hainstock, Elizabeth G. *The Essential Montessori.* New York: New American Library, 1978.

Hall, Vernon C. "Educational Psychology from 1800 to 1920." In *Educational Psychology: A Century of Contributions,* ed. Barry J. Zimmerman and Dale H. Schunk. New York: Lawrence Erlbaum, 2003: 3–39.

Halsey, Walter N. "A Valuation of the Montessori Experiments." *Journal of Education* 77 (January 1913): 63.

Harrison, Elizabeth. "The Montessori Method and the Kindergarten." *U.S. Bureau of Education Bulletin*, no. 28 (1914).

Holmes, Henry R. "Introduction." In *The Montessori Method*, by Maria Montessori. Translated by Anne E. George. New York: Frederick A. Stokes, 1912.

Hunt, J. M. "Introduction: Revisiting Montessori." In *The Montessori Method,* by Maria Montessori. New York: Schocken Books, 1964.

"Information about the Montessori Method." *McClure's Magazine* 37 (October 1911): 702–4.

Itard, Jean Marc Gaspard. *The Wild Boy of Aveyron.* New York: McGraw-Hill/Appleton & Lange, 1962.

Justman, Joseph. *The Italian People and Their Schools.* Tiffin, Ohio: Kappa Delta Pi, 1958.

Kilpatrick, William H. *The Montessori System Examined.* Boston: Houghton Mifflin, 1914.

——. "The Project Method." *Teachers College Record* 19 (September 1918): 319–35.

Kramer, Rita. *Maria Montessori: A Biography.* Reading, Mass.: Perseus Books, 1988.

——. *Maria Montessori: A Biography.* Reading, Mass.: Perseus Books, 1988.

McClure Manuscripts. Manuscript Collections. Lilly Library, Indiana University, Bloomington, Indiana.

"The Montessori American Committee." *McClure's Magazine* 39 (June 1912): 238.

Montessori, Maria. *The Absorbent Mind.* Foreword by John Chattin-McNichols. New York: Henry Holt, 1995.

——. *The Advanced Montessori Method.* Translated by F. Simmonds and I. Hutchinson. London: Heinemann, 1919.

——. "Disciplining Children." *McClure's Magazine* 39 (May 1912): 95–102.

——. *The Discovery of the Child.* Trans. Mary A. Johnstone. Madras, India: Vasanta Press, l948.

——. *Dr. Montessori's Own Handbook.* New York: Frederick A. Stokes, 1914.

——. *Education and Peace.* Trans. Helen R. Lane. Chicago: Henry Regnery Press, 1949.

——. *From Childhood to Adolescence.* New York: Schocken Books, 1948.

——. *The Montessori Method.* Trans. Anne E. George. New York: Frederick A. Stokes, 1912.

——. *Pedagogical Anthropology.* Translated by Frederick T. Cooper. New York: Frederick A. Stokes, 1913.

——. "Plan for an International Institute." *McClure's Magazine* 40 (March 1913): 221.

——. *The Secret of Childhood.* Trans. Barbara Barclay Carter. New York: Frederick A. Stokes, l939.

——. *Spontaneous Activity in Education.* Trans. Florence Simmonds. New York: Frederick A. Stokes, 1917.

Mussolini, Benito. *Fascism: Doctrine and Institution.* Rome: Ardita, 1935.

Myers, Kathrina. "Seguin's Principles of Education as Related to the Montessori Method." *Journal of Education* 77 (May 1913): 538–41.

Lillard, Paula P. *Montessori: A Modern Approach.* New York: Schocken Books, 1972.

Oren, R.C., ed. *Montessori, Her Method and the Movement, What You Need to Know.* New York: G. P. Putnam's Sons, 1974.

Parker, Francis W. *Talks on Pedagogics.* New York: E. L. Kellogg, 1894.

Pestalozzi, Johann Heinrich. *How Gertrude Teaches Her Children.* Syracuse, N.Y.: Bardeen, 1900.

Rambusch, Nancy McCormick. *Learning How to Learn.* Baltimore: Helicon Press, 1962.

Rousseau, Jean-Jacques. *Emile, or On Education.* Trans. Allan Bloom. New York: Basic Books, 1979.

Seldin, Timothy D. "Montessori." *Encyclopedia of Education.* 2nd ed. Vol. 5. Edited by James Guthrie (New York: Macmillan Reference USA/Thomson Gale, 2003).

Standing, E. M. *Maria Montessori: Her Life and Work.* New York: Penguin Putnam, 1998.

Stevens, Ellen Yale. "The Montessori Method and the American Kindergarten." *McClure's Magazine* 40 (November 1912): 77–82.

——. "The Montessori Movement: A New McClure Department." *McClure's Magazine* 40 (March 1913): 221.

——. "The Montessori Movement: A McClure Department, Answers to Correspondents." *McClure's Magazine* 40 (July 1913): 222–27.

——. "The Montessori Movement in America: A New McClure Department." *McClure's Magazine* 40 (February 1913): 222–27.

Suzzallo, Henry. "Editor's Introduction." In *The Montessori System Examined,* by William H. Kilpatrick. Boston: Houghton Mifflin, 1914.

Tanner, Laurel N. *Dewey's Laboratory School: Lessons for Today.* New York: Teachers College Press, 1997.

Tenebaum, Samuel. *William Heard Kilpatrick: Trail Blazer in Education.* New York: Harper and Brothers, 1951.

Ward, Florence E. *The Montessori Method and the American School.* New York: Macmillan, 1913.

Washington, Ida H. *Dorothy Canfield Fisher: A Biography.* Shelburne, Vt.: New England Press, 1982.

I

AN ANNOTATED EDITION OF MARIA MONTESSORI'S *THE MONTESSORI METHOD*

1

A Critical Consideration of the New Pedagogy in Its Relation to Modern Science

It is not my intention to present a treatise on scientific pedagogy. The modest design of these incomplete notes is to give the results of an experiment that apparently opens the way for putting into practice those new principles of science which in these last years are tending to revolutionize the work of education.

Much has been said in the past decade concerning the tendency of pedagogy, following in the footsteps of medicine, to pass beyond the purely speculative stage and base its conclusions on the positive results of experimentation. Physiological or experimental psychology which, from Weber and Fechner to Wundt, has become organized into a new science, seems destined to furnish to the new pedagogy that fundamental preparation which the old-time metaphysical psychology furnished to philosophical pedagogy.[1] Morphological anthropology applied to the physical study of children is also a strong element in the growth of the new pedagogy.[2]

But in spite of all these tendencies, scientific pedagogy has never yet been definitely constructed nor defined. It is something vague of which we speak, but which does not, in reality, exist. We might say that it has been, up to the present time, the mere intuition or suggestion of a science which, by the aid of the positive and experimental sciences that have renewed the thought of the nineteenth century, must emerge from the mist and clouds that have surrounded it. For man, who has formed a new world through scientific progress, must himself be prepared and developed through a new pedagogy. But I will not attempt to speak of this more fully here.

Several years ago, a well-known physician established in Italy a *School of Scientific Pedagogy*, the object of which was to prepare teachers to follow the new movement which had begun to be felt in the pedagogical world. This school had, for two or three years, a great success, so great, indeed, that teachers from all over Italy flocked to it, and it was endowed by the City of Milan with a splendid equipment of scientific material. Indeed, its beginnings were most propitious, and liberal help was afforded it in the hope that it might be possible to establish, through the experiments carried on there, "the science of forming man."

The enthusiasm which welcomed this school was, in a large measure, due to the warm support given it by the distinguished anthropologist, Giuseppe Sergi, who for more than thirty years had earnestly labored to spread among the teachers of Italy the principles of a new civilization based upon education.[3] "Today in the social world," said Sergi, "an imperative need makes itself felt—the reconstruction of educational methods; and he who fights for this cause, fights for human regeneration." . . .

The authority of Sergi was enough to convince many that, given such a knowledge of the individual, the art of educating him would develop naturally. This, as often happens, led to a confusion of ideas among his followers, arising now from a too literal interpretation, now from an exaggeration, of the master's ideas. The chief trouble lay in confusing the experimental study of the pupil with his education. And since the one was the road leading to the other, which should have grown from it naturally and rationally, they straightway gave the name of scientific pedagogy to what was in truth pedagogical anthropology. These new converts carried as their banner, the "Biographical Chart," believing that once this ensign was firmly planted upon the battlefield of the school, the victory would be won.

The so-called School of scientific pedagogy, therefore, instructed the teachers in the taking of anthropometric measurements, in the use of esthesiometric instruments, in the gathering of psychological data—and the army of new scientific teachers was formed.

It should be said that in this movement Italy showed herself to be abreast of the times. In France, in England, and especially in America, experiments have been made in the elementary schools, based upon a study of anthropology and pyschological pedagogy, in the hope of finding in anthropometry and psychometry, the regeneration of the school.[4] In these attempts it has rarely been the *teachers* who have carried on the research; the experiments have been, in most cases, in the hands of physicians who have taken more interest in their especial science than in education. They have usually sought to get from their experiments some contribution to psychology, or anthropology, rather than to attempt to organize their work and their results toward the formation of the long-sought scientific pedagogy. To sum up the situation briefly, anthropology and psychology have never devoted themselves to the question of educating children in the schools, nor have the scientifically trained teachers ever measured up to the standards of genuine scientists.

The truth is that the practical progress of the school demands a genuine *fusion* of these modern tendencies, in practice and thought; such a fusion as shall bring scientists directly into the important field of the school and at the same time raise teachers from the inferior intellectual level to which they are limited today. Toward this eminently practical ideal the University School of Pedagogy, founded in Italy by Credaro, is definitely working. It is the intention of this school to raise pedagogy from the inferior position it has occupied as a secondary branch of philosophy, to the dignity of a definite science, which shall, as does Medicine, cover a broad and varied field of comparative study.

And among the branches affiliated with it will most certainly be found Pedagogical Hygiene, Pedagogical Anthropology, and Experimental Psychology.

Truly, Italy, the country of Lombroso, of De-Giovanni, and of Sergi, may claim the honor of being preeminent in the organization of such a movement.[5] In fact, these three scientists may be called the founders of the new tendency in Anthropology: the first leading the way in criminal anthropology, the second in medical anthropology, and the third in pedagogical anthropology. For the good fortune of science, all three of them have been the recognized leaders of their special lines of thought, and have been so prominent in the scientific world that they have not only made courageous and valuable disciples, but have also prepared the minds of the masses to receive the scientific regeneration which they have encouraged. (For reference, see my treatise *Pedagogical Anthropology*.)[6]

Surely all this is something of which our country may be justly proud.

Today, however, those things which occupy us in the field of education are the interests of humanity at large, and of civilization, and before such great forces we can recognize only one country—the entire world. And in a cause of such great importance, all those who have given any contribution, even though it be only an attempt not crowned with success, are worthy of the respect of humanity throughout the civilized world. So, in Italy, the schools of Scientific Pedagogy and the Anthropological Laboratories, which have sprung up in the various cities through the efforts of elementary teachers and scholarly inspectors, and which have been abandoned almost before they became definitely organized, have nevertheless a great value by reason of the faith which inspired them, and because of the doors they have opened to thinking people.[7] . . .

To prepare teachers in the method of the experimental sciences is not an easy matter. When we shall have instructed them in anthropometry and psychometry in the most minute manner possible, we shall have only created machines, whose usefulness will be most doubtful. Indeed, if it is after this fashion that we are to initiate our teachers into experiment, we shall remain forever in the field of theory. The teachers of the old school, prepared according to the principles of metaphysical philosophy, understood the ideas of certain men regarded as authorities, and moved the muscles of speech in talking of them, and the muscles of the eye in reading their theories. Our scientific teachers, instead, are familiar with certain instruments and know how to move the muscles of the hand and arm in order to use these instruments; besides this, they have an intellectual preparation which consists of a series of typical tests, which they have, in a barren and mechanical way, learned how to apply.

The difference is not substantial, for profound differences cannot exist in exterior technique alone, but lie rather within the inner man. Not with all our initiation into scientific experiment have we prepared *new masters*, for, after all, we have left them standing without the door of real experimental science; we have not admitted them to the noblest and most profound phase of such study—to that experience which makes real scientists.

And, indeed, what is a scientist? Not, certainly, he who knows how to manipulate all the instruments in the physical laboratory, or who in the laboratory of the chemist handles the various reactives with deftness and security, or who in biology knows how to make ready the specimens for the microscope. Indeed, it is often the case that an assistant has a greater dexterity in experimental technique than the master scientist himself. We give the name scientist to the type of man who has felt experiment to be a means guiding him to search out the deep truth of life, to lift a veil from its fascinating secrets, and who, in this pursuit, has felt arising within him a love for the mysteries of nature, so passionate as to annihilate the thought of himself. The scientist is not the clever manipulator of instruments, he is the worshipper of nature and he bears the external symbols of his passion as does the follower of some religious order. To this body of real scientists belong those who, forgetting, like the Trappists of the Middle Ages, the world about them, live only in the laboratory, careless often in matters of food and dress because they no longer think of themselves; those who, through years of unwearied use of the microscope, become blind; those who in their scientific ardor inoculate themselves with tuberculosis germs; those who handle the excrement of cholera patients in their eagerness to learn the vehicle through which the diseases are transmitted; and those who, knowing that a certain chemical preparation may be an explosive, still persist in testing their theories at the risk of their lives. This is the spirit of the men of science, to whom nature freely reveals her secrets, crowning their labors with the glory of discovery.

There exists, then, the "spirit" of the scientist, a thing far above his mere "mechanical skill," and the scientist is at the height of his achievement when the spirit has triumphed over the mechanism. When he has reached this point, science will receive from him not only new revelations of nature, but philosophic syntheses of pure thought.

It is my belief that the thing which we should cultivate in our teachers is more the *spirit* than the mechanical skill of the scientist; that is, the *direction* of the *preparation* should be toward the spirit rather than toward the mechanism. For example, when we considered the scientific preparation of teachers to be simply the acquiring of the technique of science, we did not attempt to make these elementary teachers perfect anthropologists, expert experimental psychologists, or masters of infant hygiene; we wished only to *direct* them toward the field of experimental science, teaching them to manage the various instruments with a certain degree of skill. So now, we wish to *direct* the teacher, trying to awaken in him, in connection with his own particular field, the school, that scientific *spirit* which opens the door for him to broader and bigger possibilities. In other words, we wish to awaken in the mind and heart of the educator an *interest in natural phenomena* to such an extent that, loving nature, he shall understand the anxious and expectant attitude of one who has prepared an experiment and who awaits a revelation from it.[*]

The instruments are like the alphabet, and we must know how to manage them if we are to read nature; but as the book, which contains the revelation of the greatest thoughts of an author, uses in the alphabet the means of composing the external symbols or words, so nature, through the mechanism of the experiment, gives us an infinite series of revelations, unfolding for us her secrets.

Now one who has learned to spell mechanically all the words in his spelling-book, would be able to read in the same mechanical way the words in one of Shakespeare's plays, provided the print were sufficiently clear. He who is initiated solely into the making of the bare experiment, is like one who spells out the literal sense of the words in the spelling-book; it is on such a level that we leave the teachers if we limit their preparation to technique alone.

We must, instead, make of them worshippers and interpreters of the spirit of nature. They must be like him who, having learned to spell, finds himself, one day, able to read behind the written symbols the *thought* of Shakespeare, or Goethe, or Dante. As may be seen, the difference is great, and the road long. Our first error was, however, a natural one. The child who has mastered the spelling-book gives the impression of knowing how to read. Indeed, he does read the signs over the shop doors, the names of newspapers, and every word that comes under his eyes. It would be very natural if, entering a library, this child should be deluded into thinking that he knew how to read *the sense* of all the books he saw there. But attempting to do this, he would soon feel that "to know how to read mechanically" is nothing, and that he needs to go back to school. So it is with the teachers whom we have thought to prepare for scientific pedagogy by teaching them anthropometry and psychometry.[8] . . .

---

[*] See in my treatise on *Pedagogical Anthropology* the chapter on "The Method Used in Experimental Sciences."

It is not enough, then, to prepare in our Masters the scientific spirit. We must also make ready the *school* for their observation. The school must permit the *free*, *natural manifestations* of the *child* if in the school scientific pedagogy is to be born. This is the essential reform.

No one may affirm that such a principle already exists in pedagogy and in the school. It is true that some pedagogues, led by Rousseau, have given voice to impracticable principles and vague aspirations for the liberty of the child, but the true concept of liberty is practically unknown to educators.[9] They often have the same concept of liberty which animates a people in the hour of rebellion from slavery, or perhaps, the conception of *social liberty*, which although it is a more elevated idea, is still invariably restricted. "Social liberty" signifies always one more round of Jacob's ladder. In other words it signifies a partial liberation, the liberation of a country, of a class, or of thought.

That concept of liberty which must inspire pedagogy is, instead, universal. The biological sciences of the nineteenth century have shown it to us when they have offered us the means for studying life. If, therefore, the old-time pedagogy foresaw or vaguely expressed the principle of studying the pupil before educating him, and of leaving him free in his spontaneous manifestations, such an intuition, indefinite and barely expressed, was made possible of practical attainment only after the contribution of the experimental sciences during the last century. This is not a case for sophistry or discussion, it is enough that we state our point. He who would say that the principle of liberty informs the pedagogy of today, would make us smile as at a child who, before the box of mounted butterflies, should insist that they were alive and could fly. The principle of slavery still pervades pedagogy, and, therefore, the same principle pervades the school. I need only give one proof—the stationary desks and chairs. Here we have, for example, a striking evidence of the errors of the early materialistic scientific pedagogy which, with mistaken zeal and energy, carried the barren stones of science to the rebuilding of the crumbling walls of the school. The schools were at first furnished with the long, narrow benches upon which the children were crowded together. Then came science and perfected the bench. In this work much attention was paid to the recent contributions of anthropology. The age of the child and the length of his limbs were considered in placing the seat at the right height. The distance between the seat and the desk was calculated with infinite care, in order that the child's back should not become deformed, and, finally, the seats were separated and the width so closely calculated that the child could barely seat himself upon it, while to stretch himself by making any lateral movements was impossible. This was done in order that he might be separated from his neighbor. These desks are constructed in such a way as to render the child visible in all his immobility. One of the ends sought through this separation is the prevention of immoral acts in the schoolroom. What shall we say of such prudence in a state of society where it would be considered scandalous to give voice to principles of sex morality in education, for fear we might thus contaminate innocence? And, yet, here we have science lending itself to this hypocrisy, fabricating machines! Not only this; obliging science goes farther still, perfecting the benches in such a way as to permit to the greatest possible extent the immobility of the child, or, if you wish, to repress every movement of the child.

It is all so arranged that, when the child is well-fitted into his place, the desk and chair themselves force him to assume the position considered to be hygienically comfortable. The seat, the footrest, the desks are arranged in such a way that the child can never stand at his work. He is allotted only sufficient space for sitting in an erect position. It is in such ways that schoolroom desks and benches have advanced toward perfection. Every cult of the so-called scientific pedagogy has designed a model scientific desk. Not a few nations have become proud of their "national desk"—and in the struggle of competition these various machines have been patented.

Undoubtedly there is much that is scientific underlying the construction of these benches. Anthropology has been drawn upon in the measuring of the body and the diagnosis of the age; physiology, in the study of muscular movements; psychology, in regard to perversion of instincts; and, above all, hygiene, in the effort to prevent curvature of the spine. These desks were indeed scientific, following in their construction the anthropological study of the child. We have here, as I have said, an example of the literal application of science to the schools.

I believe that before very long we shall all be struck with great surprise by this attitude. It will seem incomprehensible that the fundamental error of the desk should not have been revealed earlier through the attention given to the study of infant hygiene, anthropology, and sociology, and through the general progress of thought. The marvel is greater when we consider that during the past years there has been stirring in almost every nation a movement toward the protection of the child.

I believe that it will not be many years before the public, scarcely believing the descriptions of these scientific benches, will come to touch with wondering hands the amazing seats that were constructed for the purpose of preventing among our school children curvature of the spine!

The development of these scientific benches means that the pupils were subjected to a régime, which, even though they were born strong and straight, made it possible for them to become humpbacked! The vertebral column, biologically the most primitive, fundamental, and oldest part of the skeleton, the most fixed portion of our body, since the skeleton is the most solid portion of the organism—the vertebral column, which resisted and was strong through the desperate struggles of primitive man when he fought against the desert-lion, when he conquered the mammoth, when he quarried the solid rock and shaped the iron to his uses, bends, and cannot resist, under the yoke of the school.

It is incomprehensible that so-called *science* should have worked to perfect an instrument of slavery in the school without being enlightened by one ray from the movement of social liberation, growing and developing throughout the world. For the age of scientific benches was also the age of the redemption of the working classes from the yoke of unjust labor.

The tendency toward social liberty is most evident, and manifests itself on every hand. The leaders of the people make it their slogan, the laboring masses repeat the cry, scientific and socialistic publications voice the same movement, our journals are full of it. The underfed workman does not ask for a tonic, but for better economic conditions which shall prevent malnutrition. The miner who, through the stooping position maintained during many hours of the day, is subject to inguinal rupture, does not ask for an abdominal support, but demands shorter hours and better working conditions, in order that he may be able to lead a healthy life like other men.

And when, during this same social epoch, we find that the children in our schoolrooms are working amid unhygienic conditions, so poorly adapted to normal development that even the skeleton becomes deformed, our response to this terrible revelation is an orthopedic bench. It is much as if we offered to the miner the abdominal brace, or arsenic to the underfed workman.

Some time ago a woman, believing me to be in sympathy with all scientific innovations concerning the school, showed me with evident satisfaction *a corset* or *brace for pupils*. She had invented this and felt that it would complete the work of the bench.

Surgery has still other means for the treatment of spinal curvature. I might mention orthopedic instruments, braces, and a method of periodically suspending the child, by the head or shoulders, in such a fashion that the weight of the body stretches and thus straightens the vertebral column. In the school, the orthopedic instrument in the shape of the desk is in great favor; today someone proposes the brace—one step farther and it will be suggested that we give the scholars a systematic course in the suspension method!

All this is the logical consequence of a material application of the methods of science to the decadent school. Evidently the rational method of combating spinal curvature in the pupils, is to change the form of their work—so that they shall no longer be obliged to remain for so many hours a day in a harmful position. It is a conquest of liberty which the school needs, not the mechanism of a bench.

Even were the stationary seat helpful to the child's body, it would still be a dangerous and unhygienic feature of the environment, through the difficulty of cleaning the room perfectly when the furniture cannot be moved. The footrests, which cannot be removed, accumulate the dirt carried in daily from the street by the many little feet. Today there is a general transformation in the matter of house furnishings. They are made lighter and simpler so that they may be easily moved, dusted, and even washed. But the school seems blind to the transformation of the social environment.

It behooves us to think of what may happen to the *spirit* of the child who is condemned to grow in conditions so artificial that his very bones may become deformed. When we speak of the redemption of the workingman, it is always understood that beneath the most apparent form of suffering, such as poverty of the blood, or ruptures, there exists that other wound from which the soul of the man who is subjected to any form of slavery must suffer. It is at this deeper wrong that we aim when we say that the workman must be redeemed through liberty. We know only too well that when a man's very blood has been consumed or his intestines wasted away through his work, his soul must have lain oppressed in darkness, rendered insensible, or, it may be, killed within him. The *moral* degradation of the slave is, above all things, the weight that opposes the progress of humanity—humanity striving to rise and held back by this great burden. The cry of redemption speaks far more clearly for the souls of men than for their bodies.

What shall we say then, when the question before us is that of *educating children*?

We know only too well the sorry spectacle of the teacher who, in the ordinary schoolroom, must pour certain cut and dried facts into the heads of the scholars. In order to succeed in this barren task, she finds it necessary to discipline her pupils into immobility and to force their attention. Prizes and punishments are every-ready and efficient aids to the master who must force into a given attitude of mind and body those who are condemned to be his listeners.

It is true that today it is deemed expedient to abolish official whippings and habitual blows, just as the awarding of prizes has become less ceremonious. These partial reforms are another prop approved of by science, and offered to the support of the decadent school. Such prizes and punishments are, if I may be allowed the expression, the *bench* of the soul, the instrument of slavery for the spirit. Here, however, these are not applied to lessen deformities, but to provoke them. The prize and the punishment are incentives toward unnatural or forced effort, and, therefore we certainly cannot speak of the natural development of the child in connection with them. The jockey offers a piece of sugar to his horse before jumping into the saddle, the coachman beats his horse that he may respond to the signs given by the reins; and, yet, neither of these runs so superbly as the free horse of the plains.

And here, in the case of education, shall man place the yoke upon man?

True, we say that social man is natural man yoked to society. But if we give a comprehensive glance to the moral progress of society, we shall see that little by little, the yoke is being made easier, in other words, we shall see that nature, or life, moves gradually toward triumph. The yoke of the slave yields to that of the servant, and the yoke of the servant to that of the workman.

All forms of slavery tend little by little to weaken and disappear, even the sexual slavery of woman. The history of civilization is a history of conquest and of liberation. We should ask in what stage of civilization we find ourselves and if, in truth, the good of prizes and of punishments be necessary to our advancement. If we have indeed gone beyond this point, then to apply such a form of education would be to draw the new generation back to a lower level, not to lead them into their true heritage of progress.

Something very like this condition of the school exists in society, in the relation between the government and the great numbers of the men employed in its administrative departments. These clerks work day after day for the general national good, yet they do not feel or see the advantage of their work in any immediate reward. That is, they do not realize that the state carries on its great business through their daily tasks, and that the whole nation is benefited by their work. For them the immediate good is promotion, as passing to a higher class is for the child in school. The man who loses sight of the really big aim of his work is like a child who has been placed in a class below his real standing: like a slave, he is cheated of something which is his right. His dignity as a man is reduced to the limits of the dignity of a machine which must be oiled if it is to be kept going, because it does not have within itself the impulse of life. All those petty things such as the desire for decorations or medals, are but artificial stimuli, lightening for the moment the dark, barren path in which he treads.

In the same way we give prizes to school children. And the fear of not achieving promotion withholds the clerk from running away, and binds him to his monotonous work, even as the fear of not passing into the next class drives the pupil to his book. The reproof of the superior is in every way similar to the scolding of the teacher. The correction of badly executed clerical work is equivalent to the bad mark placed by the teacher upon the scholar's poor composition. The parallel is almost perfect.[10] . . .

As for punishments, the soul of the normal man grows perfect through expanding, and punishment as commonly understood is always a form of *repression*. It may bring results with those inferior natures who grow in evil, but these are very few, and social progress is not affected by them. The penal code threatens us with punishment if we are dishonest within the limits indicated by the laws. But we are not honest through fear of the laws; if we do not rob, if we do not kill, it is because we love peace, because the natural trend of our lives leads us forward, leading us ever farther and more definitely away from the peril of low and evil acts.

Without going into the ethical or metaphysical aspects of the question, we may safely affirm that the delinquent before he transgresses the law, has, *if he knows of the existence of a punishment*, felt the threatening weight of the criminal code upon him. He has defied it, or he has been lured into the crime, deluding himself with the idea that he would be able to avoid the punishment of the law. But there has occurred within his mind, *a struggle between the crime and the punishment*. Whether it be efficacious in hindering crime or not, this penal code is undoubtedly made for a very limited class of individuals; namely, criminals. The enormous majority of citizens are honest without any regard whatever to the threats of the law.

The real punishment of normal man is the loss of the consciousness of that individual power and greatness which are the sources of his inner life. Such a punishment often falls upon men in the fullness of success. A man whom we would consider crowned by happiness and fortune may be suffering from this form of punishment. Far too often man does not see the real punishment which threatens him.

And it is just here that education may help.

Today we hold the pupils in school, restricted by those instruments so degrading to body and spirit, the desk—and material prizes and punishments. Our aim in all this is to reduce them to the discipline of immobility and silence—to lead them—where? Far too often toward no definite end.

Often the education of children consists in pouring into their intelligence the intellectual content of school programs. And often these programs have been compiled in the official department of education, and their use is imposed by law upon the teacher and the child.[11] . . .

EDITOR'S NOTES

1. Montessori emphasized the need to base education on science rather than speculative metaphysics. Here, she identified three founding figures of physiological or experimental psychology. Ernst H. Weber (1795–1878), who studied the sensitivity of sensory systems by conducting experimentation on sensory phenomenon. He is noted for "Weber's Law," the possibility of establishing relationships between variations in physical and mental events. Weber also coined the phrase, "JND," which denoted the smallest perceptible difference between two sensations. Gustav Theodor Fechner (1801–1887), who developed psychophysics, which he believed was a scientific means of examining and measuring the functional relationships between the mind and body and established methods of measuring these relationships. Wilhelm Max Wundt (1832–1920), who is credited

with developing experimental psychology that emphasized the relationships between psychology and physiology and the use of scientific methods in psychology. In her quest to develop a "scientific pedagogy," Montessori emphasized the relationships between the child's mental powers and sensation of external phenomenon.

2. Montessori uses the term "morphological anthropology" to mean the scientific study of the development, functions, and relationships between human mental and physical structures and organs. Her emphasis is on the relationships between physiology and psychology in human development rather than on the study of racial and group classifications and cultures.

3. Giuseppe Sergi (1841–1936) was a pioneer Italian anthropologist who established the first psychological laboratory at the University of Rome. His Educazione ed Istruzione (1892) emphasized the use of anthropology and experimental psychology in education. Montessori's quotes from Giuseppe Sergi's book on pages 2–3, where he urged using pedagogical anthropology and experimental psychology to create a new method of education are deleted.

4. Anthropometry refers to the science of measuring the human body and its parts and functional capacities; Psychometry refers to the branch of psychology relating to the empirical mental measurements to elicit quantitative data.

5. Montessori is referring to the contributions to experimental psychology made by Achille de Giovanni, a professor of medicine, who emphasized clinical observation and the use of anthropometry in medical education in Italy. Cesare Lombroso, a physician and surgeon, developed the field of criminal anthropology in Italy and used a variety of anthropological and physiological measurements to identify the criminal type. Sergi, a professor of anthropology, was one of Montessori's teachers at the University of Rome.

6. Montessori is referring to her book, *L'Antropolgia Pedagogica*. An English-language version was *Maria Montessori, Pedagogical Anthropology* (New York: Frederick A. Stokes, 1913).

7. The section, pp. 6–7, where Montessori praises St. Francis as a person who achieved a great cause after suffering repeated failures is deleted.

8. Montessori's inspirational exhortations and examples about the need of the directress to go beyond mechanics to respect of the child's spiritual nature that appear on pp. 11–14 are deleted.

9. Montessori is distinguishing her approach from that of Jean-Jacques Rousseau (1712–1778), the French philosopher, who wrote *Emile*, a didactic novel about the education of a boy according to natural principles, who lives on a country estate, and is guided by a highly permissive tutor. Rousseau's version of child freedom was one in which the child learned by direct experience and observation of the environment with little adult intervention. Rousseau's theory of child freedom and education based on sensation appealed to many educators, such as the Swiss pedagogue, Johann Heinrich Pestalozzi, and to child-centered progressives in the United States. Montessori rejects Rousseau's romanticized view of the child as a "noble savage" and argued that true child freedom takes place within the structured environment.

10. Montessori's several examples on the use of prizes and punishments in society and the military on pp. 23–25 are deleted.

11. A short quote from Sergi about the need to reconstruct methods of education is deleted on p. 11.

2

History of Methods

If we are to develop a system of scientific pedagogy, we must, then, proceed along lines very different from those that have been followed up to the present time. The transformation of the school must be contemporaneous with the preparation of the teacher. For if we make of the teacher an observer, familiar with the experimental methods, then we must make it possible for her to observe and to experiment in the school. The fundamental principle of scientific pedagogy must be, indeed, the *liberty of the pupil*—such liberty as shall permit a development of individual, spontaneous manifestations of the child's nature. If a new and scientific pedagogy is to arise from the *study of the individual*, such study must occupy itself with the observation of *free* children. In vain should we await a practical renewing of pedagogical methods from methodical examinations of pupils made under the guidance offered today by pedagogy, anthropology, and experimental psychology.

Every branch of experimental science has grown out of the application of a method peculiar to itself. Bacteriology owes its scientific content to the method of isolation and culture of microbes. Criminal, medical, and pedagogical anthropology owe their progress to the application of anthropological methods to individuals of various classes, such as criminals, the insane, the sick of the clinics, scholars. So experimental psychology needs as its starting point an exact definition of the technique to be used in making the experiment.

To put it broadly, it is important to define *the method, the technique*, and from its application to *await* the definite result, which must be gathered entirely from actual experience. One of the characteristics of experimental sciences is to proceed to the making of an experiment *without preconceptions of any sort* as to the final result of the experiment itself. For example, should we wish to make scientific observations concerning the development of the head as related to varying degrees of intelligence, one of the conditions of such an experiment would be to ignore, in the taking of the measurements, which were the most intelligent and which the most backward among the scholars examined. And this because the preconceived idea that the most intelligent should have the head more fully developed will inevitably alter the results of the research.

He who experiments must, while doing so, divest himself of every preconception. It is clear then that if we wish to make use of a method of experimental psychology, the first thing necessary is to renounce all former creeds and to proceed by means of the *method* in the search for truth.

We must not start, for example, from any dogmatic ideas which we may happen to have held upon the subject of child psychology. Instead, we must proceed by a method which shall tend to make possible to the child complete liberty. This we must do if we are to draw from the observation of his spontaneous manifestations conclusions which shall lead to the establishment of a truly scientific child psychology. It may be that such a method holds for us great surprises, unexpected possibilities.

Child psychology and pedagogy must establish their content by successive conquests arrived at through the method of experimentation.

Our problem then, is this: to establish the *method peculiar* to experimental pedagogy. It cannot be that used in other experimental sciences. It is true that scientific pedagogy is rounded out by hygiene, anthropology, and psychology, and adopts in part the technical method characteristic of all three, although limiting itself to a special study of the individual to be educated. But in pedagogy this study of the individual, though it must accompany the very different work of *education*, is a limited and secondary part of the science as a whole.

This present study deals in part with the *method* used in experimental pedagogy, and is the result of my experiences during two years in the "Children's Houses." I offer only a beginning of the method, which I have applied to children between the ages of three and six. But I believe that these tentative experiments, because of the surprising results which they have given, will be the means of inspiring a continuation of the work thus undertaken.

Indeed, although our educational system, which experience has demonstrated to be excellent, is not yet entirely completed, it nevertheless constitutes a system well enough established to be practical in all institutions where young children are cared for, and in the first elementary classes.

Perhaps I am not exact when I say that the present work springs from two years of experience. I do not believe that these later attempts of mine could alone have rendered possible all that I set forth in this book. The origin of the educational system in use in the "Children's Houses" is much more remote, and if this experience with normal children seems indeed rather brief, it should be remembered that it sprang from preceding pedagogical experiences with abnormal children, and that considered in this way, it represents a long and thoughtful endeavor.

About fifteen years ago, being assistant doctor at the Psychiatric Clinic of the University of Rome, I had occasion to frequent the insane asylums to study the sick and to select subjects for the clinics. In this way I became interested in the idiot children who were at that time housed in the general insane asylums. In those days thyroid organotherapy[1] was in full development, and this drew the attention of physicians to deficient children. I myself, having completed my regular hospital services, had already turned my attention to the study of children's diseases.

It was thus that, being interested in the idiot children, I became conversant with the special method of education devised for these unhappy little ones by Edouard Seguin, and was led to study thoroughly the idea, then beginning to be prevalent among the physicians, of the efficacy of "pedagogical treatment" for various morbid forms of disease such as deafness, paralysis, idiocy, rickets, etc. The fact that pedagogy must join with medicine in the treatment of disease was the practical outcome of the thought of the time. And because of this tendency the method of treating disease by gymnastics became widely popular. I, however, differed from my colleagues in that I felt that mental deficiency presented chiefly a pedagogical, rather than mainly a medical, problem. Much was said in the medical congresses of the medico-pedagogic method for the treatment and education of the feeble minded, and I expressed my differing opinion in an address on *Moral Education* at the Pedagogical Congress of Turin in 1898. I believe that I touched a chord already vibrant, because the idea, making its way among the physicians and elementary teachers, spread in a flash as presenting a question of lively interest to the school.

In fact I was called upon by my master, Guido Baccelli, the great Minister of Education, to deliver to the teachers of Rome a course of lectures on the education of feeble-minded children.[2] This course soon developed into the State Orthophrenic School, which I directed for more than two years.

In this school we had an all-day class of children composed of those who in the elementary schools were considered hopelessly deficient. Later on, through the help of a philanthropic organization, there was founded a Medical Pedagogic Institute where, besides the children from the public schools, we brought together all of the idiot children from the insane asylums in Rome.

I spent these two years with the help of my colleagues in preparing the teachers of Rome for a special method of observation and education of feeble-minded children. Not only did I train teachers, but what was much more important, after I had been in London and Paris for the purpose of studying in a practical way the education of deficients, I gave myself over completely to the actual teaching of the children, directing at the same time the work of the other teachers in our institute.

I was more than an elementary teacher, for I was present, or directly taught the children, from eight in the morning to seven in the evening without interruption. These two years of practice are my first and indeed my true degree in pedagogy. From the very beginning of my work with deficient children (1898 to 1900) I felt that the methods which I used had in them nothing peculiarly limited to the instruction of idiots. I believed that they contained educational principles *more rational* than those in use, so much more so, indeed, that through their means an inferior mentality would be able to grow and develop. This feeling, so deep as to be in the nature of an intuition, became my controlling idea after I had left the school for deficients, and, little by little, I became convinced that similar methods applied to normal children would develop or set free their personality in a marvelous and surprising way.

It was then that I began a genuine and thorough study of what is known as remedial pedagogy, and, then, wishing to undertake the study of normal pedagogy and of the principles upon which it is based, I registered as a student of philosophy at the University. A great faith animated me, and although I did not know that I should ever be able to test the truth of my idea, I gave up every other occupation to deepen and broaden its conception. It was almost as if I prepared myself for an unknown mission.

The methods for the education of deficients had their origin at the time of the French Revolution in the work of a physician whose achievements occupy a prominent place in the history of medicine, as he was the founder of that branch of medical science which today is known as Otiatria (diseases of the ear).

He was the first to attempt a methodical education of the sense of hearing. He made these experiments in the institute for deaf mutes founded in Paris by Pereire, and actually succeeded in making the semi-deaf hear clearly. Later on, having in charge for eight years the idiot boy known as "the wild boy of Aveyron," he extended to the treatment of all the senses those educational methods which had already given such excellent results in the treatment of the sense of hearing. A student of Pinel, Itard was the first educator to practice *the observation* of the pupil in the way in which the sick are observed in the hospitals, especially those suffering from diseases of the nervous system.[3]

The pedagogic writings of Itard are most interesting and minute descriptions of educational efforts and experiences, and anyone reading them today must admit that they were practically the first attempts at experimental psychology. But the merit of having completed a genuine educational system for deficient children was due to Edouard Seguin, first a teacher and then a physician. He took the experiences of Itard as his starting point, applying these methods, modifying and completing them during a period of ten years' experience with children taken from the insane asylums and placed in a little school in Rue Pigalle in Paris. This method was described for the first time in a volume of more than six hundred pages, published in Paris in 1846, with the title: *Traitement Moral, Hygiène et Education des Idiots*.[4] Later Seguin emigrated to the United States of America where he founded many institutions for deficients, and where, after another twenty years of experience, he published the second edition of his method, under a very different title: *Idiocy and its Treatment by the Physiological Method*. This volume was published in New York in 1866, and in it Seguin had carefully defined his method of education, calling it the *physiological method*. He no longer referred in the title to a method for the "education of idiots" as if the method were special to them, but spoke now of idiocy treated by a physiological method. If we consider that pedagogy always had psychology as its base, and that Wundt defines a "physiological psychology," the coincidence of these ideas must strike us, and lead us to suspect in the physiological method some connection with physiological psychology.

While I was assistant at the Psychiatric Clinic, I had read Edouard Seguin's French book, with great interest. But the English book which was published in New York twenty years later, although it was quoted in the works about special education by Bourneville, was not to be found in any library. I made a vain quest for it, going from house to house of nearly all the English physicians, who were known to be specially interested in deficient children, or who were superintendents of special schools. The fact that this book was unknown in England, although it had been published in the English language, made me think that the Seguin system had never been understood. In fact, although Seguin was constantly quoted in all the publications dealing with institutions for deficients, the educational *applications* described, were quite different from the applications of Seguin's system.

Almost everywhere the methods applied to deficients are more or less the same as those in use for normal children. In Germany, especially, a friend who had gone there in order to help me in my researches, noticed that although special materials existed here and there in the pedagogical museums of the schools for deficients, these materials were rarely used. Indeed, the German educators hold the principle that it is well to adapt to the teaching of backward children, the same method used for normal ones; but these methods are much more objective in Germany than with us.

At the Bicêtre, where I spent some time, I saw that it was the didactic apparatus of Seguin far more than his *method* which was being used, although the French text was in the hands of the educators. The teaching there was purely mechanical, each teacher following the rules according to the letter. I found, however, wherever I went, in London as well as in Paris, a desire for fresh counsel and for new experiences, since far too often Seguin's claim that with his methods the education of idiots was actually possible, had proved only a delusion.

After this study of the methods in use throughout Europe, I concluded my experiments upon the deficients of Rome, and taught them throughout two years. I followed Seguin's book, and also derived much help from the remarkable experiments of Itard.

Guided by the work of these two men, I had manufactured a great variety of didactic material. These materials, which I have never seen complete in any institution, became in the hands of those who knew how to apply them, a most remarkable and efficient means, but unless rightly presented, they failed to attract the attention of the deficients.

I felt that I understood the discouragement of those working with feeble-minded children, and could see why they had, in so many cases, abandoned the method. The prejudice that the educator must place himself on a level with the one to be educated, sinks the teacher of deficients into a species of apathy. He accepts the fact that he is educating an inferior personality, and for that very reason he does not succeed. Even so those who teach little children too often have the idea that they are educating babies and seek to place themselves on the child's level by approaching him with games, and often with foolish stories. Instead of all this, we must know how to call to the *man* which lies dormant within the soul of the child. I felt this, intuitively, and believed that not the didactic material, but my voice which called to them, *awakened* the children, and encouraged them to use the didactic material, and through it, to educate themselves. I was guided in my work by the deep respect which I felt for their misfortune, and by the love which these unhappy children know how to awaken in those who are near them.

Seguin, too, expressed himself in the same way on this subject. Reading his patient attempts, I understand clearly that the first didactic material used by him was *spiritual*. Indeed, at the close of the French volume, the author, giving a résumé of his work, concludes by saying rather sadly, that all he has established will be lost or useless, if the *teachers* are not prepared for their work. He holds rather original views concerning the preparation of teachers of deficients. He would have them good to look upon, pleasant voiced, careful in every detail of their personal appearance, doing everything possible to make themselves attractive. They must, he says, render themselves attractive in voice and manner, since it is their task to awaken souls which are frail and weary, and to lead them forth to lay hold upon the beauty and strength of life.

This belief that we must act upon the spirit, served as a sort of *secret key*, opening to me the long series of didactic experiments so wonderfully analyzed by Edouard Seguin—experiments which, properly understood, are really most efficacious in the education of idiots. I myself obtained most surprising results through their application, but I must confess that, while my efforts showed themselves in the intellectual progress of my pupils, a peculiar form of exhaustion prostrated me. It was as if I gave to them some vital force from within me. Those things which we call encouragement, comfort, love, respect, are drawn from the soul of man, and the more freely we give of them, the more do we renew and reinvigorate the life about us. . . .

Thus prepared, I was able to proceed to new experiments on my own account. This is not the place for a report of these experiments, and I will only note that at this time I attempted an original method for the teaching of reading and writing, a part of the education of the child which was most imperfectly treated in the works of both Itard and Seguin.

I succeeded in teaching a number of the idiots from the asylums both to read and to write so well that I was able to present them at a public school for an examination together with normal children. And they passed the examination successfully.

These results seemed almost miraculous to those who saw them. To me, however, the boys from the asylums had been able to compete with the normal children only because they had been taught in a different way. They had been helped in their psychic development, and the normal children had, instead, been suffocated, held back. I found myself thinking that if, some day, the special education which had developed these idiot children in such a marvelous fashion, could be applied to the development of normal children, the "miracle" of which my friends talked would no longer be possible. The abyss between the inferior mentality of the idiot and that of the normal brain can never be bridged if the normal child has reached his full development.

While everyone was admiring the progress of my idiots, I was searching for the reasons which could keep the happy healthy children of the common schools on so low a plane that they could be equaled in tests of intelligence by my unfortunate pupils![5] . . .

It was thus that Seguin taught the idiots how to walk, how to maintain their equilibrium in the most difficult movements of the body—such as going up stairs, jumping, etc., and finally, to feel, beginning the education of the muscular sensations by touching, and reading the difference of temperature, and ending with the education of the particular senses.

But if the training goes no further than this, we have only led these children to adapt themselves to a low order of life (almost a vegetable existence). "Call to the Spirit," says the prophecy, and the spirit shall enter into them, and they shall have life. Seguin, indeed, led the idiot from the vegetative to the intellectual life, "from the education of the senses to general notions, from general notions to abstract thought, from abstract thought to morality." But when this wonderful work is accomplished, and by means of a minute physiological analysis and of a gradual progression in method, the idiot has become a man, he is still an inferior in the midst of his fellow men, an individual who will never be able fully to adapt himself to the social environment: "Our bones are dried, and our hope is lost; we are cut off for our parts."

This gives us another reason why the tedious method of Seguin was so often abandoned; the tremendous difficulty of the means, did not justify the end. Everyone felt this, and many said, "There is still so much to be done for normal children!"

Having through actual experience justified my faith in Seguin's method, I withdrew from active work among deficients, and began a more thorough study of the works of Itard and Seguin. I felt the need of mediation. I did a thing which I had not done before, and which perhaps few students have been willing to do—I translated into Italian and copied out with my own hand, the writings of these men, from beginning to end, making for myself books as the old Benedictines used to do before the diffusion of printing.

I chose to do this by hand, in order that I might have time to weigh the sense of each word, and to read, in truth, the *spirit* of the author. I had just finished copying the 600 pages of Seguin's French volume when I received from New York a copy of the English book published in 1866. This old volume had been found among the books discarded from the private library of a New York physician. I translated it with the help of an English friend. This volume did not add much in the way of new pedagogical experiments, but dealt with the philosophy of the experiences described in the first volume. The man who had studied abnormal children for thirty years expressed the idea that the physiological method, which has as its base the individual study of the pupil and which forms its educative methods upon the analysis of physiological and psychological phenomena, must come also to be applied to normal children. This step, he believed, would show the way to a complete human regeneration.

The voice of Seguin seemed to be like the voice of the forerunner crying in the wilderness, and my thoughts were filled with the immensity and importance of a work which should be able to reform the school and education.

At this time I was registered at the University as a student of philosophy, and followed the courses in experimental psychology, which had only recently been established in Italian universities, namely, at Turin, Rome, and Naples. At the same time I made researches in Pedagogic Anthropology in the elementary schools, studying in this way the methods in organization used for the education of normal children. This work led to the teaching of Pedagogic Anthropology in the University of Rome.

I had long wished to experiment with the methods for deficients in a first elementary class of normal children, but I had never thought of making use of the homes or institutions where very young children were cared for. It was pure chance that brought this new idea to my mind.

It was near the end of the year 1906, and I had just returned from Milan, where I had been one of a committee at the International Exhibition for the assignment of prizes in the subjects of scientific pedagogy and Experimental Psychology. A great opportunity came to me, for I was invited by Edoardo Talamo,[6] the Director General of the Roman Association for Good Building, to undertake the organization of infant schools in its model tenements. It was Signor Talamo's happy idea to gather together in a large room all the little ones between the ages of three and seven belonging to the families living in the tenement. The play and work of these children was to be carried on under the guidance of a teacher who should have her own apartment in the tenement house. It was intended that every house should have its school, and as the Association for Good Building already owned more than 400 tenements in Rome the work seemed to offer tremendous possibilities of development. The first school was to be established in January, 1907, in a large tenement house in the Quarter of San Lorenzo. In the same Quarter the Association already owned fifty-eight buildings, and according to Signor Talamo's plans we should soon be able to open sixteen of these "schools within the house."

This new kind of school was christened by Signora Olga Lodi, a mutual friend of Signor Talamo and myself, under the fortunate title of *Casa dei Bambini* or "The Children's House." Under this name the first of our schools was opened on the sixth of January, 1907, at 58 Via dei Marsi. It was confided to the care of Candida Nuccitelli and was under my guidance and direction.

From the very first I perceived, in all its immensity, the social and pedagogical importance of such institutions, and while at that time my visions of a triumphant future seemed exaggerated, today many are beginning to understand that what I saw before was indeed the truth.

On the seventh of April of the same year, 1907, a second "Children's House" was opened in the Quarter of San Lorenzo; and on the eighteenth of October, 1908, another was inaugurated by the Humanitarian Society in Milan in the Quarter inhabited by workingmen. The workshops of this same society undertook the manufacture of the materials which we used.

On the fourth of November following, a third "Children's House" was opened in Rome, this time not in the people's Quarter, but in a modern building for the middle classes, situated in Via Famagosta, in that part of the city known as the Prati di Castello; and in January, 1909, Italian Switzerland began to transform its orphan asylums and children's homes in which the Froebel system had been used, into "Children's Houses" adopting our methods and materials.

The "Children's House" has a twofold importance: the social importance which it assumes through its peculiarity of being a school within the house, and its purely pedagogic importance gained through its methods for the education of very young children, of which I now made a trial.

As I have said, Signor Talamo's invitation gave me a wonderful opportunity for applying the methods used with deficients to normal children, not of the elementary school age, but of the age usual in infant asylums.

If a parallel between the deficient and the normal child is possible, this will be during the period of early infancy *when the child who has not the force to develop* and *he who is not yet developed* are in some ways alike.

The very young child has not yet acquired a secure coordination of muscular movements, and, therefore, walks imperfectly, and is not able to perform the ordinary acts of life, such as fastening and unfastening its garments. The sense organs, such as the power of accommodation of the eye, are not yet completely developed; the language is primordial and shows those defects common to the speech of the very young child. The difficulty of fixing the attention, the general instability, etc., are characteristics which the normal infant and the deficient child have in common. Preyer, also, in his psychological study of children has turned aside to illustrate the parallel between pathological linguistic defects, and those of normal children in the process of developing.[7]

Methods which made growth possible to the mental personality of the idiot ought, therefore, to *aid the development of young children*, and should be so adapted as to constitute a hygienic education of the entire personality of a normal human being. Many defects which become permanent, such as speech defects, the child acquires through being neglected during the most important period of his age, the period between three and six, at which time he forms and establishes his principal functions.

Here lies the significance of my pedagogical experiment in the "Children's Houses." It represents the results of a series of trials made by me, in the education of young children, with methods already used with deficients. My work has not been in any way an application, pure and simple, of the methods of Seguin to young children, as anyone who will consult the works of the author will readily see. But it is none the less true that, underlying these two years of trial, there is a basis of experiment which goes back to the days of the French Revolution, and which represents the earnest work of the lives of Itard and Seguin.

As for me, thirty years after the publication of Seguin's second book, I took up again the ideas and, I may even say, the work of this great man, with the same freshness of spirit with which he received the inheritance of the work and ideas of his master Itard. For *ten years* I not only made practical experiments according to their methods, but through reverent meditation absorbed the works of these noble and consecrated men, who have left to humanity most vital proof of their obscure heroism.

Thus my ten years of work may in a sense be considered as a summing up of the forty years of work done by Itard and Seguin. Viewed in this light, fifty years of active work preceded and prepared for this apparently brief trial of only two years, and I feel that I am not wrong in saying that these experiments represent the successive work of three physicians, who from Itard to me show in a greater or less degree the first steps along the path of psychiatry.

As definite factors in the civilization of the people, the "Children's Houses" deserve a separate volume. They have, in fact, solved so many of the social and pedagogic problems in ways which have seemed to be Utopian, that they are a part of that modern transformation of the home which must most surely be realized before many years have passed. In this way they touch directly the most important side of the social question—that which deals with the intimate or home life of the people.

It is enough here to reproduce the inaugural discourse delivered by me on the occasion of the opening of the second "Children's House" in Rome, and to present the rules and regulations which I arranged in accordance with the wishes of Signor Talamo.

It will be noticed that the club to which I refer, and the dispensary which is also an out-patients' institution for medical and surgical treatment (all such institutions being free to the inhabitants) have already been established. In the modern tenement—Casa Moderna in the Prati di Castello, opened November 4, 1908, through the philanthropy of Signor Talamo—they are also planning to annex a "communal kitchen."

EDITOR'S NOTES

1. Thyroid organotherapy refers to medical efforts to treat the endocrine gland that stimulates human growth and development.

2. Guido Baccelli was a professor of clinical medicine and head of the medical faculty at the University of Rome when Montessori was a student. A member of the Chamber of Deputies, Bacelli served as Minister of Education in several cabinets during the 1880s and 1890s. In 1899, Baccelli commissioned Montessori to present a lecture series at the Scuole Normali di Magistero, the teacher education school of the Collegio Romano on the methods of educating mentally retarded children.

3. Jean Marc Gaspard Itard (1775–1838) was a French educator, who served as physician at the Institution for Deaf Mutes in Paris, where he specialized in diseases of the ear. In 1779, Itard undertook the education of a deaf-mute feral boy, about age twelve, who had been found living with animals in a forest. Itard's efforts to train the child, known as the "Sauvage de l'Aveyron," attracted considerable attention in Europe. A report about Itard's work with the boy, *de l'education d'un homme sauvage ou des premiers developpements phyiques et moraux du jeunce sauvage de l'Averyon*

was published in 1801. Itard had some limited success in the boy's training and he concluded that it was possible to educate children with severe handicaps. Itard's major work, *Traite des maladies de l'oreille et de l'audition* was published in 1821. In several sections of *The Montessori Method*, Montessori acknowledges Itard's work and its influence on her.

4. Edouard Seguin (1812–1880), a French physician, specialized in the training and education of children with mental handicaps. Based on his physiological observations of children, he believed that they could be trained by specific activities involving specially designed apparatus such as texture boards, swing boards, stacking blocks, and climbing stools. In 1843, he applied his methods at the Hospice de la Veilleiuse (Bicetre). His books, *Hygiene et education des idiots* (1843) and *Traitement moral, hygiene et education des idiots et des autres enfants arrieres ouretardes* (1846), established his reputation as a leading authority on the education of children with mental handicaps. In 1848, Seguin immigrated to the United States where he continued his work. An English translation of his work, *Idiocy and its Treatment by the Physiological Method* (1866), attracted considerable attention in the United States. Seguin's main ideas were: (1) idiocy and a many other mental handicaps were caused by neurological impairment; (2) mentally impaired children could be educated and many of the methods used in their education also applied to the education of normal children. Montessori was highly influenced by Seguin's work, especially his use of didactic apparatus and materials and his argument that the training of children with handicaps could be used in the education of all children.

5. The passage on pp. 39–40 in which Montessori refers to prophecy of Ezekiel about flesh coming on dry bones as example of Seguin's method of education is deleted.

6. Edoardo Talamo was the Director General of the Roman Association for Good Building, a philanthropic organization established to improve living and housing conditions of Rome's urban poor. In 1910, disagreements between Talamo and Montessori caused her to leave the original Casa dei Bambini.

7. Wilhelm Preyer (1841–1897), a German psychologist, was one of the founders of the child study movement. His book, *The Mind of the Child* examined children's development and their learning processes. Like Montessori, Preyer emphasized the need to develop child psychology as a scientific field that used tests and measurements and clinical observation.

3

Inaugural Address Delivered on the Occasion of the Opening of One of the "Children's Houses"

It may be that the life lived by the very poor is a thing which some of you here today have never actually looked upon in all its degradation. You may have only felt the misery of deep human poverty through the medium of some great book, or some gifted actor may have made your soul vibrate with its horror.[1] . . .

The Quarter of San Lorenzo is celebrated, for every newspaper in the city is filled with almost daily accounts of its wretched happenings. Yet there are many who are not familiar with the origin of this portion of our city.

It was never intended to build up here a tenement district for the people. And indeed San Lorenzo is not the *People's* Quarter, it is the Quarter of the *poor*. It is the Quarter where lives the underpaid, often unemployed workingman, a common type in a city which has no factory industries. It is the home of him who undergoes the period of surveillance to which he is condemned after his prison sentence is ended. They are all here, mingled, huddled together.

The district of San Lorenzo sprang into being between 1884 and 1888 at the time of the great building fever. No standards either social or hygienic guided these new constructions. The aim in building was simply to cover with walls square foot after square foot of ground. The more space covered, the greater the gain of the interested banks and companies. All this with a complete disregard of the disastrous future which they were preparing. It was natural that no one should concern himself with the stability of the building he was creating, since in no case would the property remain in the possession of him who built it.

When the storm burst, in the shape of the inevitable building panic of 1888 to 1890, these unfortunate houses remained for a long time untenanted. Then, little by little, the need of dwelling places began to make itself felt, and these great houses began to fill. Now, those speculators who had been so unfortunate as to remain possessors of these buildings could not, and did not wish to add fresh capital to that already lost, so the houses constructed in the first place in utter disregard of all laws of hygiene, and rendered still worse by having been used as temporary habitations, came to be occupied by the poorest class in the city.

The apartments not being prepared for the working class, were too large, consisting of five, six, or seven rooms. These were rented at a price which, while exceedingly low in relation to the size, was yet too high for any one family of very poor people. This led to the evil of subletting. The tenant who has taken a six-room apartment at eight dollars a month sublets rooms at one dollar and a half or two dollars a month to those who can pay so much, and a corner of a room, or a corridor, to a poorer tenant, thus making an income of fifteen dollars or more, over and above the cost of his own rent.

This means that the problem of existence is in great part solved for him, and that in every case he adds to his income through usury. The one who holds the lease traffics in the misery of his fellow tenants, lending small sums at a rate which generally corresponds to twenty cents a week for the loan of two dollars, equivalent to an annual rate of 500 percent.

Thus we have in the evil of subletting the most cruel form of usury: that which only the poor know how to practice upon the poor.

To this we must add the evils of crowded living, promiscuousness, immorality, crime. Every little while the newspapers uncover for us one of these *intérieurs:* a large family, growing boys and girls, sleep in one room; while one corner of the room is occupied by an outsider, a woman who receives the nightly visits of men. This is seen by the girls and the boys; evil passions are kindled that lead to the crime and bloodshed which unveil for a brief instant before our eyes, in some lurid paragraph, this little detail of the mass of misery.

Whoever enters, for the first time, one of these apartments is astonished and horrified. For this spectacle of genuine misery is not at all like the garish scene he has imagined. We enter here a world of shadows, and that which strikes us first is the darkness which, even though it be midday, makes it impossible to distinguish any of the details of the room.

When the eye has grown accustomed to the gloom, we perceive, within, the outlines of a bed upon which lies huddled a figure—someone ill and suffering. If we have come to bring money from some society for mutual aid, a candle must be lighted before the sum can be counted and the receipt signed. Oh, when we talk of social problems, how often we speak vaguely, drawing upon our fancy for details instead of preparing ourselves to judge intelligently through a personal investigation of facts and conditions.

We discuss earnestly the question of home study for school children, when for many of them home means a straw pallet thrown down in the corner of some dark hovel. We wish to establish circulating libraries that the poor may read at home. We plan to send among these people books which shall form their domestic literature—books through whose influence they shall come to higher standards of living. We hope through the printed page to educate these poor people in matters of hygiene, of morality, of culture, and in this we show ourselves profoundly ignorant of their most crying needs. For many of them have no light by which to read! . . .

In speaking of the children born in these places, even the conventional expressions must be changed, for they do not "first see the light of day"; they come into a world of gloom. They grow among the poisonous shadows which envelope over-crowded humanity. These children cannot be other than filthy in body, since the water supply in an apartment originally intended to be occupied by three or four persons, when distributed among twenty or thirty is scarcely enough for drinking purposes!

We Italians have elevated our word "casa" to the almost sacred significance of the English word "home," the enclosed temple of domestic affection, accessible only to dear ones.

Far removed from this conception is the condition of the many who have no "casa," but only ghastly walls within which the most intimate acts of life are exposed upon the pillory. Here, there can be no privacy, no modesty, no gentleness; here, there is often not even light, nor air, nor water! It seems a cruel mockery to introduce here our idea of the home as essential to the education of the masses, and as furnishing, along with the family, the only solid basis for the social structure. In doing this we would be not practical reformers but visionary poets.

Conditions such as I have described make it more decorous, more hygienic, for these people to take refuge in the street and to let their children live there. But how often these streets are the scene of bloodshed, of quarrel, of sights so vile as to be almost inconceivable. The papers tell us of women pursued and killed by drunken husbands! Of young girls with the fear of worse than death, stoned by low men. Again, we see untellable things—a wretched woman thrown, by the drunken men who have preyed upon her, forth into the gutter. There, when day has come, the children of the neighborhood crowd about her like scavengers about their dead prey, shouting and laughing at the sight of this wreck of womanhood, kicking her bruised and filthy body as it lies in the mud of the gutter!

Such spectacles of extreme brutality are possible here at the very gate of a cosmopolitan city, the mother of civilization and queen of the fine arts, because of a new fact which was unknown to past centuries, namely, *the isolation of the masses of the poor.*

In the Middle Ages, leprosy was isolated: the Catholics isolated the Hebrews in the Ghetto; but poverty was never considered a peril and an infamy so great that it must be isolated. The homes of the poor were scattered among those of the rich and the contrast between these was commonplace in literature up to our own times. Indeed, when I was a child in school, teachers, for the purpose of moral education, frequently resorted to the illustration of the kind princess who sends help to the poor cottage next door, or of the good children from the great house who carry food to the sick woman in the neighboring attic.

Today all this would be as unreal and artificial as a fairy tale. The poor may no longer learn from their more fortunate neighbors lessons in courtesy and good breeding, they no longer have the hope of help from them in cases of extreme need. We have herded them together far from us, without the walls, leaving them to learn of each other, in the abandon of desperation, the cruel lessons of brutality and vice. Anyone in whom the social conscience is awake must see that we have thus created infected regions that threaten with deadly peril the city which, wishing to make all beautiful and shining according to an æsthetic and aristocratic ideal, has thrust without its walls whatever is ugly or diseased. . . .

But what indeed is benevolence? Little more than an expression of sorrow; it is pity translated into action. The benefits of such a form of charity cannot be great, and through the absence of any continued income and the lack of organization it is restricted to a small number of persons. The great and widespread peril of evil demands, on the other hand, a broad and comprehensive work directed toward the redemption of the entire community. Only such an organization, as, working for the good of others, shall itself grow and prosper through the general prosperity which it has made possible, can make a place for itself in this quarter and accomplish a permanent good work.

It is to meet this dire necessity that the great and kindly work of the Roman Association of Good Building has been undertaken. The advanced and highly modern way in which this work is being carried on is due to Edoardo Talamo, Director General of the Association. His plans, so original, so comprehensive, yet so practical, are without counterpart in Italy or elsewhere.

This Association was incorporated three years ago in Rome, its plan being to acquire city tenements, remodel them, put them into a productive condition, and administer them as a good father of a family would.

The first property acquired comprised a large portion of the Quarter of San Lorenzo, where today the Association possesses fifty-eight houses, occupying a ground space of about 30,000 square meters, and containing, independent of the ground floor, 1,600 small apartments. Thousands of people will in this way receive the beneficent influence of the protective reforms of the Good Building Association. Following its beneficent program, the Association set about transforming these old houses, according to the most modern standards, paying as much attention to questions related to hygiene and morals as to those relating to buildings. The constructional changes would make the property of real and lasting value, while the hygienic and moral transformation would, through the improved condition of the inmates, make the rent from these apartments a more definite asset.

The Association of Good Building therefore decided upon a program which would permit of a gradual attainment of their ideal. It is necessary to proceed slowly because it is not easy to empty a tenement house at a time when houses are scarce, and the humanitarian principles which govern the entire movement make it impossible to proceed more rapidly in this work of regeneration. So it is, that the Association has up to the present time transformed only three houses in the Quarter of San Lorenzo.[2] . . .

The division of the house into small apartments has done much toward this moral regeneration. Each family is thus set apart, *homes* are made possible, while the menacing evil of subletting together with all its disastrous consequences of overcrowding and immorality is checked in the most radical way.

On one side this arrangement lessens the burden of the individual lease holders, and on the other increases the income of the proprietor, who now receives those earnings which were the unlawful gain of the system of subletting. When the proprietor who originally rented an apartment of six rooms for a monthly rental of eight dollars, makes such an apartment over into three small, sunny, and airy suites consisting of one room and a kitchen, it is evident that he increases his income.

The moral importance of this reform as it stands today is tremendous, for it has done away with those evil influences and low opportunities which arise from crowding and from promiscuous contact, and has brought to life among these people, for the first time, the gentle sentiment of feeling themselves free within their own homes, in the intimacy of the family.

But the project of the Association goes beyond even this. The house which it offers to its tenants is not only sunny and airy, but in perfect order and repair, almost shining, and as if perfumed with purity and freshness. These good things, however, carry with them a responsibility which the tenant must assume if he wishes to enjoy them. He must pay an actual tax of *care* and *good will*. The tenant who receives a clean house must keep it so, must respect the walls from the big general entrance to the interior of his own little apartment. He who keeps his house in good condition receives the recognition and consideration due such a tenant. Thus all the tenants unite in an ennobling warfare for practical hygiene, an end made possible by the simple task of *conserving* the already perfect conditions.

Here indeed is something new! So far only our great national buildings have had a continued *maintenance fund*. Here, in these houses offered to the people, the maintenance is confided to a hundred or so workingmen, that is, to all the occupants of the building. This care is almost perfect. The people keep the house in perfect condition, without a single spot. The building in which we find ourselves today has been for two years under the sole protection of the tenants, and the work of maintenance has been left entirely to them. Yet few of our houses can compare in cleanliness and freshness with this home of the poor.

The experiment has been tried and the result is remarkable. The people acquire together with the love of homemaking, that of cleanliness. They come, moreover, to wish to beautify their homes. The Association helps this by placing growing plants and trees in the courts and about the halls.

Out of this honest rivalry in matters so productive of good, grows a species of pride new to this quarter; this is the pride which the entire body of tenants takes in having the best-cared-for building and in having risen to a higher and more civilized plane of living. They not only live in a house, but they *know how to live*, they *know how to respect* the house in which they live.

This first impulse has led to other reforms. From the clean home will come personal cleanliness. Dirty furniture cannot be tolerated in a clean house, and those persons living in a permanently clean house will come to desire personal cleanliness.

One of the most important hygienic reforms of the Association is that of *the baths*. Each remodeled tenement has a place set apart for bathrooms, furnished with tubs or shower, and having hot and cold water. All the tenants in regular turn may use these baths, as, for example, in various tenements the occupants go according to turn, to wash their clothes in the fountain in the court. This is a great convenience which invites the people to be clean. These hot and cold baths *within the house* are a great improvement upon the general public baths. In this way we make possible to these people, at one and the same time, health and refinement, opening not only to the sun, but to progress, those dark habitations once the *vile caves* of misery.

But in striving to realize its ideal of a semi-gratuitous maintenance of its buildings, the Association met with a difficulty in regard to those children under school age, who must often be left alone during the entire day while their parents went out to work. These little ones, not being able to understand the educative motives which taught their parents to respect the house, became ignorant little vandals, defacing the walls and stairs. And here we have another reform the expense of which may be considered as indirectly assumed by the tenants as was the care of the building. This reform may be considered as the most brilliant transformation of a tax which progress and civilization have as yet devised. The "Children's House" is earned by the parents through the care of the building. Its expenses are met by the sum that the Association would have otherwise been forced to spend upon repairs. A wonderful climax, this, of moral benefits received! Within the "Children's House," which belongs exclusively to those children under school age, working mothers may safely leave their little ones, and may proceed with a feeling of great relief and freedom to their own work. But this benefit, like that of the care of the house, is not conferred without a tax of care and of good will. The Regulations posted on the walls announce it thus:

"The mothers are obliged to send their children to the 'Children's House' clean, and to co-operate with the Directress in the educational work."

Two obligations: namely, the physical and moral care of their own children. If the child shows through its conversation that the educational work of the school is being undermined by the attitude taken in his home, he will be sent back to his parents, to teach them thus how to take advantage of their good opportunities. Those who give themselves over to low-living, to fighting, and to brutality, shall feel upon them the weight of those little lives, so needing care. They shall feel that they themselves have once more cast into the darkness of neglect those little creatures who are the dearest part of the family. In other words, the parents must learn to *deserve* the benefit of having within the house the great advantage of a school for their little ones.

"Good will," a willingness to meet the demands of the Association is enough, for the directress is ready and willing to teach them how. The regulations say that the mother must go at least once a week, to confer with the directress, giving an account of her child, and accepting any helpful advice which the directress may be able to give. The advice thus given will undoubtedly prove most illuminating in regard to the child's health and education, since to each of the "Children's Houses" is assigned a physician as well as a directress.

The directress is always at the disposition of the mothers, and her life, as a cultured and educated person, is a constant example to the inhabitants of the house, for she is obliged to live in the tenement and to be therefore a cohabitant with the families of all her little pupils. This is a fact of immense importance. Among these almost savage people, into these houses where at night no one dared go about unarmed, there has come not only to teach, *but to live the very life they live,* a gentlewoman of culture, an educator by profession, who dedicates her time and her life to helping those about her! A true missionary, a moral queen among the people, she may, if she be possessed of sufficient tact and heart, reap an unheard-of harvest of good from her social work.

This house is verily *new;* it would seem a dream impossible of realization, but it has been tried. It is true that there have been before this attempts made by generous persons to go and live among the poor to civilize them. But such work is not practical, unless the house of the poor is hygienic, making it possible for people of better standards to live there. Nor can such work succeed in its purpose unless some common advantage or interest unites all of the tenants in an effort toward better things.

This tenement is new also because of the pedagogical organization of the "Children's House." This is not simply a place where the children are kept, not just an *asylum*, but a true school for their education, and its methods are inspired by the rational principles of scientific pedagogy.

The physical development of the children is followed, each child being studied from the anthropological standpoint. Linguistic exercises, a systematic sense-training, and exercises which directly fit the child for the duties of practical life, form the basis of the work done. The teaching is decidedly objective, and presents an unusual richness of didactic material.

It is not possible to speak of all this in detail. I must, however, mention that there already exists in connection with the school a bathroom, where the children may be given hot or cold baths and where they may learn to take a partial bath, hands, face, neck, ears. Wherever possible the Association has provided a piece of ground in which the children may learn to cultivate the vegetables in common use.

It is important that I speak here of the pedagogical progress attained by the "Children's House" as an institution. Those who are conversant with the chief problems of the school know that today much attention is given to a great principle, one that is ideal and almost beyond realization—the union of the family and the school in the matter of educational aims. But the family is always something far away from the school, and is almost always regarded as rebelling against its ideals. It is a species of phantom upon which the school can never lay its hands. The home is closed not only to pedagogical progress, but often to social progress. We see here for the first time the possibility of realizing the long-talked-of pedagogical ideal. We have put *the school within the house;* and this is not all. We have placed it within the house as the *property of the collectivity,* leaving under the eyes of the parents the whole life of the teacher in the accomplishment of her high mission.

This idea of the collective ownership of the school is new and very beautiful and profoundly educational.

The parents know that the "Children's House" is their property, and is maintained by a portion of the rent they pay. The mothers may go at any hour of the day to watch, to admire, or to meditate upon the life there. It is in every way a continual stimulus to reflection, and a fount of evident blessing and help to their own children. We may say that the mothers *adore* the "Children's House," and the directress. How many delicate and thoughtful attentions these good mothers show the teacher of their little ones! They often leave sweets or flowers upon the sill of the schoolroom window, as a silent token, reverently, almost religiously, given.

And when after three years of such a novitiate, the mothers send their children to the common schools, they will be excellently prepared to cooperate in the work of education, and will have acquired a sentiment, rarely found even among the best classes; namely, the idea that they must *merit* through their own conduct and with their own virtue, the possession of an educated son.

Another advance made by the "Children's Houses" as an institution is related to scientific pedagogy. This branch of pedagogy, heretofore, being based upon the anthropological study of the pupil whom it is to educate, has touched only a few of the positive questions which tend to transform education. For a man is not only a biological but a social product, and the social environment of individuals in the process of education, is the home. Scientific pedagogy will seek in vain to better the new generation if it does not succeed in influencing also the environment within which this new generation grows! I believe, therefore, that in opening the house to the light of new truths, and to the progress of civilization we have solved the problem of being able to modify directly, the *environment* of the new generation, and have thus made it possible to apply, in a practical way, the fundamental principles of scientific pedagogy.

The "Children's House" marks still another triumph; it is the first step toward the *socialization of the house*. The inmates find under their own roof the convenience of being able to leave their little ones in a place, not only safe, but where they have every advantage.

And let it be remembered that *all* the mothers in the tenement may enjoy this privilege, going away to their work with easy minds. Until the present time only one class in society might have this advantage. Rich women were able to go about their various occupations and amusements, leaving their children in the hands of a nurse or a governess. Today the women of the people who live in these remodeled houses, may say, like the great lady, "I have left my son with the governess and the nurse." More than this, they may add, like the princess of the blood, "And the house physician watches over them and directs their sane and sturdy growth." These women, like the most advanced class of English and American mothers, possess a "Biographical Chart," which, filled for the mother by the directress and the doctor, gives her the most practical knowledge of her child's growth and condition.

We are all familiar with the ordinary advantages of the communistic transformation of the general environment. For example, the collective use of railway carriages, of street lights, of the telephone, all these are great advantages. The enormous production of useful articles, brought about by industrial progress, makes possible to all, clean clothes, carpets, curtains, table delicacies, better tableware, etc. The making of such benefits generally tends to level social caste. All this we have seen in its reality. But the communizing of *persons* is new. That the collectivity shall benefit from the services of the servant, the nurse, the teacher—this is a modern ideal.

We have in the "Children's Houses" a demonstration of this ideal which is unique in Italy or elsewhere. Its significance is most profound, for it corresponds to a need of the times. We can no longer say that the convenience of leaving their children takes away from the mother a natural social duty of first importance; namely, that of caring for and educating her tender offspring. No, for today the social and economic evolution calls the working woman to take her place among wage earners, and takes away from her by force those duties which would be most dear to her! The mother must, in any event, leave her child, and often with the pain of knowing him to be abandoned. The advantages furnished by such institutions are not limited to the laboring classes, but extend also to the general middle class, many of whom work with the brain. Teachers, professors, often obliged to give private lessons after school hours, frequently leave their children to the care of some rough and ignorant maid-of-all-work. Indeed, the first announcement of the "Children's House" was followed by a deluge of letters from persons of the better class demanding that these helpful reforms be extended to their dwellings.

We are, then, communizing a "maternal function," a feminine duty, within the house. We may see here in this practical act the solving of many of woman's problems which have seemed to many impossible of solution. What then will become of the home, one asks, if the woman goes away from it? The home will be transformed and will assume the functions of the woman.

I believe that in the future of society other forms of communistic life will come.[3]

Take, for example, the infirmary; woman is the natural nurse for the dear ones of her household. But who does not know how often in these days she is obliged to tear herself unwillingly from the bedside of her sick to go to her work? Competition is great, and her absence from her post threatens the tenure of the position from which she draws the means of support. To be able to leave the sick one in a "house-infirmary," to which she may have access any free moments she may have, and where she is at liberty to watch during the night, would be an evident advantage to such a woman.

And how great would be the progress made in the matter of family hygiene, in all that relates to isolation and disinfection! Who does not know the difficulties of a poor family when one child is ill of some contagious disease, and should be isolated from the others? Often such a family may have no kindred or friends in the city to whom the other children may be sent.

Much more distant, but not impossible, is the communal kitchen, where the dinner ordered in the morning is sent at the proper time, by means of a dumb-waiter, to the family dining room. Indeed, this has been successfully tried in America. Such a reform would be of the greatest advantage to those families of the middle class who must confide their health and the pleasures of the table to the hands of an ignorant servant who ruins the food. At present, the only alternative in such cases is to go outside the home to some café where a cheap table d'hôte may be had.

Indeed, the transformation of the house must compensate for the loss in the family of the presence of the woman who has become a social wage earner.

In this way the house will become a center, drawing unto itself all those good things which have hitherto been lacking: schools, public baths, hospitals, etc.

Thus the tendency will be to change the tenement houses, which have been places of vice and peril, into centers of education, of refinement, of comfort. This will be helped if, besides the schools for the children, there may grow up also *clubs* and reading rooms for the inhabitants, especially for the men, who will find there a way to pass the evening pleasantly and decently. The tenement club, as possible and as useful in all social classes as is the "Children's House," will do much toward closing the gambling houses and saloons to the great moral advantage of the people. And I believe that the Association of Good Building will before long establish such clubs in its reformed tenements here in the Quarter of San Lorenzo; clubs where the tenants may find newspapers and books, and where they may hear simple and helpful lectures.

We are, then, very far from the dreaded dissolution of the home and of the family, through the fact that woman has been forced by changed social and economic conditions to give her time and strength to remunerative work. The home itself assumes the gentle feminine attributes of the domestic housewife. The day may come when the tenant, having given to the proprietor of the house a certain sum, shall receive in exchange whatever is necessary to the *comfort* of life; in other words, the administration shall become the *steward* of the family.

The house, thus considered, tends to assume in its evolution a significance more exalted than even the English word "home" expresses. It does not consist of walls alone, though these walls be the pure and shining guardians of that intimacy which is the sacred symbol of the family. The home shall become more than this. It lives! It has a soul. It may be said to embrace its inmates with the tender, consoling arms of woman. It is the giver of moral life, of blessings; it cares for, it educates and feeds the little ones. Within it, the tired workman shall find rest and newness of life. He shall find there the intimate life of the family, and its happiness.

The new woman, like the butterfly come forth from the chrysalis, shall be liberated from all those attributes which once made her desirable to man only as the source of the material blessings of existence. She shall be, like man, an individual, a free human being, a social worker; and, like man, she shall seek blessing and repose within the house, the house which has been reformed and communized.

She shall wish to be loved for herself and not as a giver of comfort and repose. She shall wish a love free from every form of servile labor. The goal of human love is not the egotistical end of assuring its own satisfaction—it is the sublime goal of multiplying the forces of the free spirit, making it almost Divine, and, within such beauty and light, perpetuating the species.[4] . . .

To better the species consciously, cultivating his own health, his own virtue, this should be the goal of man's married life. It is a sublime concept of which, as yet, few think. And the socialized home of the future, living, provident, kindly; educator and comforter; is the true and worthy home of those human mates who wish to better the species, and to send the race forward triumphant into the eternity of life!

RULES AND REGULATIONS OF THE "CHILDREN'S HOUSES"

The Roman Association of Good Building hereby establishes within its tenement house number, a "Children's House," in which may be gathered together all children under common school age, belonging to the families of the tenants.

The chief aim of the "Children's House" is to offer, free of charge, to the children of those parents who are obliged to absent themselves for their work, the personal care which the parents are not able to give.

In the "Children's House" attention is given to the education, the health, the physical and moral development of the children. This work is carried on in a way suited to the age of the children.

There shall be connected with the "Children's House" a Directress, a Physician, and a Caretaker.

The program and hours of the "Children's House" shall be fixed by the Directress.

There may be admitted to the "Children's House" all the children in the tenement between the ages of three and seven.

The parents who wish to avail themselves of the advantages of the "Children's House" pay nothing. They must, however, assume these binding obligations:

(a) To send their children to the "Children's House" at the appointed time, clean in body and clothing, and provided with a suitable apron.
(b) To show the greatest respect and deference toward the Directress and toward all persons connected with the "Children's House," and to cooperate with the Directress herself in the education of the children. Once a week, at least, the mothers may talk with the Directress, giving her information concerning the home life of the child, and receiving helpful advice from her.

There shall be expelled from the "Children's House":

(a) Those children who present themselves unwashed, or in soiled clothing.

(b) Those who show themselves to be incorrigible.

(c) Those whose parents fail in respect to the persons connected with the "Children's House," or who destroy through bad conduct the educational work of the institution.

EDITOR'S NOTES

1. The section on pp. 54–55 where Montessori continues her recital of the ills of the San Lorenzo district is deleted.

2. Montessori discussion of some architectural details about building plans of the Association of Good Building on p. 57 is deleted.

3. Montessori's term "communistic" was not used in a Marxist or political sense. For her, it meant communal or shared human association.

4. Montessori reference to ideal love as portrayed by the woman in Nietzsche's *Zarathustra* on p. 69 is deleted.

4

Pedagogical Methods Used in the "Children's Houses"

As soon as I knew that I had at my disposal a class of little children, it was my wish to make of this school a field for scientific experimental pedagogy and child psychology. I started with a view in which Wundt concurs; namely, that child psychology does not exist. Indeed, experimental researches in regard to childhood, as, for example, those of Preyer and Baldwin, have been made upon not more than two or three subjects, children of the investigators.[1] Moreover, the instruments of psychometry must be greatly modified and simplified before they can be used with children, who do not lend themselves passively as subjects for experimentation. Child psychology can be established only through the method of external observation. We must renounce all idea of making any record of internal states, which can be revealed only by the introspection of the subject himself. The instruments of psychometric research, as applied to pedagogy, have up to the present time been limited to the esthesiometric phase of the study.

My intention was to keep in touch with the researches of others, but to make myself independent of them, proceeding to my work without preconceptions of any kind. I retained as the only essential, the affirmation, or, rather, the definition of Wundt, that "all methods of experimental psychology may be reduced to one; namely, carefully recorded observation of the subject."

Treating of children, another factor must necessarily intervene: the study of the development. Here too, I retained the same general criterion, but without clinging to any dogma about the activity of the child according to age.

ANTHROPOLOGICAL CONSIDERATION

In regard to physical development, my first thought was given to the regulating of anthropometric observations, and to the selection of the most important observations to be made.[2] . . .

Having thus facilitated the technique of the researches, I decided to take the measurements of the children's stature, seated and standing, every month, and in order to have these regulated as exactly as possible in their relation to development, and also to give greater regularity to the research work of the teacher, I made a rule that the measurements should be taken on the day on which the child completed each month of his age.[3] . . .

I have found that the usual questions asked patients who present themselves at the clinics, are not adapted for use in our schools, as the members of the families living in these tenements are for the greater part perfectly normal.

I therefore encourage the directress of the school to gather from her conversations with the mothers information of a more practical sort. She informs herself as to the education of the parents, their habits, the wages earned, the money spent for household purposes, etc., and from all this she outlines a history of each family, much on the order of those used by Le-Play. This method is, of course, practical only where the directress lives among the families of her scholars.

In every case, however, the physician's advice to the mothers concerning the hygienic care of each particular child, as well as his directions concerning hygiene in general, will prove most helpful. The directress should act as the go-between in these matters, since she is in the confidence of the mothers, and since from her, such advice comes naturally.

ENVIRONMENT: SCHOOLROOM FURNISHINGS

The method of *observation* must undoubtedly include the *methodical observation* of the morphological growth of the pupils. But let me repeat that, while this element necessarily enters, it is not upon this particular kind of observation that the method is established.

The method of observation is established upon one fundamental base—*the liberty of the pupils in their spontaneous manifestations.*

With this in view, I first turned my attention to the question of environment, and this, of course, included the furnishing of the schoolroom. In considering an ample playground with space for a garden as an important part of this school environment, I am not suggesting anything new.

The novelty lies, perhaps, in my idea for the use of this open-air space, which is to be in direct communication with the schoolroom, so that the children may be free to go and come as they like, throughout the entire day. I shall speak of this more fully later on.

The principal modification in the matter of school furnishings is the abolition of desks, and benches or stationary chairs. I have had tables made with wide, solid, octagonal legs, spreading in such a way that the tables are at the same time solidly firm and very light, so light, indeed, that two four-year-old children can easily carry them about. These tables are rectangular and sufficiently large to accommodate two children on the long side, there being room for three if they sit rather close together. There are smaller tables at which one child may work alone.

I also designed and had manufactured little chairs. My first plan for these was to have them cane seated, but experience has shown the wear on these to be so great, that I now have chairs made entirely of wood. These are very light and of an attractive shape. In addition to these, I have in each schoolroom a number of comfortable little armchairs, some of wood and some of wicker.

Another piece of our school furniture consists of a little washstand, so low that it can be used by even a three-year-old child. This is painted with a white waterproof enamel and, besides the broad, upper and lower shelves which hold the little white enameled basins and pitchers, there are small side shelves for the soap dishes, nailbrushes, towels, etc. There is also a receptacle into which the basins may be emptied. Wherever possible, a small cupboard provides each child with a space where he may keep his own soap, nailbrush, toothbrush, and so forth.

In each of our schoolrooms we have provided a series of long low cupboards, especially designed for the reception of the didactic materials. The doors of these cupboards open easily, and the care of the materials is confided to the children. The tops of these cases furnish room for potted plants, small aquariums, or for the various toys with which the children are allowed to play freely. We have ample blackboard space, and these boards are so hung as to be easily used by the smallest child. Each blackboard is provided with a small case in which are kept the chalk, and the white cloths which we use instead of the ordinary erasers.

Above the blackboards are hung attractive pictures, chosen carefully, representing simple scenes in which children would naturally be interested. Among the pictures in our "Children's Houses" in Rome we have hung a copy of Raphael's "Madonna della Seggiola," and this picture we have chosen as the emblem of the "Children's Houses." For indeed, these "Children's

Houses" represent not only social progress, but universal human progress, and are closely related to the elevation of the idea of motherhood, to the progress of woman and to the protection of her offspring.[4] . . .

This, then, is the environment which I have selected for the children we wish to educate.

I know the first objection which will present itself to the minds of persons accustomed to the old-time methods of discipline;—the children in these schools, moving about, will overturn the little tables and chairs, producing noise and disorder; but this is a prejudice which has long existed in the minds of those dealing with little children, and for which there is no real foundation.

Swaddling clothes have for many centuries been considered necessary to the newborn babe, walking chairs to the child who is learning to walk. So in the school, we still believe it necessary to have heavy desks and chairs fastened to the floor. All these things are based upon the idea that the child should grow in immobility, and upon the strange prejudice that, in order to execute any educational movement, we must maintain a special position of the body—as we believe that we must assume a special position when we are about to pray.

Our little tables and our various types of chairs are all light and easily transported, and we permit the child to *select* the position which he finds most comfortable. He can *make himself comfortable* as well as seat himself in his own place. And this freedom is not only an external sign of liberty, but a means of education. If by an awkward movement a child upsets a chair, which falls noisily to the floor, he will have an evident proof of his own incapacity; the same movement had it taken place amid stationary benches would have passed unnoticed by him. Thus the child has some means by which he can correct himself, and having done so he will have before him the actual proof of the power he has gained: the little tables and chairs remain firm and silent each in its own place. It is plainly seen that the *child has learned to command his movements*.

In the old method, the proof of discipline attained lay in a fact entirely contrary to this; that is, in the immobility and silence of the child himself. Immobility and silence which *hindered* the child from learning to move with grace and with discernment, and left him so untrained, that, when he found himself in an environment where the benches and chairs were not nailed to the floor, he was not able to move about without overturning the lighter pieces of furniture. In the "Children's Houses" the child will not only learn to move gracefully and properly, but will come to understand the reason for such deportment. The ability to move which he acquires here will be of use to him all his life. While he is still a child, he becomes capable of conducting himself correctly, and yet, with perfect freedom.

The Directress of the Casa dei Bambini at Milan constructed under one of the windows a long, narrow shelf upon which she placed the little tables containing the metal geometric forms used in the first lessons in design. But the shelf was too narrow, and it often happened that the children in selecting the pieces which they wished to use would allow one of the little tables to fall to the floor, thus upsetting with great noise all the metal pieces which it held. The directress intended to have the shelf changed, but the carpenter was slow in coming, and while waiting for him she discovered that the children had learned to handle these materials so carefully that in spite of the narrow and sloping shelf, the little tables no longer fell to the floor.

The children, by carefully directing their movements, had overcome the defect in this piece of furniture. The simplicity or imperfection of external objects often serves to develop the *activity* and the dexterity of the pupils. This has been one of the surprises of our method as applied in the "Children's Houses."

It all seems very logical, and now that it has been actually tried and put into words, it will no doubt seem to everyone as simple as the egg of Christopher Columbus.

EDITOR'S NOTES

1. J. M. Baldwin (1861–1934), an American psychologist, had studied with Wundt in Germany. He pioneered in developing experimental psychology and established a psychological laboratory at the University of Toronto. He was a leading figure in psychology, was one of the founders of the American Psychological Association in 1892, and served the Association's President in 1897. His major work was *Mental Development in the Child and the Race* (New York: Macmillan, 1896). Influenced by Darwin's theory of evolution, Baldwin believed that the human mind was a growing and developing activity and that intellectual processes evolved through three stages: (1) the pre-logical in which young children deal with concrete objects; (2) the logical during which older children construct more abstract concepts and generalize and reflect on their thoughts and experiences; (3) the hyperlogical in which abstract ideas and moral issues are considered and weighed by the mind. For him, learning was a process in which new activities and experiences were accommodated to and assimilated with previous ones. Montessori's comments about Wundt, Preyer, Baldwin, and other experimental and laboratory psychologists show that she was well read and knowledgeable in the field.

2. Montessori's detailed description on p. 73 of an instrument, she designed, called an anthropometer, to take children's measurements, is deleted.

3. Montessori's detailed instructions on filling in physician and other charts and discussion of children's bathing that appears on pp. 74–79 are deleted.

4. Montessori's discussion of Raphael's painting, *Madonna della Seggiola*, the *Madonna of the Chair*, which appears on pp. 82–83, is deleted.

5

Discipline

The pedagogical method of *observation* has for its base the *liberty* of the child; and *liberty is activity*.

Discipline must come through liberty. Here is a great principle which is difficult for followers of common-school methods to understand. How shall one obtain *discipline* in a class of free children? Certainly in our system, we have a concept of discipline very different from that commonly accepted. If discipline is founded upon liberty, the discipline itself must necessarily be *active*. We do not consider an individual disciplined only when he has been rendered as artificially silent as a mute and as immovable as a paralytic. He is an individual *annihilated*, not *disciplined*.

We call an individual disciplined when he is master of himself, and can, therefore, regulate his own conduct when it shall be necessary to follow some rule of life. Such a concept of *active discipline* is not easy either to comprehend or to apply. But certainly it contains a great *educational* principle, very different from the old-time absolute and undiscussed coercion to immobility.

A special technique is necessary to the teacher who is to lead the child along such a path of discipline, if she is to make it possible for him to continue in this way all his life, advancing indefinitely toward perfect self-mastery. Since the child now learns to *move* rather than to *sit still*, he prepares himself not for the school, but for life; for he becomes able, through habit and through practice, to perform easily and correctly the simple acts of social or community life. The discipline to which the child habituates himself here is, in its character, not limited to the school environment but extends to society.

The liberty of the child should have as its *limit* the collective interest; as its *form*, what we universally consider good breeding. We must, therefore, check in the child whatever offends or annoys others, or whatever tends toward rough or ill-bred acts. But all the rest—every manifestation having a useful scope—whatever it be, and under whatever form it expresses itself, must not only be permitted, but must be *observed* by the teacher. Here lies the essential point; from her scientific preparation, the teacher must bring not only the capacity, but the desire, to observe natural phenomena. In our system, she must become a passive, much more than an active, influence, and her passivity shall be composed of anxious scientific curiosity, and of absolute *respect* for the phenomenon which she wishes to observe. The teacher must understand and *feel* her position of *observer*: the *activity* must lie in the *phenomenon*.

Such principles assuredly have a place in schools for little children who are exhibiting the first psychic manifestations of their lives. We cannot know the consequences of suffocating a *spontaneous action* at the time when the child is just beginning to be active: perhaps we suffocate *life itself*. Humanity shows itself in all its intellectual splendor during this tender age as the sun shows itself at the dawn, and the flower in the first unfolding of the petals; and we must *respect* religiously, reverently, these first indications of individuality. If any educational act is to be efficacious, it will be only that which tends to *help* toward the complete unfolding of this life. To be thus helpful it is necessary rigorously to avoid the *arrest of spontaneous movements and the imposition of arbitrary tasks*. It is of course understood, that here we do not speak of useless or dangerous acts, for these must be *suppressed, destroyed*.

Actual training and practice are necessary to fit for this method teachers who have not been prepared for scientific observation, and such training is especially necessary to those who have been accustomed to the old domineering methods of the common school. My experiences in training teachers for the work in my schools did much to convince me of the great distance between these methods and those. Even an intelligent teacher, who understands the principle, finds much difficulty in putting it into practice. She cannot understand that her new task is apparently *passive*, like that of the astronomer who sits immovable before the telescope while the worlds whirl through space. This idea, that *life acts of itself*, and that in order to study it, to divine its secrets or to direct its activity, it is necessary to observe it and to understand it without intervening—this idea, I say, is very difficult for anyone to *assimilate* and to *put into practice*.

The teacher has too thoroughly learned to be the one free activity of the school; it has for too long been virtually her duty to suffocate the activity of her pupils. When in the first days in one of the "Children's Houses" she does not obtain order and silence, she looks about her embarrassed as if asking the public to excuse her, and calling upon those present to testify to her innocence. In vain do we repeat to her that the disorder of the first moment is necessary. And finally, when we oblige her to do nothing but *watch*, she asks if she had not better resign, since she is no longer a teacher.

But when she begins to find it her duty to discern which are the acts to hinder and which are those to observe, the teacher of the old school feels a great void within herself and begins to ask if she will not be inferior to her new task. In fact, she who is not prepared finds herself for a long time abashed and impotent; whereas the broader the teacher's scientific culture and practice in experimental psychology, the sooner will come for her the marvel of unfolding life, and her interest in it.[1] . . .

Thus I saw my teachers act in the first days of my practice school in the "Children's Houses." They almost involuntarily recalled the children to immobility without *observing* and *distinguishing* the nature of the movements they repressed. There was, for example, a little girl who gathered her companions about her and then, in the midst of them, began to talk and gesticulate. The teacher at once ran to her, took hold of her arms, and told her to be still; but I, observing the child, saw that she was playing at being teacher or mother to the others, and teaching them the morning prayer, the invocation to the saints, and the sign of the cross: she already showed herself as a *director*. Another child, who continually made disorganized and misdirected movements, and who was considered abnormal, one day, with an expression of intense attention, set about moving the tables. Instantly they were upon him to make him stand still because he made too much noise. Yet this was one of the *first manifestations*, in this child, of *movements* that were *coordinated* and *directed toward a useful end*, and it was therefore an action that should have been respected. In fact, after this the child began to be quiet and happy like the others whenever he had any small objects to move about and to arrange upon his desk.

It often happened that while the directress replaced in the boxes various materials that had been used, a child would draw near, picking up the objects, with the evident desire of imitating the teacher. The first impulse was to send the child back to her place with the remark, "Let it alone; go to your seat." Yet the child expressed by this act a desire to be useful; the time, with her, was ripe for a lesson in order.

One day, the children had gathered themselves, laughing and talking, into a circle about a basin of water containing some floating toys. We had in the school a little boy barely two and a half years old. He had been left outside the circle, alone, and it was easy to see that he was filled with intense curiosity. I watched him from a distance with great interest; he first drew near to the other children and tried to force his way among them, but he was not strong enough to do this, and he then stood looking about him. The expression of thought on his little face was intensely interesting. I wish that I had had a camera so that I might have photographed him. His eye lighted upon a little chair, and evidently he made up his mind to place it behind the group of children and then to climb up on it. He began to move toward the chair, his face illuminated with hope, but at that moment the teacher seized him brutally (or, perhaps, she would have said, gently) in her arms, and lifting him up above the heads of the other children showed him the basin of water, saying, "Come, poor little one, you shall see too!"

Undoubtedly the child, seeing the floating toys, did not experience the joy that he was about to feel through conquering the obstacle with his own force. The sight of those objects could be of no advantage to him, while his intelligent efforts would have developed his inner powers. The teacher *hindered* the child, in this case, from educating himself, without giving him any compensating good in return. The little fellow had been about to feel himself a conqueror, and he found himself held within two imprisoning arms, impotent. The expression of joy, anxiety, and hope, which had interested me so much faded from his face and left on it the stupid expression of the child who knows that others will act for him.

When the teachers were weary of my observations, they began to allow the children to do whatever they pleased. I saw children with their feet on the tables, or with their fingers in their noses, and no intervention was made to correct them. I saw others push their companions, and I saw dawn in the faces of these an expression of violence; and not the slightest attention on the part of the teacher. Then I had to intervene to show with what absolute rigor it is necessary to hinder, and little by little suppress, all those things which we must not do, so that the child may come to discern clearly between good and evil.

If discipline is to be lasting, its foundations must be laid in this way and these first days are the most difficult for the directress. The first idea that the child must acquire, in order to be actively disciplined, is that of the difference between *good* and *evil*; and the task of the educator lies in seeing that the child does not confound *good* with *immobility*, and *evil* with *activity*, as often happens in the case of the old-time discipline. And all this because our aim is to discipline *for activity, for work, for good*; not for *immobility*, not for *passivity*, not for *obedience*.

A room in which all the children move about usefully, intelligently, and voluntarily, without committing any rough or rude act, would seem to me a classroom very well disciplined indeed.

To seat the children in rows, as in the common schools, to assign to each little one a place, and to propose that they shall sit thus quietly observant of the order of the whole class as an assemblage—this can be attained later, as *the starting place of collective education*. For also, in life, it sometimes happens that we must all remain seated and quiet; when, for example, we attend a concert or a lecture. And we know that even to us, as grown people, this costs no little sacrifice.

If we can, when we have established individual discipline, arrange the children, sending each one to *his own place, in order*, trying to make them understand the idea that thus placed they look well, and that it is a *good thing* to be thus placed in order, that it is a *good and pleasing arrangement in the room*, this ordered and tranquil adjustment of theirs—then their remaining in their places, *quiet* and *silent*, is the result of a species of *lesson*, not an *imposition*. To make them understand the idea, without calling their attention too forcibly to the practice, to have them *assimilate a principle of collective order*—that is the important thing.

If, after they have understood this idea, they rise, speak, change to another place, they no longer do this without knowing and without thinking, but they do it because they *wish* to rise, to speak, etc.; that is, from that *state of repose and order*, well understood, they depart in order to undertake *some voluntary action*; and knowing that there are actions which are prohibited, this will give them a new impulse to remember to discriminate between good and evil.

The movements of the children from the state of order become always more coordinated and perfect with the passing of the days; in fact, they learn to reflect upon their own acts. Now (with the idea of order understood by the children) the observation of the way in which the children pass from the first disordered movements to those which are spontaneous and ordered—this is the book of the teacher; this is the book which must inspire her actions; it is the only one in which she must read and study if she is to become a real educator.

For the child with such exercises makes, to a certain extent, a selection of his own *tendencies*, which were at first confused in the unconscious disorder of his movements. It is remarkable how clearly *individual differences* show themselves, if we proceed in this way; the child, conscious and free, *reveals himself*.

There are those who remain quietly in their seats, apathetic, or drowsy; others who leave their places to quarrel, to fight, or to overturn the various blocks and toys, and then there are those others who set out to fulfill a definite and determined act—moving a chair to some particular spot and sitting down in it, moving one of the unused tables and arranging upon it the game they wish to play.

Our idea of liberty for the child cannot be the simple concept of liberty we use in the observation of plants, insects, etc.

The child, because of the peculiar characteristics of helplessness with which he is born, and because of his qualities as a social individual is circumscribed by *bonds* which *limit* his activity.

An educational method that shall have *liberty* as its basis must intervene to help the child to a conquest of these various obstacles. In other words, his training must be such as shall help him to diminish, in a rational manner, the *social bonds*, which limit his activity.

Little by little, as the child grows in such an atmosphere, his spontaneous manifestations will become more *clear, with the clearness of truth*, revealing his nature. For all these reasons, the first form of educational intervention must tend to lead the child toward independence.

INDEPENDENCE

No one can be free unless he is independent: therefore, the first, active manifestations of the child's individual liberty must be so guided that through this
activity he may arrive at independence. Little children, from the moment in
which they are weaned, are making their way toward independence.

What is a weaned child? In reality it is a child that has become independent
of the mother's breast. Instead of this one source of nourishment he will find
various kinds of food; for him the means of existence are multiplied, and he
can to some extent make a selection of his food, whereas he was at first limited absolutely to one form of nourishment.

Nevertheless, he is still dependent, since he is not yet able to walk, and cannot wash and dress himself, and since he is not yet able to *ask* for things in a
language which is clear and easily understood. He is still in this period to a
great extent the *slave* of everyone. By the age of three, however, the child
should have been able to render himself to a great extent *independent* and free.

That we have not yet thoroughly assimilated the highest concept of the
term *independence*, is due to the fact that the social form in which we live is
still *servile*. In an age of civilization where servants exist, the concept of that
form of life which is *independence* cannot take root or develop freely. Even
so in the time of slavery, the concept of liberty was distorted and darkened.

Our servants are not our dependents, rather it is we who are dependent
upon them.

It is not possible to accept universally as a part of our social structure such
a deep human error without feeling the general effects of it in the form of
moral inferiority. We often believe ourselves to be independent simply because no one commands us, and because we command others; but the noble-
man who needs to call a servant to his aid is really a dependent through his
own inferiority. The paralytic who cannot take off his boots because of a
pathological fact, and the prince who dare not take them off because of a social fact, are in reality reduced to the same condition.

Any nation that accepts the idea of servitude and believes that it is an advantage for man to be served by man, admits servility as an instinct, and indeed we all too easily lend ourselves to *obsequious service*, giving to it such
complimentary names as *courtesy, politeness, charity*.

In reality, *he who is served is limited* in his independence. This concept will
be the foundation of the dignity of the man of the future; "I do not wish to be
served, *because* I am not an impotent." And this idea must be gained before
men can feel themselves to be really free.

Any pedagogical action, if it is to be efficacious in the training of little children, must tend to *help* the children to advance upon this road of indepen-

dence. We must help them to learn to walk without assistance, to run, to go up and down stairs, to lift up fallen objects, to dress and undress themselves, to bathe themselves, to speak distinctly, and to express their own needs clearly. We must give such help as shall make it possible for children to achieve the satisfaction of their own individual aims and desires. All this is a part of education for independence.

We habitually *serve* children; and this is not only an act of servility toward them, but it is dangerous, since it tends to suffocate their useful, spontaneous activity. We are inclined to believe that children are like puppets, and we wash them and feed them as if they were dolls. We do not stop to think that the child *who does not do, does not know how to do.* He must, nevertheless, do these things, and nature has furnished him with the physical means for carrying on these various activities, and with the intellectual means for learning how to do them. And our duty toward him is, in every case, that of *helping him* to make a conquest of such useful acts as nature intended he should perform for himself. The mother who feeds her child without making the least effort to teach him to hold the spoon for himself and to try to find his mouth with it, and who does not at least eat herself, inviting the child to look and see how she does it, is not a good mother. She offends the fundamental human dignity of her son—she treats him as if he were a doll, when he is, instead, a man confided by nature to her care.

Who does not know that to *teach* a child to feed himself, to wash and dress himself, is a much more tedious and difficult work, calling for infinitely greater patience, than feeding, washing and dressing the child one's self? But the former is the work of an educator, the latter is the easy and inferior work of a servant. Not only is it easier for the mother, but it is very dangerous for the child, since it closes the way and puts obstacles in the path of the life which is developing.[2] . . .

ABOLITION OF PRIZES AND OF EXTERNAL FORMS OF PUNISHMENT

Once we have accepted and established such principles, the abolition of prizes and external forms of punishment will follow naturally. Man, disciplined through liberty, begins to desire the true and only prize which will never belittle or disappoint him—the birth of human power and liberty within that inner life of his from which his activities must spring.

In my own experience I have often marveled to see how true this is. During our first months in the "Children's Houses," the teachers had not yet learned to put into practice the pedagogical principles of liberty and discipline. One of them, especially, busied herself, when I was absent, in *remedying* my ideas by introducing a few of those methods to which she had been accustomed. So, one day when I came in unexpectedly, I found one of the most intelligent of the children wearing a large Greek cross of silver, hung from his neck by a fine piece of white ribbon, while another child was seated in an armchair which had been conspicuously placed in the middle of the room.

The first child had been rewarded, the second was being punished. The teacher, at least while I was present, did not interfere in any way, and the situation remained as I had found it. I held my peace, and placed myself where I might observe quietly.

The child with the cross was moving back and forth, carrying the objects with which he had been working, from his table to that of the teacher, and bringing others in their place. He was busy and happy. As he went back and forth he passed by the armchair of the child who was being punished. The silver cross slipped from his neck and fell to the floor, and the child in the armchair picked it up, dangled it on its white ribbon, looking at it from all sides, and then said to his companion: "Do you see what you have dropped?" The child turned and looked at the trinket with an air of indifference; his expression seemed to say; "Don't interrupt me," his voice replied "I don't care." "Don't you care, really?" said the punished one calmly. "Then I will put it on myself." And the other replied, "Oh, yes, put it on," in a tone that seemed to add, "and leave me in peace!"

The boy in the armchair carefully arranged the ribbon so that the cross lay upon the front of his pink apron where he could admire its brightness and its pretty form, then he settled himself more comfortably in his little chair and rested his arms with evident pleasure upon the arms of the chair. The affair remained thus, and was quite just. The dangling cross could satisfy the child who was being punished, but not the active child, content and happy with his work.[3] . . .

As to punishments, we have many times come in contact with children who disturbed the others without paying any attention to our corrections. Such children were at once examined by the physician. When the case proved to be that of a normal child, we placed one of the little tables in a corner of the room, and in this way isolated the child; having him sit in a comfortable little armchair, so placed that he might see his companions at work, and giving him those games and toys to which he was most attracted. This isolation almost always succeeded in calming the child; from his position he could see the entire assembly of his companions, and the way in which they carried on their work was an *object lesson* much more efficacious than any words of the teacher could possibly have been. Little by little, he would come to see the advantages of being one of the company working so busily before his eyes, and he would really wish to go back and do as the others did. We have in this way led back again to discipline all the children who at first seemed to rebel against it. The isolated child was always made the object of special care, almost as if he were ill. I myself, when I entered the room, went first of all directly to him, caressing him, as if he were a very little child. Then I turned my attention to the others, interesting myself in their work, asking questions about it as if they had been little men. I do not know what happened in the soul of these children whom we found it necessary to discipline, but certainly the conversion was always very complete and lasting. They showed great pride in learning how to work and how to conduct themselves, and always showed a very tender affection for the teacher and for me.

THE BIOLOGICAL CONCEPT OF LIBERTY IN PEDAGOGY

From a biological point of view, the concept of *liberty* in the education of the child in his earliest years must be understood as demanding those conditions adapted to the most favorable *development* of his entire individuality. So, from the physiological side as well as from the mental side, this includes the free development of the brain. The educator must be as one inspired by a deep *worship of life*, and must, through this reverence, *respect*, while he observes with human interest, the *development* of the child life. Now, child life is not an abstraction; *it is the life of individual children.* There exists only one real biological manifestation: the *living individual;* and toward single individuals, one by one observed, education must direct itself. By education must be understood the active *help* given to the normal expansion of the life of the child. The child is a body which grows, and a soul which de-develops—these two forms, physiological and psychic, have one eternal font, life itself. We must neither mar nor stifle the mysterious powers which lie within these two forms of growth, but we must *await from them* the manifestations which we know will succeed one another.

Environment is undoubtedly a *secondary* factor in the phenomena of life; it can modify in that it can help or hinder, but it can never *create*. The modern theories of evolution, from Naegeli to De Vries, consider throughout the development of the two biological branches, animal and vegetable, this interior factor as the essential force in the transformation of the species and in the transformation of the individual.[4] The origins of the *development*, both in the species and in the individual, *lie within*. The child does not grow *because* he is nourished, *because* he breathes, *because* he is placed in conditions of temperature to which he is adapted; he grows because the potential life within him develops, making itself visible; because the fruitful germ from which his life has come develops itself according to the biological destiny which was fixed for it by heredity. Adolescence does not come *because* the child laughs, or dances, or does gymnastic exercises, or is well nourished; but because he has arrived at that particular physiological state. Life makes itself manifest— life creates, life gives—and is in its turn held within certain limits and bound by certain laws which are insuperable. The *fixed* characteristics of the species do not change—they can only vary.

This concept, so brilliantly set forth by De Vries in his Mutation Theory, illustrates also the limits of education. We can act on the *variations* which are in relation to the environment, and whose limits vary slightly in the species and in the individual, but we cannot act upon the *mutations*. The mutations are bound by some mysterious tie to the very font of life itself, and their power rises superior to the modifying elements of the environment.

A species, for example, cannot *mutate* or change into another species through any phenomenon of *adaptation*, as, on the other hand, a great human genius cannot be suffocated by any limitation, nor by any false form of education.

The *environment* acts more strongly upon the individual life the less fixed and strong this individual life may be. But environment can act in two opposite senses, favoring life, and stifling it. Many species of palm, for example, are splendid in the tropical regions, because the climatic conditions are favorable to their development, but many species of both animals and plants have become extinct in regions to which they were not able to adapt themselves.

Life is a superb goddess, always advancing, overthrowing the obstacles which environment places in the way of her triumph. This is the basic or fundamental truth—whether it be a question of species or of individuals, there persists always the forward march of those victorious ones in whom this mysterious life force is strong and vital.

It is evident that in the case of humanity, and especially in the case of our civil humanity, which we call society, the important and imperative question is that of the *care*, or perhaps we might say, the *culture* of human life.

EDITOR'S NOTES

1. Montessori's example and long quote from Notari's *My Millionaire Uncle* to illustrate how a teacher interferes with characters in the novel on pp. 89–90 is deleted.

2. Montessori's examples to illustrate the concept of dependency on pp. 98–101, which repeat earlier examples, are deleted.

3. Montessori's story of children resisting the awarding of prizes or rewards on pp. 102–3 is deleted.

4. Montessori cites the work of Karl Wilhelm von Naegeli (1817–1891), a Swiss botanist and biologist and Hugo De Vries (1848–1935), a Dutch botanist who revived and conducted experiments to verify Mendel's theory of mutation. De Vries developed the theory of mutation in which changes favorable to the survival of an individual persist until more favorable mutations occur. Montessori uses the reference to point out her belief that the environment cannot change the nature of the human being but can shape how the individual responds to that environment.

6

How the Lessons Should Be Given

"Let all thy words be counted."

Dante, Inf., canto X.

Given the fact that, through the régime of liberty the pupils can manifest their natural tendencies in the school, and that with this in view we have prepared the environment and the materials (the objects with which the child is to work), the teacher must not limit her action to *observation*, but must proceed to *experiment*.

In this method the lesson corresponds to an *experiment*. The more fully the teacher is acquainted with the methods of experimental psychology, the better will she understand how to give the lesson. Indeed, a special technique is necessary if the method is to be properly applied. The teacher must at least have attended the training classes in the "Children's Houses," in order to acquire a knowledge of the fundamental principles of the method and to understand their application. The most difficult portion of this training is that which refers to the method for discipline.

In the first days of the school the children do not learn the idea of collective order; this idea follows and comes as a result of those disciplinary exercises through which the child learns to discern between good and evil. This being the case, it is evident that, at the outset the teacher *cannot give* collective lessons. Such lessons, indeed, will always be *very rare*, since the children being free are not obliged to remain in their places quiet and ready to listen to the teacher, or to watch what she is doing. The collective lessons, in fact, are of very secondary importance, and have been almost abolished by us.

CHARACTERISTICS OF THE INDIVIDUAL LESSONS—
CONCISENESS, SIMPLICITY, OBJECTIVITY

The lessons, then, are individual, and *brevity* must be one of their chief characteristics. Dante gives excellent advice to teachers when he says, "Let thy words be counted." The more carefully we cut away useless words, the more perfect will become the lesson. And in preparing the lessons which she is to give, the teacher must pay special attention to this point, counting and weighing the value of the words which she is to speak.

Another characteristic quality of the lesson in the "Children's Houses" is its *simplicity*. It must be stripped of all that is not absolute truth. That the teacher must not lose herself in vain words, is included in the first quality of conciseness; this second, then, is closely related to the first: that is, the carefully chosen words must be the most simple it is possible to find, and must refer to the truth.

The third quality of the lesson is its *objectivity*. The lesson must be presented in such a way that the personality of the teacher shall disappear. There shall remain in evidence only the *object* to which she wishes to call the attention of the child. This brief and simple lesson must be considered by the teacher as an explanation of the object and of the use which the child can make of it.

In the giving of such lessons the fundamental guide must be the *method of observation*, in which is included and understood the liberty of the child. So the teacher shall *observe* whether the child interests himself in the object, how he is interested in it, for how long, etc., even noticing the expression of his face. And she must take great care not to offend the principles of liberty. For, if she provokes the child to make an unnatural effort, she will no longer know what is the *spontaneous* activity of the child. If, therefore, the lesson rigorously prepared in this brevity, simplicity, and truth is not understood by the child, is not accepted by him as an explanation of the object—the teacher must be warned of two things—first, not to *insist* by repeating the lesson; and second, *not to make the child feel that he has made a mistake*, or that he has not understood, because in doing so she will cause him to make an effort to understand, and will thus alter the natural state which must be used by her in making her psychological observation. A few examples may serve to illustrate this point.

Let us suppose, for example, that the teacher wishes to teach to a child the two colors, red and blue. She desires to attract the attention of the child to the object. She says, therefore, "Look at this." Then, in order to teach the colors, she says, showing him the red, "This is *red*," raising her voice a little and pronouncing the word "red" slowly and clearly; then showing him the other color, "This is *blue*." In order to make sure that the child has understood, she says to him, "Give me the red—Give me the blue." Let us suppose that the child in following this last direction makes a mistake. The teacher does not repeat and does not insist; she smiles, gives the child a friendly caress and takes away the colors.

Teachers ordinarily are greatly surprised at such simplicity. They often say, "But everybody knows how to do that!" Indeed, this again is a little like the egg of Christopher Columbus, but the truth is that not everyone knows how to do this simple thing (to give a lesson with such simplicity). To *measure* one's own activity, to make it conform to these standards of clearness, brevity, and truth, is practically a very difficult matter. Especially is this true of teachers prepared by the old-time methods, who have learned to labor to deluge the child with useless, and often, false words. For example, a teacher who had taught in the public schools often reverted to collectivity. Now in giving a collective lesson much importance is necessarily given to the simple thing which is to be taught, and it is necessary to oblige all the children to follow the teacher's explanation, when perhaps not all of them are disposed to give their attention to the particular lesson in hand. The teacher has perhaps commenced her lesson in this way: "Children, see if you can guess what I have in my hand!" She knows that the children cannot guess, and she therefore attracts their attention by means of a falsehood. Then she probably says, "Children, look out at the sky. Have you ever looked at it before? Have you never noticed it at night when it is all shining with stars? No! Look at my apron. Do you know what color it is? Doesn't it seem to you the same color as the sky? Very well then, look at this color I have in my hand. It is the same color as the sky and my apron. It is *blue*. Now look around you a little and see if you can find something in the room which is blue. And do you know what color cherries are, and the color of the burning coals in the fireplace, etc., etc."

Now in the mind of the child after he has made the useless effort of trying to guess there revolves a confused mass of ideas—the sky, the apron, the cherries, etc. It will be difficult for him to extract from all this confusion the idea which it was the scope of the lesson to make clear to him; namely, the recognition of the two colors, blue and red. Such a work of selection is almost impossible for the mind of a child who is not yet able to follow a long discourse.

I remember being present at an arithmetic lesson where the children were being taught that two and three make five. To this end, the teacher made use of a counting board having colored beads strung on its thin wires. She arranged, for example, two beads on the top line, then on a lower line three, and at the bottom five beads. I do not remember very clearly the development of this lesson, but I do know that the teacher found it necessary to place beside the two beads on the upper wire a little cardboard dancer with a blue skirt, which she christened on the spot the name of one of the children in the class, saying, "This is Mariettina." And then beside the other three beads she placed a little dancer dressed in a different color, which she called "Gigina." I do not know exactly how the teacher arrived at the demonstration of the sum, but certainly she talked for a long time with these little dancers, moving them about, etc. If *I* remember the dancers more clearly than I do the arithmetic process, how must it have been with the children? If by such a method they were able to learn that two and three make five, they must have made a tremendous mental effort, and the teacher must have found it necessary to talk with the little dancers for a long time.[1] . . .

To obtain a *simple lesson* from a teacher who has been prepared according to the ordinary methods, is a very difficult task. I remember that, after having explained the material fully and in detail, I called upon one of my teachers to teach, by means of the geometric insets, the difference between a square and a triangle. The task of the teacher was simply to fit a square and a triangle of wood into the empty spaces made to receive them. She should then have shown the child how to follow with his finger the contours of the wooden pieces and of the frames into which they fit, saying, meanwhile, "This is a square—this is a triangle." The teacher whom I had called upon began by having the child touch the square, saying, "This is a line—another—another—and another. There are four lines: count them with your little finger and tell me how many there are. And the corners—count the corners, feel them with your little finger. See, there are four corners too. Look at this piece well. It is a square." I corrected the teacher, telling her that in this way she was not teaching the child to recognize a form, but was giving him an idea of sides, of angles, of number, and that this was a very different thing from that which she was to teach in this lesson. "But," she said, trying to justify herself, "it is the same thing." It is not, however, the same thing. It is the geometric analysis and the mathematics of the thing. It would be possible to have an idea of the form of the quadrilateral without knowing how to count to four, and, therefore, without appreciating the number of sides and angles. The sides and the angles are abstractions which in themselves do not exist; that which does exist is this piece of wood of a determined form. The elaborate explanations of the teacher not only confused the child's mind, but bridged over the distance that lies between the concrete and the abstract, between the form of an object and the mathematics of the form.[2] . . .

To stimulate life—leaving it then free to develop, to unfold—herein lies the first task of the educator. In such a delicate task, a great art must suggest the moment, and limit the intervention, in order that we shall arouse no perturbation, cause no deviation, but rather that we shall help the soul which is coming into the fullness of life, and which shall live from its *own forces*. This *art* must accompany the *scientific method*.

When the teacher shall have touched, in this way, soul for soul, each one of her pupils, awakening and inspiring the life within them as if she were an invisible spirit, she will then possess each soul, and a sign, a single word from her shall suffice; for each one will feel her in a living and vital way, will recognize her and will listen to her. There will come a day when the directress herself shall be filled with wonder to see that all the children obey her with gentleness and affection, not only ready, but intent, at a sign from her. They will look toward her who has made them live, and will hope and desire to receive from her, new life.

Experience has revealed all this, and it is something which forms the chief source of wonder for those who visit the "Children's Houses." Collective discipline is obtained as if by magic force. Fifty or sixty children from two and a half years to six years of age, all together, and at a single time know how to hold their peace so perfectly that the absolute silence seems that of a desert. And, if the teacher, speaking in a low voice, says to the children, "Rise, pass several times around the room on the tips of your toes and then come back to your place in silence" all together, as a single person, the children rise, and follow the order with the least possible noise. The teacher with that one voice has spoken to each one; and each child hopes from her intervention to receive some light and inner happiness. And feeling so, he goes forth intent and obedient like an anxious explorer, following the order in his own way.

In this matter of discipline we have again something of the egg of Christopher Columbus. A concert master must prepare his scholars one by one in order to draw from their collective work great and beautiful harmony; and each artist must perfect himself as an individual before he can be ready to follow the voiceless commands of the master's baton.

How different is the method which we follow in the public schools! It is as if a concert master taught the same monotonous and sometimes discordant rhythm contemporaneously to the most diverse instruments and voices.

Thus we find that the most disciplined members of society are the men who are best trained, who have most thoroughly perfected themselves, but this is the training or the perfection acquired through contact with other people. The perfection of the collectivity cannot be that material and brutal solidarity which comes from mechanical organization alone.

In regard to infant psychology, we are more richly endowed with prejudices than with actual knowledge bearing upon the subject. We have, until the present day, wished to dominate the child through force, by the imposition of external laws, instead of making an interior conquest of the child, in order to direct him as a human soul. In this way, the children have lived beside us without being able to make us know them. But if we cut away the artificiality with which we have enwrapped them, and the violence through which we have foolishly thought to discipline them, they will reveal themselves to us in all the truth of child nature.

Their gentleness is so absolute, so sweet, that we recognize in it the infancy of that humanity which can remain oppressed by every form of yoke, by every injustice; and the child's love of *knowledge* is such that it surpasses every other love and makes us think that in very truth humanity must carry within it that passion which pushes the minds of men to the successive conquest of thought, making easier from century to century the yokes of every form of slavery.

EDITOR'S NOTES

1. Montessori's reiteration of her point on auditory training by using an example of how a teacher unnecessarily confuses children in making distinctions between sound and noise on pp. 111–13 is deleted.

2. Montessori's example of a lesson that confuses children by over complicating the relationship between geometry and architecture on pp. 114–15 is deleted.

Exercises of Practical Life

PROPOSED WINTER SCHEDULE OF HOURS IN THE "CHILDREN'S HOUSES"

Opening at Nine O'Clock—Closing at Four O'Clock

9:00–10:00   Entrance. Greeting. Inspection as to personal cleanliness. Exercises of practical life; helping one another to take off and put on the aprons. Going over the room to see that everything is dusted and in order. Language: Conversation period: Children give an account of the events of the day before. Religious exercises.

10:00–11:00   Intellectual exercises. Objective lessons interrupted by short rest periods. Nomenclature, Sense exercises.

11:00–11:30   Simple gymnastics: Ordinary movements done gracefully, normal position of the body, walking, marching in line, salutations, movements for attention, placing of objects gracefully.

11:30–12:00   Luncheon: Short prayer.

12:00–1:00   Free games.

1:00–2:00   Directed games, if possible, in the open air. During this period the older children in turn go through with the exercises of practical life, cleaning the room, dusting, putting the material in order. General inspection for cleanliness: Conversation.

2:00–3:00   Manual work. Clay modeling, design, etc.

3:00–4:00   Collective gymnastics and songs, if possible in the open air. Exercises to develop forethought: Visiting, and caring for, the plants and animals.

As soon as a school is established, the question of schedule arises. This must be considered from two points of view; the length of the school day and the distribution of study and of the activities of life.

I shall begin by affirming that in the "Children's Houses," as in the school for deficients, the hours may be very long, occupying the entire day. For poor children, and especially for the "Children's Houses" annexed to working-men's tenements, I should advise that the school day should be from nine in the morning to five in the evening in winter, and from eight to six in summer. These long hours are necessary, if we are to follow a directed line of action which shall be helpful to the growth of the child. It goes without saying, that in the case of little children such a long school day should be interrupted by at least an hour's rest in bed. And here lies the great practical difficulty. At present we must allow our little ones to sleep in their seats in a wretched po-sition, but I foresee a time, not distant, when we shall be able to have a quiet, darkened room where the children may sleep in low-swung hammocks. I should like still better to have this nap taken in the open air.

In the "Children's Houses" in Rome we send the little ones to their own apartments for the nap, as this can be done without their having to go out into the streets.

It must be observed that these long hours include not only the nap, but the luncheon. This must be considered in such schools as the "Children's Houses," whose aim is to help and to direct the growth of children in such an important period of development as that from three to six years of age.

The "Children's House" is a garden of child culture, and we most certainly do not keep the children for so many hours in school with the idea of making students of them!

The first step which we must take in our method is to *call* to the pupil. We call now to his attention, now to his interior life, now to the life he leads with others. Making a comparison which must not be taken in a literal sense—it is necessary to proceed as in experimental psychology or anthropology when one makes an experiment—that is, after having prepared the instrument (to which in this case the environment may correspond) we prepare the subject. Consid-ering the method as a whole, we must begin our work by preparing the child for the forms of social life, and we must attract his attention to these forms.

In the schedule which we outlined when we established the first "Chil-dren's House," but which we have never followed entirely, (a sign that a schedule in which the material is distributed in arbitrary fashion is not adapted to the régime of liberty) we begin the day with a series of exercises of practical life, and I must confess that these exercises were the only part of the program which proved thoroughly stationary. These exercises were such a success that they formed the beginning of the day in all of the "Children's Houses." First:

Cleanliness
Order
Poise
Conversation

As soon as the children arrive at school we make an inspection for cleanliness. If possible, this should be carried on in the presence of the mothers, but their attention should not be called to it directly. We examine the hands, the nails, the neck, the ears, the face, the teeth; and care is given to the tidiness of the hair. If any of the garments are torn or soiled or ripped, if the buttons are lacking, or if the shoes are not clean, we call the attention of the child to this. In this way, the children become accustomed to observing themselves and take an interest in their own appearance.

The children in our "Children's Houses" are given a bath in turn, but this, of course, cannot be done daily. In the class, however, the teacher, by using a little washstand with small pitchers and basins, teaches the children to take a partial bath: for example, they learn how to wash their hands and clean their nails. Indeed, sometimes we teach them how to take a footbath. They are shown especially how to wash their ears and eyes with great care. They are taught to brush their teeth and rinse their mouths carefully. In all of this, we call their attention to the different parts of the body which they are washing, and to the different means which we use in order to cleanse them: clear water for the eyes, soap and water for the hands, the brush for the teeth, etc. We teach the big ones to help the little ones, and, so, encourage the younger children to learn quickly to take care of themselves.

After this care of their persons, we put on the little aprons. The children are able to put these on themselves, or, with the help of each other. Then we begin our visit about the schoolroom. We notice if all of the various materials are in order and if they are clean. The teacher shows the children how to clean out the little corners where dust has accumulated, and shows them how to use the various objects necessary in cleaning a room—dust cloths, dust brushes, little brooms, etc. All of this, when the children are allowed *to do it by themselves*, is very quickly accomplished. Then the children go each to his own place. The teacher explains to them that the normal position is for each child to be seated in his own place, in silence, with his feet together on the floor, his hands resting on the table, and his head erect. In this way she teaches them poise and equilibrium. Then she has them rise on their feet in order to sing the hymn, teaching them that in rising and sitting down it is not necessary to be noisy. In this way the children learn to move about the furniture with poise and with care. After this we have a series of exercises in which the children learn to move gracefully, to go and come, to salute each other, to lift objects carefully, to receive various objects from each other politely. The teacher calls attention with little exclamations to a child who is clean, a room which is well ordered, a class seated quietly, a graceful movement, etc.

From such a starting point we proceed to the free teaching. That is, the teacher will no longer make comments to the children, directing them how to move from their seats, etc., she will limit herself to correcting the disordered movements.

After the directress has talked in this way about the attitude of the children and the arrangement of the room, she invites the children to talk with her. She questions them concerning what they have done the day before, regulating her inquiries in such a way that the children need not report the intimate happenings of the family but their individual behavior, their games, attitude to parents, etc. She will ask if they have been able to go up the stairs without getting them muddy, if they have spoken politely to their friends who passed, if they have helped their mothers, if they have shown in their family what they have learned at school, if they have played in the street, etc. The conversations are longer on Monday after the vacation, and on that day the children are invited to tell what they have done with the family; if they have gone away from home, whether they have eaten things not usual for children to eat, and if this is the case we urge them not to eat these things and try to teach them that they are bad for them. Such conversations as these encourage the *unfolding* or development of language and are of great educational value, since the directress can prevent the children from recounting happenings in the house or in the neighborhood, and can select, instead, topics which are adapted to pleasant conversation, and in this way can teach the children those things which it is desirable to talk about; that is, things with which we occupy ourselves in life, public events, or things which have happened in the different houses, perhaps, to the children themselves—as baptism, birthday parties, any of which may serve for occasional conversation. Things of this sort will encourage children to describe, themselves. After this morning talk we pass to the various lessons.

8

Refection—The Child's Diet

In connection with the exercises of practical life, it may be fitting to consider the matter of refection.

In order to protect the child's development, especially in neighborhoods where standards of child hygiene are not yet prevalent in the home, it would be well if a large part at least of the child's diet could be entrusted to the school. It is well known today that the diet must be adapted to the physical nature of the child; and as the medicine of children is not the medicine of adults in reduced doses, so the diet must not be that of the adult in lesser quantitative proportions. For this reason I should prefer that even in the "Children's Houses" which are situated in tenements and from which little ones, being at home, can go up to eat with the family, school refection should be instituted. Moreover, even in the case of rich children, school refection would always be advisable until a scientific course in cooking shall have introduced into the wealthier families the habit of specializing in children's food.[1]

EDITOR'S NOTE

1. Montessori's discussion of food and children's diet—preparation of meals for children, degree of spiciness, and seasoning which is highly specific to Italy and to the historical period that appears on pp. 125–36 is deleted.

9

Muscular Education—Gymnastics

The generally accepted idea of gymnastics is, I consider, very inadequate. In the common schools we are accustomed to describe as gymnastics a species of collective muscular discipline which has as its aim that children shall learn to follow definite ordered movements given in the form of commands. The guiding spirit in such gymnastics is coercion, and I feel that such exercises repress spontaneous movements and impose others in their place. I do not know what the psychological authority for the selection of these imposed movements is. Similar movements are used in medical gymnastics in order to restore a normal movement to a torpid muscle or to give back a normal movement to a paralyzed muscle. A number of chest movements which are given in the school are advised, for example, in medicine for those who suffer from intestinal torpidity, but truly I do not well understand what office such exercises can fulfill when they are followed by squadrons of normal children. In addition to these formal gymnastics we have those which are carried on in a gymnasium, and which are very like the first steps in the training of an acrobat. However, this is not the place for criticism of the gymnastics used in our common schools. Certainly in our case we are not considering such gymnastics. Indeed, many who hear me speak of gymnastics for infant schools very plainly show disapprobation and they will disapprove more heartily when they hear me speak of a gymnasium for little children. Indeed, if the gymnastic exercises and the gymnasium were those of the common schools, no one would agree more heartily than I in the disapproval expressed by these critics.

We must understand by *gymnastics* and in general by muscular education a series of exercises tending to *aid* the normal development of physiological movements (such as walking, breathing, speech), to protect this development, when the child shows himself backward or abnormal in any way, and to encourage in the children those movements which are useful in the achievement of the most ordinary acts of life; such as dressing, undressing, buttoning their clothes and lacing their shoes, carrying such objects as balls, cubes, etc. If there exists an age in which it is necessary to protect a child by means of a series of gymnastic exercises, between three and six years is undoubtedly the age. The special gymnastics necessary, or, better still, hygienic, in this period of life, refer chiefly to walking. A child in the general morphological growth of his body is characterized by having a torso greatly developed in comparison with the lower limbs.[1] . . .

We cannot, if we consider all these things, judge the manner of walking in little children by the standard set for our own equilibrium. If a child is not strong, the erect posture and walking are really sources of fatigue for him, and the long bones of the lower limbs, yielding to the weight of the body, easily become deformed and usually bowed. This is particularly the case among the badly nourished children of the poor, or among those in whom the skeleton structure, while not actually showing the presence of rickets, still seems to be slow in attaining normal ossification.

We are wrong then if we consider little children from this physical point of view as *little men*. They have, instead, characteristics and proportions that are entirely special to their age. The tendency of the child to stretch out on his back and kick his legs in the air is an expression of physical needs related to the proportions of his body. The baby loves to walk on all fours just because, like the quadruped animals, his limbs are short in comparison with his body. Instead of this, we divert these natural manifestations by foolish habits which we impose on the child. We hinder him from throwing himself on the earth, from stretching, etc., and we oblige him to walk with grown people and to keep up with them; and excuse ourselves by saying that we don't want him to become capricious and think he can do as he pleases! It is indeed a fatal error and one which has made bowlegs common among little children. It is well to enlighten the mothers on these important particulars of infant hygiene. Now we, with the gymnastics, can, and, indeed, should, help the child in his development by making our exercises correspond to the movement which he *needs to make*, and in this way save his limbs from fatigue.

One very simple means for helping the child in his activity was suggested to me by my observation of the children themselves. The teacher was having the children march, leading them about the courtyard between the walls of the house and the central garden. This garden was protected by a little fence made of strong wires which were stretched in parallel lines, and were supported at intervals by wooden palings driven into the ground. Along the fence, ran a little ledge on which the children were in the habit of sitting down when they were tired of marching. In addition to this, I always brought out little chairs, which I placed against the wall. Every now and then, the little ones of two and one half and three years would drop out from the marching line, evidently being tired; but instead of sitting down on the ground or on the chairs, they would run to the little fence and catching hold of the upper line of wire they would walk along sideways, resting their feet on the wire which was nearest the ground. That this gave them a great deal of pleasure, was evident from the way in which they laughed as, with bright eyes, they watched their larger companions who were marching about. The truth was that these little ones had solved one of my problems in a very practical way. They moved themselves along on the wires, pulling their bodies sideways. In this way, they moved their limbs *without throwing upon them the weight of the body*. Such an apparatus placed in the gymnasium for little children, will enable them to fulfill the need which they feel of throwing themselves on the floor and kicking their legs in the air; for the movements they make on the little fence correspond even more correctly to the same physical needs. Therefore, I advise the manufacture of this little fence for use in children's playrooms. It can be constructed of parallel bars supported by upright poles firmly fixed on to the heavy base. The children, while playing upon this little fence, will be able to look out and see with great pleasure what the other children are doing in the room.

Other pieces of gymnasium apparatus can be constructed upon the same plan, that is, having as their aim the furnishing of the child with a proper outlet for his individual activities. One of the things invented by Seguin to develop the lower limbs, and especially to strengthen the articulation of the knee in weak children, is the trampoline.

This is a kind of swing, having a very wide seat, so wide, indeed, that the limbs of the child stretched out in front of him are entirely supported by this broad seat. This little chair is hung from strong cords and is left swinging. The wall in front of it is reinforced by a strong smooth board against which the children press their feet in pushing themselves back and forth in the swing. The child seated in this swing exercises his limbs, pressing his feet against the board each time that he swings toward the wall. The board against which he swings may be erected at some distance from the wall, and may be so low that the child can see over the top of it. As he swings in this chair, he strengthens his limbs through the species of gymnastics limited to the lower limbs, and this he does without resting the weight of his body upon his legs. Other pieces of gymnastic apparatus, less important from the hygienic standpoint, but very amusing to the children, may be described briefly. "The Pendulum," a game which may be played by one child or by several, consists of rubber balls hung on a cord. The children seated in their little armchairs strike the ball, sending it from one to another. It is an exercise for the arms and for the spinal column, and is at the same time an exercise in which the eye gauges the distance of bodies in motion. Another game, called "The Cord," consists of a line, drawn on the earth with chalk, along which the children walk. This helps to order and to direct their free movements in a given direction. A game like this is very pretty, indeed, after a snowfall, when the little path made by the children shows the regularity of the line they have traced, and encourages a pleasant war among them in which each one tries to make his line in the snow the most regular.

The little round stair is another game, in which a little wooden stairway, built on the plan of the spiral, is used. This little stair is enclosed on one side by a balustrade on which the children can rest their hands. The other side is open and circular. This serves to habituate the children to climbing and descending stairs without holding on to the balustrade, and teaches them to move up and down with movements that are poised and self-controlled. The steps must be very low and very shallow. Going up and down on this little stair, the very smallest children can learn movements which they cannot follow properly in climbing ordinary stairways in their homes, in which the proportions are arranged for adults.

Another piece of gymnasium apparatus, adapted for the broad jump, consists of a low wooden platform painted with various lines, by means of which the distance jumped may be gauged. There is a small flight of stairs which may be used in connection with this plane, making it possible to practice and to measure the high jump.

I also believe that rope ladders may be so adapted as to be suitable for use in schools for little children. Used in pairs, these would, it seems to me, help to perfect a great variety of movements, such as kneeling, rising, bending forward and backward, and so forth.; movements which the child, without the help of the ladder, could not make without losing his equilibrium. All of these movements are useful in that they help the child to acquire, first, equilibrium, then that coordination of the muscular movements necessary to him. They are, moreover, helpful in that they increase the chest expansion. Besides all this, such movements as I have described, reinforce the *hand* in its most primitive and essential action, *prehension*—the movement which necessarily precedes all the finer movements of the hand itself. Such apparatus was successfully used by Seguin to develop the general strength and the movement of prehension in his idiotic children.

The gymnasium, therefore, offers a field for the most varied exercises, tending to establish the coordination of the movements common in life, such as walking, throwing objects, going up and down stairs, kneeling, rising, jumping, and so forth.

FREE GYMNASTICS

By free gymnastics I mean those which are given without any apparatus. Such gymnastics are divided into two classes: directed and required exercises, and free games. In the first class, I recommend the march, the object of which should be not rhythm, but poise only. When the march is introduced, it is well to accompany it with the singing of little songs, because this furnishes a breathing exercise very helpful in strengthening the lungs. Besides the march, many of the games of Froebel which are accompanied by songs, very similar to those which the children constantly play among themselves, may be used. In the free games, we furnish the children with balls, hoops, bean bags, and kites. The trees readily offer themselves to the game of "Pussy wants a corner," and many simple games of tag.

EDUCATIONAL GYMNASTICS

Under the name of educational gymnastics, we include two series of exercises which really form a part of other school work, as, for instance, the cultivation of the earth, the care of plants and animals (watering and pruning the plants, carrying the grain to the chickens, etc.). These activities call for various coordinated movements, as, for example, in hoeing, in getting down to plant things, and in rising; the trips which children make in carrying objects to some definite place, and in making a definite practical use of these objects, offer a field for very valuable gymnastic exercises. The scattering of minute objects, such as corn and oats, is valuable, and also the exercise of opening and closing the gates to the garden and to the chicken yard. All of these exercises are the more valuable in that they are carried on in the open air. Among our educational gymnastics we have exercises to develop coordinated movements of the fingers, and these prepare the children for the exercises of practical life, such as dressing and undressing themselves. The didactic material which forms the basis of these last named gymnastics is very simple, consisting of wooden frames, each mounted with two pieces of cloth, or leather, to be fastened and unfastened by means of the buttons and buttonholes, hooks and eyes, eyelets and lacings, or automatic fastenings.

In our "Children's Houses" we use ten of these frames, so constructed that each one of them illustrates a different process in dressing or undressing.

One: mounted with heavy pieces of wool which are to be fastened by means of large bone buttons—corresponds to children's dresses.

Two: mounted with pieces of linen to be fastened with pearl buttons—corresponds to a child's underwear.

Three: leather pieces mounted with shoe buttons—in fastening these leather pieces the children make use of the buttonhook—corresponds to a child's shoes.

Four: pieces of leather which are laced together by means of eyelets and shoe laces.

Five: two pieces of cloth to be laced together. (These pieces are boned and therefore correspond to the little bodices worn by the peasants in Italy.)

Six: two pieces of stuff to be fastened by means of large hooks and eyes.

Seven: two pieces of linen to be fastened by means of small hooks and worked eyelets.

Eight: two pieces of cloth to be fastened by means of broad colored ribbon, which is to be tied into bows.

Nine: pieces of cloth laced together with round cord, on the same order as the fastenings on many of the children's underclothes.

Ten: two pieces to be fastened together by means of the modern automatic fasteners.

Through the use of such toys, the children can practically analyze the movements necessary in dressing and undressing themselves, and can prepare themselves separately for these movements by means of repeated exercises. We succeed in teaching the child to dress himself without his really being aware of it, that is, without any direct or arbitrary command we have led him to this mastery. As soon as he knows how to do it, he begins to wish to make a practical application of his ability, and very soon he will be proud of being sufficient unto himself, and will take delight in an ability which makes his body free from the hands of others, and which leads him the sooner to that modesty and activity which develops far too late in those children of today who are deprived of this most practical form of education. The fastening games are very pleasing to the little ones, and often when ten of them are using the frames at the same time, seated around the little tables, quiet and serious, they give the impression of a workroom filled with tiny workers.

RESPIRATORY GYMNASTICS

The purpose of these gymnastics is to regulate the respiratory movements: in other words, to teach the *art of breathing*. They also help greatly the correct formation of the child's *speech habits*. The exercises which we use were introduced into school literature by Professor Sala. We have chosen the simple exercises described by him in his treatise, "Cura della Balbuzie." These include a number of respiratory gymnastic exercises with which are coordinated muscular exercises. I give here an example:

Mouth wide open, tongue held flat, hands on hips.
Breathe deeply, lift the shoulders rapidly, lowering the diaphragm.
Expel breath slowly, lowering shoulders slowly, returning to normal position.

The directress should select or devise simple breathing exercises, to be accompanied with arm movements, and so forth.

Exercises for proper use of *lips, tongue, and teeth*. These exercises teach the movements of the lips and tongue in the pronunciation of certain fundamental consonant sounds, reinforcing the muscles, and making then ready for these movements. These gymnastics prepare the organs used in the formation of language.

In presenting such exercises we begin with the entire class, but finish by testing the children individually. We ask the child to pronounce, *aloud* and with *force*, the first syllable of a word. When all are intent upon putting the greatest possible force into this, we call each child separately, and have him repeat the word. If he pronounces it correctly, we send him to the right, if badly, to the left. Those who have difficulty with the word, are then encouraged to repeat it several times. The teacher takes note of the age of the child, and of the particular defects in the movements of the muscles used in articulating. She may then touch the muscles which should be used, tapping, for example, the curve of the lips, or even taking hold of the child's tongue and placing it against the dental arch, or showing him clearly the movements which she herself makes when pronouncing the syllable. She must seek in every way to aid the normal development of the movements necessary to the exact articulation of the word.[2] . . .

EDITOR'S NOTES

1. Montessori's detailed discussion of the physiological development of limbs on pp. 138–39 is deleted.

2. Montessori's precise instructions for pronouncing the Italian words—*pane, fame, lana, sina, stella, rana, gatto*—on p. 148 is deleted.

10

Nature in Education—Agricultural Labor: Culture of Plants and Animals

Itard, in a remarkable pedagogical treatise: "*Des premiers développements du jeune sauvage de l'Aveyron,*" expounds in detail the drama of a curious, gigantic education which attempted to overcome the psychical darkness of an idiot and at the same time to snatch a man from primitive nature.

The savage of the Aveyron was a child who had grown up in the natural state: criminally abandoned in a forest where his assassins thought they had killed him, he was cured by natural means, and had survived for many years free and naked in the wilderness, until, captured by hunters, he entered into the civilized life of Paris, showing by the scars with which his miserable body was furrowed the story of the struggles with wild beasts, and of lacerations caused by falling from heights.

The child was, and always remained, mute; his mentality, diagnosed by Pinel as idiotic, remained forever almost inaccessible to intellectual education.[1]

To this child are due the first steps of positive pedagogy. Itard, a physician of deaf-mutes and a student of philosophy, undertook his education with methods which he had already partially tried for treating defective hearing—believing at the beginning that the savage showed characteristics of inferiority, not because he was a degraded organism, but for want of education. He was a follower of the principles of Helvetius: "Man is nothing without the work of man";[2] that is, he believed in the omnipotence of education, and was opposed to the pedagogical principle which Rousseau had promulgated before the Revolution: "*Tout est bien sortant des mains de l'Auteur des choses, tout dégénère dans les mains de l'homme,*"—that is, the work of education is deleterious and spoils the man.[3]

143

The savage, according to the erroneous first impression of Itard, demonstrated experimentally by his characteristics the truth of the former assertion. When, however, he perceived, with the help of Pinel, that he had to do with an idiot, his philosophical theories gave place to the most admirable, tentative, experimental pedagogy.

Itard divides the education of the savage into two parts. In the first, he endeavors to lead the child from natural life to social life; and in the second, he attempts the intellectual education of the idiot. The child in his life of frightful abandonment had found one happiness; he had, so to speak, immersed himself in, and unified himself with, nature, taking delight in it—rains, snow, tempests, boundless space, had been his sources of entertainment, his companions, his love. Civil life is a renunciation of all this: but it is an acquisition beneficent to human progress. In Itard's pages we find vividly described the moral work which led the savage to civilization, multiplying the needs of the child and surrounding him with loving care.[4] . . .

But the advantages which we prepare for him in this social life, in a great measure escape the little child, who at the beginning of his life is a predominantly vegetative creature.

To soften this transition in education, by giving a large part of the educative work to nature itself, is as necessary as it is not to snatch the little child suddenly and violently from its mother and to take him to school; and precisely this is done in the "Children's Houses," which are situated within the tenements where the parents live, where the cry of the child reaches the mother and the mother's voice answers it.

Nowadays, under the form of child hygiene, this part of education is much cultivated: children are allowed to grow up in the open air, in the public gardens, or are left for many hours half naked on the seashore, exposed to the rays of the sun. It has been understood, through the diffusion of marine and Apennine colonies, that the best means of invigorating the child is to immerse him in nature.

Short and comfortable clothing for children, sandals for the feet, nudity of the lower extremities, are so many liberations from the oppressive shackles of civilization.

It is an obvious principle that we should sacrifice to natural liberties in education only as much as is *necessary* for the acquisition of the greater pleasures which are offered by civilization without *useless sacrifices*.

But in all this progress of modern child education, we have not freed ourselves from the prejudice which denies children spiritual expression and spiritual needs, and makes us consider them only as amiable vegetating bodies to be cared for, kissed, and set in motion. The *education* which a good mother or a good modern teacher gives today to the child who, for example, is running about in a flower garden is the counsel *not to touch the flowers*, not to tread on the grass; as if it were sufficient for the child to satisfy the physiological needs of his body by moving his legs and breathing fresh air.

But if for the physical life it is necessary to have the child exposed to the vivifying forces of nature, it is also necessary for his psychical life to place the soul of the child in contact with creation, in order that he may lay up for himself treasure from the directly educating forces of living nature. The method for arriving at this end is to set the child at agricultural labor, guiding him to the cultivation of plants and animals, and so to the intelligent contemplation of nature.[5] . . .

First. The child is initiated into observation of the phenomena of life. He stands with respect to the plants and animals in relations analogous to those in which the *observing* teacher stands towards him. Little by little, as interest and observation grow, his zealous care for the living creatures grows also, and in this way, the child can logically be brought to appreciate the care which the mother and the teacher take of him.

Second. The child is initiated into *foresight* by way of *auto-education*; when he knows that the life of the plants that have been sown depends upon his care in watering them, and that of the animals, upon his diligence in feeding them, without which the little plant dries up and the animals suffer hunger, the child becomes vigilant, as one who is beginning to feel a mission in life. Moreover, a voice quite different from that of his mother and his teacher calling him to his duties, is speaking here, exhorting him never to forget the task he has undertaken. It is the plaintive voice of the needy life which lives by his care. Between the child and the living creatures which he cultivates there is born a mysterious correspondence which induces the child to fulfill certain determinate acts without the intervention of the teacher, that is, leads him to an *auto-education*.

The rewards which the child reaps also remain between him and nature: one fine day after long patient care in carrying food and straw to the brooding pigeons, Behold the little ones! Behold a number of chickens peeping about the setting hen which yesterday sat motionless in her brooding place! Behold one day the tender little rabbits in the hutch where formerly dwelt in solitude the pair of big rabbits to which he had not a few times lovingly carried the green vegetables left over in his mother's kitchen![6] . . .

Third. The children are initiated into the virtue of *patience and into confident expectation*, which is a form of faith and of philosophy of life.

When the children put a seed into the ground, and wait until it fructifies, and see the first appearance of the shapeless plant, and wait for the growth and the transformations into flower and fruit, and see how some plants sprout sooner and some later, and how the deciduous plants have a rapid life, and the fruit trees a slower growth, they end by acquiring a peaceful equilibrium of conscience, and absorb the first germs of that wisdom which so characterized the tillers of the soil in the time when they still kept their primitive simplicity.

Fourth. The children are inspired with a feeling for nature, which is maintained by the marvels of creation—that creation which *rewards* with a generosity not measured by the labor of those who help it to evolve the life of its creatures.[7] . . .

But what most develops a feeling of nature is the *cultivation* of the *living* things, because they by their natural development give back far more than they receive, and show something like infinity in their beauty and variety. When the child has cultivated the iris or the pansy, the rose or the hyacinth, has placed in the soil a seed or a bulb and periodically watered it, or has planted a fruit-bearing shrub, and the blossomed flower and the ripened fruit offer themselves as a *generous gift* of nature, a rich reward for a small effort; it seems almost as if nature were answering with her gifts to the feeling of desire, to the vigilant love of the cultivator, rather than striking a balance with his material efforts.

It will be quite different when the child has to gather the *material* fruits of his labor: motionless, uniform objects, which are consumed and dispersed rather than increased and multiplied.

The difference between the products of nature and those of industry, between divine products and human products—it is this that must be born spontaneously in the child's conscience, like the determination of a fact.

But at the same time, as the plant must give its fruit, so man must give his labor.

Fifth. The child follows the natural way of development of the human race. In short, such education makes the evolution of the individual harmonize with that of humanity. Man passed from the natural to the artificial state through agriculture: when he discovered the secret of intensifying the production of the soil, he obtained the reward of civilization.

The same path must be traversed by the child who is destined to become a civilized man.

The action of educative nature so understood is very practically accessible. Because, even if the vast stretch of ground and the large courtyard necessary for physical education are lacking, it will always be possible to find a few square yards of land that may be cultivated, or a little place where pigeons can make their nest, things sufficient for spiritual education. Even a pot of flowers at the window can, if necessary, fulfill the purpose.

In the first "Children's House" in Rome we have a vast courtyard, cultivated as a garden, where the children are free to run in the open air—and, besides, a long stretch of ground, which is planted on one side with trees, has a branching path in the middle, and on the opposite side, has broken ground for the cultivation of plants. This last, we have divided into so many portions, reserving one for each child.

While the smaller children run freely up and down the paths, or rest in the shade of the trees, the *possessors of the earth* (children from four years of age up), are sowing, or hoeing, watering or examining, the surface of the soil watching for the sprouting of plants. It is interesting to note the following fact: the little reservations of the children are placed along the wall of the tenement, in a spot formerly neglected because it leads to a blind road; the inhabitants of the house, therefore, had the habit of throwing from those windows every kind of offal, and at the beginning our garden was thus contaminated.

But, little by little, without any exhortation on our part, solely through the respect born in the people's mind for the children's labor, nothing more fell from the windows, except the loving glances and smiles of the mothers upon the soil which was the beloved possession of their little children.

EDITOR'S NOTES

1. Phillippe Pinel, regarded as an authority on the insane, was called upon by Itard to diagnose the wild boy.

2. Claude Adrien Helvetius (1715–1771), a French rationalist philosopher, wrote *De l'Esprit* (1758) and *De l'Homme, de ses facultes intellectuelles et de son education* (1772) in which he argued that: (1) sensation was the source of all intellectual activities; (2) human actions, though motivated by self-interest, can be brought into conformity with the good of the larger community by legislation and education; (3) all people can be educated; (4) human process was possible through education. Like Montessori, Helvetius argued that it was possible to develop a science of education.

3. Montessori is quoting the opening sentence of Book I of Jean-Jacque Rousseau's *Emile*, "Everything is good as it leaves the hands of the Author of things; everything degenerates in the hands of man." Montessori somewhat misinterprets Rousseau's statement. He is referring to the political, social, economic as well as the educational institutions and processes that limit human freedom to develop naturally. Rousseau is not arguing against all education but is advocating a natural education in contrast to a socially directed ornamental and artificial one.

Throughout her book, Montessori distinguished her concept of the child's freedom within the structures of the prepared environment from Rousseau's romanticized version of children freedom.

4. Montessori's series of quotes from Itard's discussion of his efforts to educate the wild boy of Aveyron on pp. 150–53 is deleted. Earlier in her book, Montessori described the influence of Itard on her method of education.

5. Montessori's critique of a Mrs. Latter, an English educator who developed nature and agricultural studies for children and Guido Baccelli's educative gardens on p. 156 is deleted. Montessori critiqued these approaches as being overly intellectual and failing to develop children's physical, sensory, and psychic potentials.

6. Montessori's several examples of the pleasure children get from caring for pigeons in letters she has received from teachers on pp. 157–59 that repeats earlier examples is deleted.

7. Montessori's discussion of Mrs. Latter's comments that children do not fear earthworms and other small creatures that some adults do on p. 159 is deleted.

11

Manual Labor—The Potter's Art and Building

Manual labor is distinguished from manual gymnastics by the fact that the object of the latter is to exercise the hand, and the former, to *accomplish a determinate work*, being, or simulating, a socially useful object. The one perfects the individual, the other enriches the world; the two things are, however, connected because, in general, only one who has perfected his own hand can produce a useful product.

I have thought wise, after a short trial, to exclude completely Froebel's exercises, because weaving and sewing on cardboard are ill adapted to the physiological state of the child's visual organs where the powers of the accommodation of the eye have not yet reached complete development; hence, these exercises cause an *effort* of the organ which may have a fatal influence on the development of the sight. The other little exercises of Froebel, such as the folding of paper, are exercises of the hand, not work.

There is still left plastic work—the most rational among all the exercises of Froebel—which consists in making the child reproduce determinate objects in clay.[1]

In consideration, however, of the system of liberty which I proposed, I did not like to make the children *copy* anything, and, in giving them clay to fashion in their own manner, I did not direct the children to *produce useful things;* nor was I accomplishing an educative result, inasmuch as plastic work, as I shall show later, serves for the study of the psychic individuality of the child in his spontaneous manifestations, but not for his education.[2] . . .

Thus, when once the handicraft leading to the construction of vases has been learned (and this is the part of the progress in the work, learned from the direct and graduated instruction of the teacher), anyone can modify it according to the inspiration of his own aesthetic taste and this is the artistic, individual part of the work. Besides this, in Randone's school the use of the potter's wheel is taught, and also the composition of the mixture for the bath of majolica ware, and baking the pieces in the furnace, stages of manual labor which contain an industrial culture.

Another work in the School of Educative Art is the manufacture of diminutive bricks, and their baking in the furnace, and the construction of diminutive *walls* built by the same processes which the masons use in the construction of houses, the bricks being joined by means of mortar handled with a trowel. After the simple construction of the wall—which is very amusing for the children who build it, placing brick on brick, superimposing row on row—the children pass to the construction of real *houses*—first, resting on the ground, and, then, really constructed with foundations, after a previous excavation of large holes in the ground by means of little hoes and shovels. These little houses have openings corresponding to windows and doors, and are variously ornamented in their façades by little tiles of bright and multicolored majolica: the tiles themselves being manufactured by the children.

Thus the children learn to *appreciate* the objects and constructions which surround them, while a real manual and artistic labor gives them profitable exercise.

Such is the manual training which I have adopted in the "Children's Houses"; after two or three lessons the little pupils are already enthusiastic about the construction of vases, and they preserve very carefully their own products, in which they take pride. With their plastic art they then model little objects, eggs or fruits, with which they themselves fill the vases. One of the first undertakings is the simple vase of red clay filled with eggs of white clay; then comes the modeling of the vase with one or more spouts, of the narrow-mouthed vase, of the vase with a handle, of that with two or three handles, of the tripod, of the amphora.

For children of the age of five or six, the work of the potter's wheel begins. But what most delights the children is the work of building a wall with little bricks, and seeing a little house, the fruit of their own hands, rise in the vicinity of the ground in which are growing plants, also cultivated by them. Thus the age of childhood epitomizes the principal primitive labors of humanity, when the human race, changing from the nomadic to the stable condition, demanded of the earth its fruit, built itself shelter, and devised vases to cook the foods yielded by the fertile earth.

EDITOR'S NOTES

1. Montessori's comments about Froebel made some important distinctions between the Froebelian kindergarten and the Montessori method. Friedrich Wilhelm August Froebel (1782–1852), a German educator, developed the kindergarten as a distinct approach to early childhood education. He developed a series of gifts; objects used to stimulate the child's consciousness of concepts, and occupations, materials upon with children could work. Froebel also stressed the importance of songs, stories, games, and play to connect the children to their broader culture. While Montessori shared many ideas with Froebel, there were important differences between them on how they constructed the educational environment. In this passage, Montessori excludes Froebel's exercises on weaving and sewing on cardboard as ill adapted to child's physiological and visual readiness. However, she retains his plastic work—clay modeling. When Montessori's method was introduced, there was some rivalry between orthodox kindergarten educators and those who favored Montessori's method. Some, however, tried to fuse certain aspects of Montessori's method into the kindergarten.

2. Montessori's discussion of Radone's School of Educative Art, the Wall of Beilisarius in Rome, and the relationship of the vase to the degree of a culture's civilization on pp. 163–65 are deleted.

12

Education of the Senses

In a pedagogical method which is experimental the education of the senses must undoubtedly assume the greatest importance. Experimental psychology also takes note of movements by means of sense measurements.

Pedagogy, however, although it may profit by psychometry is not designed to *measure* the sensations, but *educate* the senses. This is a point easily understood, yet one which is often confused. While the proceedings of esthesiometry are not to any great extent applicable to little children, the *education* of the *senses* is entirely possible.

We do not start from the conclusions of experimental psychology. That is, it is not the knowledge of the average sense conditions according to the age of the child which leads us to determine the educational applications we shall make. We start essentially from a method, and it is probable that psychology will be able to draw its conclusions from pedagogy so understood, and not *vice versa*.

The method used by me is that of making a pedagogical experiment with a didactic object and awaiting the spontaneous reaction of the child. This is a method in every way analogous to that of experimental psychology.

I make use of a material which, at first glance, may be confused with psychometric material. Teachers from Milan who had followed the course in the Milan school of experimental psychology, seeing my material exposed, would recognize among it, measures of the perception of color, hardness, and weight, and would conclude that, in truth, I brought no new contribution to pedagogy since these instruments were already known to them.[1] . . .

Much of the material used for deficients is abandoned in the education of the normal child—and much that is used has been greatly modified. I believe, however, that I have arrived at a *selection of objects* (which I do not here wish

153

to speak of in the technical language of psychology as stimuli) representing the minimum *necessary* to a practical sense education.

These objects constitute the *didactic system* (or set of didactic materials) used by me. They are manufactured by the House of Labour of the Humanitarian Society at Milan.

A description of the objects will be given as the educational scope of each is explained. Here I shall limit myself to the setting forth of a few general considerations.

First. The difference in the reaction between deficient and normal children, in the presentation of didactic material made up of graded stimuli. This difference is plainly seen from the fact that the same didactic material used with deficients *makes education possible,* while with normal children it *provokes auto-education.*

This fact is one of the most interesting I have met with in all my experience, and it inspired and rendered possible the method of *observation* and *liberty.*

Let us suppose that we use our first object—a block in which solid geometric forms are set. Into corresponding holes in the block are set ten little wooden cylinders, the bases diminishing gradually about two millimeters. The game consists in taking the cylinders out of their places, putting them on the table, mixing them, and then putting each one back in its own place. The aim is to educate the eye to the differential perception of dimensions.

With the deficient child, it would be necessary to begin with exercises in which the stimuli were much more strongly contrasted, and to arrive at this exercise only after many others had preceded it.

With normal children, this is, on the other hand, the first object which we may present, and out of all the didactic material this is the game preferred by the very little children of two and a half and three years. Once we arrived at this exercise with a deficient child, it was necessary continually and actively to recall his attention, inviting him to look at the block and showing him the various pieces. And if the child once succeeded in placing all the cylinders properly, he stopped, and the game was finished. Whenever the deficient child committed an error, it was necessary to correct it, or to urge him to correct it himself, and when he was able to correct an error he was usually quite indifferent.

Now the normal child, instead, takes spontaneously a lively interest in this game. He pushes away all who would interfere, or offer to help him, and wishes to be alone before his problem.

It had already been noted that little ones of two or three years take the greatest pleasure in arranging small objects, and this experiment in the "Children's Houses" demonstrates the truth of this assertion.

Now, and here is the important point, the normal child attentively observes the relation between the size of the opening and that of the object which he is to place in the mold, and is greatly interested in the game, as is clearly shown by the expression of attention on the little face.

If he mistakes, placing one of the objects in an opening that is small for it, he takes it away, and proceeds to make various trials, seeking the proper opening. If he makes a contrary error, letting the cylinder fall into an opening that is a little too large for it, and then collects all the successive cylinders in openings just a little too large, he will find himself at the last with the big cylinder in his hand while only the smallest opening is empty. The didactic material *controls every error*. The child proceeds to correct himself, doing this in various ways. Most often he feels the cylinders or shakes them, in order to recognize which are the largest. Sometimes, he sees at a glance where his error lies, pulls the cylinders from the places where they should not be, and puts those left out where they belong, then replaces all the others. The normal child always repeats the exercise with growing interest.

Indeed, it is precisely in these errors that the educational importance of the didactic material lies, and when the child with evident security places each piece in its proper place, he has outgrown the exercise, and this piece of material becomes useless to him.

This self-correction leads the child to concentrate his attention upon the differences of dimensions, and to compare the various pieces. It is in just this comparison that the *psycho-sensory* exercise lies.

There is, therefore, no question here of teaching the child the *knowledge* of the dimensions, through the medium of these pieces. Neither is it our aim that the child shall know how to use, *without an error,* the material presented to him thus performing the exercises well.

That would place our material on the same basis as many others, for example that of Froebel, and would require again the *active* work of the *teacher* who busies herself furnishing knowledge, and making haste to correct every error in order that the child may *learn the use of the objects*.

Here instead it is the work of the child, the auto-correction, the auto-education which acts, for the *teacher must not interfere* in the *slightest* way. No teacher can furnish the child with the *agility which he acquires* through gymnastic *exercises:* it is necessary that the *pupil perfect himself* through his own efforts. It is very much the same with the *education of the senses*.

It might be said that the same thing is true of every form of education; a man is not what he is because of the teachers he has had, but because of what he has done.

One of the difficulties of putting this method into practice with teachers of the old school, lies in the difficulty of preventing them from intervening when the little child remains for some time puzzled before some error, and with his eyebrows drawn together and his lips puckered, makes repeated efforts to correct himself. When they see this, the old-time teachers are seized with pity, and long, with an almost irresistible force, to help the child. When we prevent this intervention, they burst into words of compassion for the little scholar, but he soon shows in his smiling face the joy of having surmounted an obstacle.

Normal children repeat such exercises many times. This repetition varies according to the individual. Some children after having completed the exercise five or six times are tired of it. Others will remove and replace the pieces at least *twenty times,* with an expression of evident interest. Once, after I had watched a little one of four years repeat this exercise sixteen times, I had the other children sing in order to distract her, but she continued unmoved to take out the cylinders, mix them up and put them back in their places.

An intelligent teacher ought to be able to make most interesting individual psychological observations, and, to a certain point, should be able to measure the length of time for which the various stimuli held the attention.

In fact, when the child educates himself, and when the control and correction of errors is yielded to the didactic material, there *remains for the teacher nothing but to observe.* She must then be more of a psychologist than a teacher, and this shows the importance of a scientific preparation on the part of the teacher.

Indeed, with my methods, the teacher teaches *little* and observes *much,* and, above all, it is her function to direct the psychic activity of the children and their physiological development. For this reason I have changed the name of teacher into that of directress.

At first this name provoked many smiles, for everyone asked whom there was for this teacher to direct, since she had no assistants, and since she must leave her little pupils *in liberty.* But her direction is much more profound and important than that which is commonly understood, for this teacher directs *the life and the soul.*

Second. The education of the senses has, as its aim, the refinement of the differential perception of stimuli by means of repeated exercises.

There exists a *sensory culture,* which is not generally taken into consideration, but which is a factor in esthesiometry.

For example, in the mental *tests* which are used in France, or in a series of tests which De Sanctis has established for the *diagnosis* of the intellectual status, I have often seen used *cubes of different sizes placed at varying distances.* The child was to select the *smallest* and the *largest,* while the chronometer measured the time of reaction between the command and the execution of the act. Account was also taken of the errors. I repeat that in such experiments the factor of *culture* is forgotten and by this I mean *sensory culture.*

Our children have, for example, among the didactic material for the education of the senses, a series of ten cubes. The first has a base of ten centimeters, and the others decrease, successively, one centimeter as to base, the smallest cube having a base of one centimeter. The exercise consists in throwing the blocks, which are pink in color, down upon a green carpet, and then building them up into a little tower, placing the largest cube as the base, and then placing the others in order of size until the little cube of one centimeter is placed at the top.

The little one must each time select, from the blocks scattered upon the green carpet, "the largest" block. This game is most entertaining to the little ones of two years and a half, who, as soon as they have constructed the little tower, tumble it down with little blows of the hand, admiring the pink cubes as they lie scattered upon the green carpet. Then, they begin again the construction, building and destroying a definite number of times.

If we were to place before these tests one of my children from three to four years, and one of the children from the first elementary (six or seven years old), my pupil would undoubtedly manifest a shorter period of reaction, and would not commit errors. The same may be said for the tests of the chromatic sense, etc.

This educational method should therefore prove interesting to students of experimental psychology as well as to teachers.

In conclusion, let me summarize briefly: Our didactic material renders auto-education possible, permits a methodical education of the senses. Not upon the ability of the teacher does such education rest, but upon the didactic system. This presents objects which, first, attract the spontaneous attention of the child, and, second, contain a rational gradation of stimuli.

We must not confuse the *education* of the senses, with the concrete ideas which may be gathered from our environment by means of the senses. Nor must this education of the senses be identical in our minds with the language through which is given the nomenclature corresponding to the concrete idea, nor with the acquisition of the abstract idea of the exercises.[2] . . .

The directress of the "Children's House" must have a clear idea of the two factors which enter into her work—the guidance of the child, and the individual exercise.

Only after she has this concept clearly fixed in her mind, may she proceed to the application of a *method* to *guide* the spontaneous education of the child and to impart necessary notions to him.

In the opportune quality and in the manner of this intervention lies the *personal art* of the *educator*.

For example, in the "Children's House" in the Prati di Castello, where the pupils belong to the middle class, I found, a month after the opening of the school, a child of five years who already knew how to compose any word, as he knew the alphabet perfectly—he had learned it in two weeks. He knew how to write on the blackboard, and in the exercises in free design he showed himself not only to be an observer, but to have some intuitive idea of perspective, drawing a house and chair very cleverly. As for the exercises of the chromatic sense, he could mix together the eight gradations of the eight colors which we

use, and from this mass of sixty-four tablets, each wound with silk of a different color or shade, he could rapidly separate the eight groups. Having done this,
he would proceed with ease to arrange each color series in perfect gradation. In
this game the child would almost cover one of the little tables with a carpet of
finely shaded colors. I made the experiment, taking him to the window and
showing him in full daylight one of the colored tablets, telling him to look at it
well, so that he might be able to remember it. I then sent him to the table on
which all the gradations were spread out, and asked him to find the tablet like
the one at which he had looked. He committed only very slight errors, often
choosing the exact shade but more often the one next it, rarely a tint two grades
removed from the right one. This boy had then a power of discrimination and a
color memory which were almost prodigious. Like all the other children, he
was exceedingly fond of the color exercises. But when I asked the name of the
white color spool, he hesitated for a long time before replying uncertainly
"white." Now a child of such intelligence should have been able, even without
the special intervention of the teacher, to learn the name of each color.

The directress told me that having noticed that the child had great difficulty
in retaining the nomenclature of the colors, she had up until that time left him
to exercise himself freely with the games for the color sense. At the same time
he had developed rapidly a power over written language, which in my method
is presented through a series of problems to be solved. These problems are
presented as sense exercises. This child was, therefore, most intelligent. In
him the discriminative sensory perceptions kept pace with great intellectual
activities—attention and judgment. But his *memory for names* was inferior.

The directress had thought best not to interfere, as yet, in the teaching of
the child. Certainly, the education of the child was a little disordered, and the
directress had left the spontaneous explanation of his mental activities exces-
sively free. However desirable it may be to furnish a sense education as a basis for intellectual ideas, it is nevertheless advisable at the same time to associate the *language* with these *perceptions*.

In this connection I have found excellent for use with normal children *the
three periods* of which the lesson according to Seguin consists:

First Period. The association of the sensory perception with the name. For
    example, we present to the child, two colors, red and blue. Presenting the
    red, we say simply, "This is red," and presenting the blue, "This is blue."
    Then, we lay the spools upon the table under the eyes of the child.
Second Period. Recognition of the object corresponding to the name. We
    say to the child, "Give me the red," and then, "Give me the blue."
Third Period. The remembering of the name corresponding to the object.
    We ask the child, showing him the object, "What is this?" and he should
    respond, "Red."

Seguin insists strongly upon these three periods, and urges that the colors be left for several instants under the eyes of the child. He also advises us never to present the color singly, but always two at a time, since the contrast helps the chromatic memory. Indeed, I have proved that there cannot be a better method for teaching color to the deficients, who, with this method were able to learn the colors much more perfectly than normal children in the ordinary schools who have had a haphazard sense education. For normal children however there exists a *period preceding* the Three Periods of Seguin—a period which contains the real *sense education*. This is the acquisition of a fineness of differential perception, which can be obtained *only* through auto-education.

This, then, is an example of the great superiority of the normal child, and of the greater effect of education which such pedagogical methods may exercise upon the mental development of normal as compared with deficient children.

The association of the name with the stimulus is a source of great pleasure to the normal child. I remember, one day, I had taught a little girl, who was not yet three years old, and who was a little tardy in the development of language, the names of three colors. I had the children place one of their little tables near a window, and seating myself in one of the little chairs, I seated the little girl in a similar chair at my right.

I had, on the table, six of the color spools in pairs, that is two reds, two blues, two yellows. In the First Period, I placed one of the spools before the child, asking her to find the one like it. This I repeated for all three of the colors, showing her how to arrange them carefully in pairs. After this I passed to the Three Periods of Seguin. The little girl learned to recognize the three colors and to pronounce the name of each.

She was so happy that she looked at me for a long time, and then began to jump up and down. I, seeing her pleasure, said to her, laughing, "Do you know the colors?" and she replied, still jumping up and down, "Yes! YES!" Her delight was inexhaustible; she danced about me, waiting joyously for me to ask her the same question, that she might reply with the same enthusiasm, "Yes! Yes!"

Another important particular in the technique of sense education lies in *isolating the sense,* whenever this is possible. So, for example, the exercises on the sense of hearing can be given more successfully in an environment not only of silence, but even of darkness.

For the education of the senses in general, such as in the tactile, thermic, baric, and stereognostic exercises, we blindfold the child. The reasons for this particular technique have been fully set forth by psychology. Here, it is enough to note that in the case of normal children the blindfold greatly increases their interest, without making the exercises degenerate into noisy fun, and without having the child's attention attracted more to the *bandage* than to the sense-stimuli upon which we wish to *focus* the attention.

For example, in order to test the acuteness of the child's sense of hearing (a most important thing for the teacher to know), I use an empiric test which is coming to be used almost universally by physicians in the making of medical examinations. This test is made by modulating the voice, reducing it to a whisper. The child is blindfolded, or the teacher may stand behind him, speaking his name, in *a whisper* and from varying distances. I establish a *solemn silence* in the schoolroom, darken the windows, have the children bow their heads upon their hands which they hold in front of their eyes. Then I call the children by name, one by one, in a whisper, lighter for those who are nearer me, and more clearly for those farther away. Each child awaits, in the darkness, the faint voice which calls him, listening intently, ready to run with keenest joy toward the mysterious and much desired call.

The normal child may be blindfolded in the games where, for example, he is to recognize various weights, for this does help him to intensify and concentrate his attention upon the baric stimuli which he is to test. The blindfold adds to his pleasure, since he is proud of having been able to guess.

The effect of these games upon deficient children is very different. When placed in darkness, they often go to sleep, or give themselves up to disordered acts. When the blindfold is used, they fix their attention upon the bandage itself, and change the exercise into a game, which does not fulfill the end we have in view with the exercise.

We speak, it is true, of *games* in education, but it must be made clear that we understand by this term a free activity, ordered to a definite end; not disorderly noise, which distracts the attention.[3] . . .

EDITOR'S NOTES

1. Montessori's extended discussion of the differences between instruments such as the esthesiometer to measure sensations and didactic materials to exercise the senses on p. 168 is deleted.

2. Montessori's reiteration of her views of sensory education by an example of piano lessons on p. 175 is deleted.

3. Montessori's long series of quotations from Itard on using sensory teaching techniques with defective children on pp. 181–84 is deleted. She discussed Itard's influence on her method earlier in the book.

13

Education of the Senses and Illustrations of the Didactic Material: General Sensibility; the Tactile, Thermic, Baric, and Stereognostic Senses

The education of the tactile and the thermic senses go together, since the warm bath, and heat in general, render the tactile sense more acute. Since to exercise the tactile sense it is necessary to *touch*, bathing the hands in warm water has the additional advantage of teaching the child a principle of cleanliness—that of not touching objects with hands that are not clean. I therefore apply the general notions of practical life, regarding the washing of the hands, care of the nails, to the exercises preparatory to the discrimination of tactile stimuli.

The limitation of the exercises of the tactile sense to the cushioned tips of the fingers, is rendered necessary by practical life. It must be made a necessary phase of *education* because it prepares for a life in which man exercises and uses the tactile sense through the medium of these finger tips. Hence, I have the child wash his hands carefully with soap, in a little basin; and in another basin I have him rinse them in a bath of tepid water. Then I show him how to dry and rub his hands gently, in this way preparing for the regular bath. I next teach the child how to *touch*, that is, the manner in which he should touch surfaces. For this it is necessary to take the finger of the child and to draw *it very, very lightly* over the surface.

Another particular of the technique is to teach the child to hold his eyes closed while he touches, encouraging him to do this by telling him that he will be able to feel the differences better, and so leading him to distinguish, without the help of sight, the change of contact. He will quickly learn, and will show that he enjoys the exercise. Often after the introduction of such exercises, it is a common thing to have a child come to you, and, closing his eyes, touch with great delicacy the palm of your hand or the cloth of your dress, especially any silken or velvet trimmings. They do verily *exercise the* tactile sense. They enjoy keenly touching any soft pleasant surface, and become exceedingly keen in discriminating between the differences in the sandpaper cards.

The Didactic Material consists of: *a*—a rectangular wooden board divided into two equal rectangles, one covered with very smooth paper, or having the wood polished until a smooth surface is obtained; the other covered with sandpaper. *b*—a tablet like the preceding covered with alternating strips of smooth paper and sandpaper.

I also make use of a collection of paper slips, varying through many grades from smooth, fine cardboard to coarsest sandpaper. The stuffs described elsewhere are also used in these lessons.

As to the Thermic Sense, I use a set of little metal bowls, which are filled with water at different degrees of temperature. These I try to measure with a thermometer, so that there may be two containing water of the same temperature.

I have designed a set of utensils which are to be made of very light metal, and filled with water. These have covers, and to each is attached a thermometer. The bowl touched from the outside gives the desired impression of heat.

I also have the children put their hands into cold, tepid, and warm water, an exercise which they find most diverting. I should like to repeat this exercise with the feet, but I have not had an opportunity to make the trial.

For the education of the baric sense (sense of weight), I use with great success little wooden tablets, six by eight centimeters, having a thickness of 1/2 centimeter. These tablets are in three different qualities of wood, wistaria, walnut, and pine. They weigh respectively, 24, 18, and 12 grams, making them differ in weight by 6 grams. These tablets should be very smooth; if possible, varnished in such a way that every roughness shall be eliminated, but so that the natural color of the wood shall remain. The child, *observing* the color, *knows* that they are of differing weights, and this offers a means of controlling the exercise. He takes two of the tablets in his hands, letting them rest upon the palm at the base of his outstretched fingers. Then he moves his hands up and down in order to gauge the weight. This movement should come to be, little by little, almost insensible. We lead the child to make his distinction purely through the difference in weight, leaving out the guide of the different colors, and closing his eyes. He learns to do this of himself, and takes great interest in "guessing."

The game attracts the attention of those near, who gather in a circle about the one who has the tablets, and who take turns in *guessing*. Sometimes the children spontaneously make use of the blindfold, taking turns, and interspersing the work with peals of joyful laughter.

EDUCATION OF THE STEREOGNOSTIC SENSE

The education of this sense leads to the recognition of objects through feeling, that is, through the simultaneous help of the tactile and muscular senses.

Taking this union as a basis, we have made experiments which have given marvelously successful educational results. I feel that for the help of teachers these exercises should be described.

The first didactic material used by us is made up of the bricks and cubes of Froebel. We call the attention of the child to the form of the two solids, have him feel them carefully and accurately, with his eyes open, repeating some phrase serving to fix his attention upon the particulars of the forms presented. After this the child is told to place the cubes to the right, the bricks to the left, always feeling them, and without looking at them. Finally the exercise is repeated, by the child blindfolded. Almost all the children succeed in the exercise, and after two or three times, are able to eliminate every error. There are twenty-four of the bricks and cubes in all, so that the attention may be held for some time through this "game"—but undoubtedly the child's pleasure is greatly increased by the fact of his being watched by a group of his companions, all interested and eager.

One day a directress called my attention to a little girl of three years, one of our very youngest pupils, who had repeated this exercise perfectly. We seated the little girl comfortably in an armchair, close to the table. Then, placing the twenty-four objects before her upon the table, we mixed them, and calling the child's attention to the difference in form, told her to place the cubes to the right and the bricks to the left. When she was blindfolded she began the exercise as taught by us, taking an object in each hand, feeling each and putting it in its right place. Sometimes she took two cubes, or two bricks, sometimes she found a brick in the right hand, a cube in the left. The child had to recognize the form, and to remember throughout the exercise the proper placing of the different objects. This seemed to me very difficult for a child of three years.

But observing her I saw that she not only performed the exercise easily, but that the movements with which we had taught her to feel the form were superfluous. Indeed the instant she had taken the two objects in her hands, if it so happened that she had taken a cube with the left hand and a brick in the right, she *exchanged* them *immediately*, and *then* began the laborious feeling the form which we had taught and which she perhaps, believed to be obligatory. But the objects had been recognized by her through *the first light touch*, that is, the *recognition* was *contemporaneous* to *the taking*.

Continuing my study of the subject, I found that this little girl was possessed of a remarkable *functional ambidexterity*—I should be very glad to make a wider study of this phenomenon having in view the desirability of a simultaneous education of both hands.

I repeated the exercise with other children and found that they *recognize* the objects before feeling their contours. This was particularly true of the *little ones*. Our educational methods in this respect furnished a remarkable exercise in associative gymnastics, leading to a rapidity of judgment which was truly surprising and had the advantage of being perfectly adapted to very young children.

These exercises of the stereognostic sense may be multiplied in many ways—they amuse the children who find delight in the recognition of a stimulus, as in the thermic exercises; for example—they may raise any small objects, toy soldiers, little balls, and, above all, the various *coins* in common use. They come to discriminate between small forms varying very slightly, such as corn, wheat, and rice.

They are very proud of *seeing without eyes*, holding out their hands and crying, "Here are my eyes!" "I can see with my hand!" Indeed, our little ones walking in the ways we have planned, make us marvel over their unforeseen progress, surprising us daily. Often, while they are wild with delight over some new conquest—we watch, in deepest wonder and meditation.

EDUCATION OF THE SENSES OF TASTE AND SMELL

This phase of sense education is most difficult, and I have not as yet had any satisfactory results to record. I can only say that the exercises ordinarily used in the tests of psychometry do not seem to me to be practical for use with young children.

The olfactory sense in children is not developed to any great extent, and this makes it difficult to attract their attention by means of this sense. We have made use of one test which has not been repeated often enough to form the basis of a method. We have the child smell fresh violets, and jessamine flowers. We then blindfold him, saying, "Now we are going to present you with flowers." A little friend then holds a bunch of violets under the child's nose, that he may guess the name of the flower. For greater or less intensity we present fewer flowers, or even one single blossom.

But this part of education, like that of the sense of taste, can be obtained by the child during the luncheon hour—when he can learn to recognize various odors.

As to taste, the method of touching the tongue with various solutions, bitter or acid, sweet, salty, is perfectly applicable. Children of four years readily lend themselves to such games, which serve as a reason for showing them how to rinse their mouths perfectly. The children enjoy recognizing various flavors, and learn, after each test, to fill a glass with tepid water, and carefully rinse their mouths. In this way the exercise for the sense of taste is also an exercise in hygiene.

EDUCATION OF THE SENSE OF VISION

I. Differential Visual Perception of Dimensions

First. Solid Insets: This material consists of three solid blocks of wood each 55 centimeters long, 6 centimeters high, and 8 centimeters wide. Each block contains ten wooden pieces, set into corresponding holes. These pieces are cylindrical in shape and are to be handled by means of a little wooden or brass button which is fixed in the center of the top. The cases of cylinders are in appearance much like the cases of weights used by chemists. In the first set of the series, the cylinders are all of equal height (55 millimeters) but differ in diameter. The smallest cylinder has a diameter of 1 centimeter, and the others increase in diameter at the rate of ½ centimeter. In the second set, the cylinders are all of equal diameter, corresponding to half the diameter of the largest cylinder in the preceding series—(27 millimeters). The cylinders in this set differ in height, the first being merely a little disk only a centimeter high, the others increase 5 millimeters each, the tenth one being 55 millimeters high. In the third set, the cylinders differ both in height and diameter, the first being 1 centimeter high and 1 centimeter in diameter and each succeeding one increasing ½ centimeter in height and diameter. With these insets, the child, working by himself, learns to differentiate objects according to *thickness*, according *to height*, and according to *size*.

In the schoolroom, these three sets may be played with by three children gathered about a table, an exchange of games adding variety. The child takes the cylinders out of the molds, mixes them upon the table, and then puts each back into its corresponding opening. These objects are made of hard pine, polished and varnished.

Second. Large pieces in graded dimensions—There are three sets of blocks which come under this head, and it is desirable to have two of each of these sets in every school.

(*a*) Thickness: this set consists of objects which vary from *thick* to *thin*. There are ten quadrilateral prisms, the largest of which has a base of 10 centimeters, the others decreasing by 1 centimeter. The pieces are of equal length, 20 centimeters. These prisms are stained a dark brown. The child mixes them, scattering them over the little carpet, and then puts them in order, placing one against the other according to the graduations of thickness, observing that the length shall correspond exactly. These blocks, taken from the first to the last, form a species of *stair*, the steps of which grow broader toward the top. The child may begin with the thinnest piece or with the thickest, as suits his pleasure. The control of the exercise is not *certain*, as it was in the solid cylindrical insets. There, the large cylinders could not enter the small opening, the taller ones would project beyond the top of the block, and so forth. In this game of the Big Stair, the *eye* of the child can easily recognize an error, since if he mistakes, the *stair* is irregular, that is, there will be a high step, behind which the step which should have ascended, decreases.

(b) Length: Long and Short Objects—This set consists of *ten rods*. These are four-sided, each face being 3 centimeters. The first rod is a meter long, and the last a decimeter. The intervening rods decrease, from first to last, 1 decimeter each. Each space of 1 decimeter is painted alternately *red* or *blue*. The rods, when placed close to each other, must be so arranged that the colors correspond, forming so many transverse stripes—the whole set when arranged has the appearance of a rectangular triangle made up of organ pipes, which decrease on the side of the hypothenuse.

The child arranges the rods which have first been scattered and mixed. He puts them together according to the graduation of length, and observes the correspondence of colors. This exercise also offers a very evident control of error, for the regularity of the decreasing length of the stairs along the hypothenuse will be altered if the rods are not properly placed.

This most important set of blocks will have its principal application in arithmetic, as we shall see. With it, one may count from one to ten and may construct the addition and other tables, and it may constitute the first steps in the study of the decimal and metric system.

(c) Size: Objects, Larger and Smaller—This set is made up of ten wooden cubes painted in rose-colored enamel. The largest cube has a base of 10 centimeters, the smallest, of 1 centimeter, the intervening ones decrease 1 centimeter each. A little green cloth carpet goes with these blocks. This may be of oilcloth or cardboard. The game consists of building the cubes up, one upon another, in the order of their dimensions, constructing a little tower of which the largest cube forms the base and the smallest the apex. The carpet is placed on the floor, and the cubes are scattered upon it. As the tower is built upon the carpet, the child goes through the exercise of kneeling, rising, etc. The control is given by the irregularity of the tower as it decreases toward the apex. A cube misplaced reveals itself, because it breaks the line. The most common error made by the children in playing with these blocks at first, is that of placing the second cube as the base and placing the first cube upon it, thus confusing the two largest blocks. I have noted that the same error was made by deficient children in the repeated trials I made with the tests of De Sanctis. At the question, "Which is the largest?" the child would take, not the largest, but that nearest it in size.

Any of these three sets of blocks may be used by the children in a slightly different game. The pieces may be mixed upon a carpet or table, and then put in order upon another table at some distance. As he carries each piece, the child must walk without letting his attention wander, since he must remember the dimensions of the piece for which he is to look among the mixed blocks.

The games played in this way are excellent for children of four or five years; while the simple work of arranging the pieces in order upon the same carpet where they have been mixed is more adapted to the little ones between three and four years of age. The construction of the tower with the pink cubes is very attractive to little ones of less than three years, who knock it down and build it up time after time.

II. Differential Visual Perception of Form and Visual-Tactile-Muscular Perception

Didactic Material. Plane geometric *insets of wood:* The idea of these insets goes back to Itard and was also applied by Seguin.

In the school for deficients I had made and applied these insets in the same form used by my illustrious predecessors. In these there were two large tablets of wood placed one above the other and fastened together. The lower board was left solid, while the upper one was perforated by various geometric figures. The game consisted in placing in these openings the corresponding wooden figures which, in order that they might be easily handled, were furnished with a little brass knob.

In my school for deficients, I had multiplied the games calling for these insets, and distinguished between those used to teach color and those used to teach form. The insets for teaching color were all circles, those used for teaching form were all painted blue. I had great numbers of these insets made in graduations of color and in an infinite variety of form. This material was most expensive and exceedingly cumbersome.

In many later experiments with normal children, I have, after many trials, completely excluded the plane geometric insets as an aid to the teaching of color, since this material offers no control of errors, the child's task being that of *covering* the forms before him.

I have kept the geometric insets, but have given them a new and original aspect. The form in which they are now made was suggested to me by a visit to the splendid manual training school in the Reformatory of St. Michael in Rome. I saw there wooden models of geometric figures, which could be set into corresponding frames or placed above corresponding forms. The scope of these materials was to lead to exactness in the making of the geometric pieces in regard to control of dimension and form; the *frame* furnishing the *control* necessary for the exactness of the work.

This led me to think of making modifications in my geometric insets, making use of the frame as well as of the inset. I therefore made a rectangular tray, which measured 30 × 20 centimeters. This tray was painted a dark blue and was surrounded by a dark frame. It was furnished with a cover so arranged that it would contain six of the square frames with their insets. The advantage of this tray is that the forms may be changed, thus allowing us to present any combination we choose. I have a number of blank wooden squares which make it possible to present as few as two or three geometric forms at a time, the other spaces being filled in by the blanks. To this material I have added a set of white cards, 10 centimeters square. These cards form a series presenting the geometric forms in other aspects. In the *first* of the series, the form is cut from blue paper and mounted upon the card. In the *second* box of cards, the *contour* of the same figures is mounted in the same blue paper, forming an outline one centimeter in width. On the *third* set of cards the contour of the geometric form is *outlined by a black line*. We have then the tray, the collection of small frames with their corresponding insets, and the set of the cards in three series.

I also designed a case containing six trays. The front of this box may be lowered when the top is raised and the trays may be drawn out as one opens the drawers of a desk. Each *drawer* contains six of the small frames with their respective insets. In the first drawer I keep the four plain wooden squares and two frames, one containing a rhomboid, and the other a trapezoid. In the second, I have a series consisting of a square, and five rectangles of the same length, but varying in width. The third drawer contains six circles which diminish in diameter. In the fourth are six triangles, in the fifth, five polygons from a pentagon to a decagon. The sixth drawer contains six curved figures (an ellipse, an oval, etc., and a flower-like figure formed by four crossed arcs).

Exercise with the Insets. This exercise consists in presenting to the child the large frame or tray in which we may arrange the figures as we wish to present them. We proceed to take out the insets, mix them upon the table, and then invite the child to put them back in place. This game may be played by even the younger children and holds the attention for a long period, though not for so long a time as the exercise with the cylinders. Indeed, I have never seen a child repeat this exercise more than five or six times. The child, in fact, expends much energy upon this exercise. He must *recognize* the form and must look at it carefully.

At first many of the children only succeed in placing the insets after many attempts, trying for example to place a triangle in a trapezoid, then in a rectangle, etc. Or when they have taken a rectangle, and recognize where it should go, they will still place it with the long side of the inset across the short side of the opening, and will only after many attempts, succeed in placing it. After three or four successive lessons, the child recognizes the geometric figures with *extreme* facility and places the insets with a security which has a tinge of nonchalance, or of *slight contempt for an exercise that is too easy*. This is the moment in which the child may be led to a methodical observation of the forms. We change the forms in the frame and pass from contrasted frames to analogous ones. The exercise is easy for the child, who habituates himself to placing the pieces in their frames without errors or false attempts.

The first period of these exercises is at the time when the child is obliged to make repeated *trials* with figures that are strongly contrasted in form. The *recognition* is greatly helped by associating with the visual sense the muscular-tactile perception of the forms. I have the child touch* the contour of the piece with the *index finger* of *his right hand*, and then have him repeat this with the contour of the frame into which the pieces must fit. We succeed in making this a *habit* with the child. This is very easily attained, since all children love to *touch* things. I have already learned, through my work with deficient children, that among the various forms of sense memory that of the muscular sense is the most precocious. Indeed, many children who have not arrived at the point of recognizing a *figure by looking at it*, could recognize it by *touching it*, that is, by computing the movements necessary to the following of its contour. The same is true of the greater number of normal children—confused as to where to place a figure, they turn it about trying in vain to fit it in, yet as soon as they have touched the two contours of the piece and its frame, they succeed in placing it perfectly. Undoubtedly, the association of the *muscular-tactile* sense with that of *vision*, aids in a most remarkable way the perception of forms and fixes them in memory.

In such exercises, the control is absolute, as it was in the solid insets. The figure can only enter the corresponding frame. This makes it possible for the child to work by himself, and to accomplish a genuine sensory auto-education, in the visual perception of form.

Exercise with the three series of cards. First series. We give the child the wooden forms and the cards upon which the blue figure is mounted. Then we mix the cards upon the table; the child must arrange them in a line upon his table (which he loves to do), and then place the corresponding wooden pieces upon the cards. Here the control lies in the eyes. The child must *recognize* this figure, and place the wooden piece upon it so perfectly that it will cover and hide the paper figure. The eye of the child here corresponds to the frame, which *materially* led him at first to bring the two pieces together. In addition to covering the figure, the child is to accustom himself to *touching* the contour of the mounted figures as a part of the exercise (the child always voluntarily follows those movements); and after he has placed the wooden inset he again touches the contour, adjusting with his finger the superimposed piece until it exactly covers the form beneath.

---

*Here and elsewhere throughout the book the word "touch" is used not only to express contact between the fingers and an object, but the moving of fingers or hand over an object or its outline.

Second Series. We give a number of cards to the child together with the corresponding wooden insets. In this second series, the figures are repeated by an outline of blue paper. The child through these exercises is passing gradually from the *concrete* to the *abstract*. At first, he handled only *solid objects*. He then passed to a *plane figure*, that is, to the plane which in itself does not exist. He is now passing to the *line*, but this line does not represent for him the abstract contour of a plane figure. It is to him the *path which he has so often followed with his index finger;* this line is the *trace* of a *movement*. Following again the contour of the figure with his finger, the child receives the impression of actually leaving a trace, for the figure is covered by his finger and appears as he moves it. It is the eye now which guides the movement, but it must be remembered that this movement was *already prepared* for when the child touched the contours of the solid pieces of wood.

Third Series. We now present to the child the cards upon which the figures are drawn in black, giving him, as before, the corresponding wooden pieces. Here, he has actually passed to the *line;* that is, to an abstraction, yet here, too, there is the idea of the result of a movement.

This cannot be, it is true, the trace left by the finger, but, for example, that of a pencil which is guided by the hand in the same movements made before. These geometric figures in simple outline *have grown out* of a gradual series of representations which were concrete to vision and touch. These representations return to the mind of the child when he performs the exercise of superimposing the corresponding wooden figures.

III. Differential Visual Perception of Colors: Education of the Chromatic Sense

In many of our *lessons on the colors*, we make use of pieces of brightly-colored stuffs, and of balls covered with wool of different colors. The didactic material for the *education of the chromatic* sense is the following, which I have established after a long series of tests made upon normal children, (in the institute for deficients, I used as I have said above, the geometric insets). The present material consists of small flat tablets, which are wound with colored wool or silk. These tablets have a little wooden border at each end which prevents the silk-covered card from touching the table. The child is also taught to take hold of the piece by these wooden extremities, so that he need not soil the delicate colors. In this way, we are able to use this material for a long time without having to renew it.

I have chosen eight tints, and each one has with it eight gradations of different intensity of color. There are, therefore, sixty-four color tablets in all. The eight tints selected are *black (from grey to white), red, orange, yellow, green, blue, violet,* and *brown.* We have duplicate boxes of these sixty-four colors, giving us two of each exercise. The entire set, therefore, consists of one hundred twenty-eight tablets. They are contained in two boxes, each divided into eight equal compartments so that one box may contain sixty-four tablets.

Exercises with the Color Tablets. For the earliest of these exercises, we select three strong colors: for example, *red, blue,* and *yellow,* in pairs. These six tablets we place upon the table before the child. Showing him one of the colors, we ask him to find its duplicate among the mixed tablets upon the table. In this way, we have him arrange the color tablets in a column, two by two, pairing them according to color.

The number of tablets in this game may be increased until the eight colors, or sixteen tablets, are given at once. When the strongest tones have been presented, we may proceed to the presentation of lighter tones, in the same way. Finally, we present two or three tablets of the same color, but of different tone, showing the child how to arrange these in order of gradation. In this way, the eight gradations are finally presented.

Following this, we place before the child the eight gradations of two different colors (red and blue); he is shown how to separate the groups and then arrange each group in gradation. As we proceed we offer groups of more nearly related colors; for example, blue and violet, yellow and orange, etc.

In one of the "Children's Houses," I have seen the following game played with the greatest success and interest, and with surprising *rapidity.* The directress places upon a table, about which the children are seated, as many color groups as there are children, for example, three. She then calls each child's attention to the color each is to select, or which she assigns to him. Then, she mixes the three groups of colors upon the table. Each child takes rapidly from the mixed heap of tablets all the gradations of his color, and proceeds to arrange the tablets, which, when thus placed in a line, give the appearance of a strip of shaded ribbon.

In another "House," I have seen the children take the entire box, empty the sixty-four color tablets upon the table and after carefully mixing them, rapidly collect them into groups and arrange them in gradation, constructing a species of little carpet of delicately colored and intermingling tints. The children very quickly acquire an ability before which we stand amazed. Children of three years are able to put all of the tints into gradation.

Experiments in Color Memory. Experiments in color memory may be made by showing the child a tint, allowing him to look at it as long as he will, and then asking him to go to a distant table upon which all of the colors are arranged and to select from among them the tint similar to the one at which he has looked. The children succeed in this game remarkably, committing only slight errors. Children of five years enjoy this immensely, taking great pleasure in comparing the two spools and judging as to whether they have chosen correctly.[1] . . .

With very young children linguistic education must occupy a most important place. Another aim of such exercises is to educate the ear of the child to noises so that he shall accustom himself to distinguish every slight noise and compare it with *sounds*, coming to resent harsh or disordered noises. Such sense education has a value in that it exercises aesthetic taste, and may be applied in a most noteworthy way to practical discipline. We all know how the younger children disturb the order of the room by shouts, and by the noise of overturned objects.

The rigorous scientific education of the sense of hearing is not practically applicable to the didactic method. This is true because the child cannot *exercise himself through his own activity* as he does for the other senses. Only one child at a time can work with any instrument producing the gradation of sounds. In other words, *absolute silence* is necessary for the discrimination of sounds.[2] . . .

For the discrimination of sounds, we use Pizzoli's series of little whistles. For the gradation of noises, we use small boxes filled with different substances, more or less fine (sand or pebbles). The noises are produced by shaking the boxes.

In the lessons for the sense of hearing I proceed as follows: I have the teachers establish silence in the usual way and then I *continue* the work, making the silence more profound. I say, "St! St!" in a series of modulations, now sharp and short, now prolonged and light as a whisper. The children, little by little, become fascinated by this. Occasionally I say, "More silent still—more silent."

I then begin the sibilant St! St! again, making it always lighter and repeating "More silent still," in a barely audible voice. Then I say still in a low whisper, "Now, I hear the clock, now I can hear the buzzing of a fly's wings, now I can hear the whisper of the trees in the garden."

The children, ecstatic with joy, sit in such absolute and complete silence that the room seems deserted; then I whisper, "Let us close our eyes." This exercise repeated, so habituates the children to immobility and to absolute silence that, when one of them interrupts, it needs only a syllable, a gesture to call him back immediately to perfect order.

In the silence, we proceeded to the production of sounds and noises, making these at first strongly contrasted, then, more nearly alike. Sometimes we present the comparisons between noise and sound. I believe that the best results can be obtained with the primitive means employed by Itard in 1805. He used the drum and the bell. His plan was a graduated series of drums for the noises—or, better, for the heavy harmonic sounds, since these belong to a musical instrument—and a series of bells. The diapason, the whistles, the boxes, are not attractive to the child, and do not educate the sense of hearing as do these other instruments. There is an interesting suggestion in the fact that the two great human institutions, that of hate (war), and that of love (religion), have adopted these two opposite instruments, the drum and the bell.

I believe that after establishing silence it would be educational to ring well-toned bells, now calm and sweet, now clear and ringing, sending their vibrations through the child's whole body. And when, besides the education of the ear, we have produced a *vibratory* education of the whole body, through these wisely selected sounds of the bells, giving a peace that pervades the very fibers of his being, then I believe these young bodies would be sensitive to crude noises, and the children would come to dislike, and to cease from making, disordered and ugly noises.

In this way one whose ear has been trained by a musical education suffers from strident or discordant notes. I need give no illustration to make clear the importance of such education for the masses in childhood. The new generation would be more calm, turning away from the confusion and the discordant sounds, which strike the ear today in one of the vile tenements where the poor live, crowded together, left by us to abandon themselves to the lower, more brutal human instincts.

Musical Education

This must be carefully guided by method. In general, we see little children pass by the playing of some great musicians as an animal would pass. They do not perceive the delicate complexity of sounds. The street children gather about the organ grinder, crying out as if to hail with joy the *noises* which will come instead of sounds.

For the musical education we must *create instruments* as well as music. The scope of such an instrument in addition to the discrimination of sounds, is to awaken a sense of rhythm, and, so to speak, to give the *impulse* toward calm and coordinate movements to those muscles already vibrating in the peace and tranquility of immobility.

I believe that stringed instruments (perhaps some very much simplified harp) would be the most convenient. The stringed instruments together with the drum and the bells form the trio of the classic instruments of humanity. The harp is the instrument of "the intimate life of the individual." Legend places it in the hand of Orpheus, folklore puts it into fairy hands, and romance gives it to the princess who conquers the heart of a wicked prince.

The teacher who turns her back upon her scholars to play, (far too often badly), will never be the *educator* of their musical sense.

The child needs to be charmed in every way, by the glance as well as by the pose. The teacher who, bending toward them, gathering them about her, and leaving them free to stay or go, touches the chords, in a simple rhythm, puts herself in communication with them, *in relation with their very souls*. So much the better if this touch can be accompanied by her *voice*, and the children left free to follow her, no one being obliged to sing. In this way she can select as "adapted to education," those songs which were followed by all the children. So she may regulate the complexity of rhythm to various ages, for she will see now only the older children following the rhythm, now, also the little ones. At any rate, I believe that simple and primitive instruments are the ones best adapted to the awakening of music in the soul of the little child.

I have tried to have the Directress of the "Children's House "in Milan, who is a gifted musician, make a number of trials, and experiments, with a view to finding out more about the muscular capacity of young children. She has made many trials with the pianoforte, observing how the children *are not sensitive* to the musical *tone*, but only to the *rhythm*. On a basis of rhythm she arranged simple little dances, with the intention of studying the influence of the rhythm itself upon the coordination of muscular movements. She was greatly surprised to discover the *educational disciplinary* effect of such music. Her children, who had been led with great wisdom and art through liberty to a *spontaneous* ordering of their acts and movements, had nevertheless lived in the streets and courts, and had an almost universal habit of jumping.

Being a faithful follower of the method of liberty, and not considering that *jumping* was a wrong act, she had never corrected them.

She now noticed that as she multiplied and repeated the rhythm exercises, the children little by little left off their ugly jumping, until finally it was a thing of the past. The directress one day asked for an explanation of this change of conduct. Several little ones looked at her without saying anything. The older children gave various replies, whose meaning was the same.

"It isn't nice to jump."

"Jumping is ugly."

"It's rude to jump."

This was certainly a beautiful triumph for our method! This experience shows that it is possible to educate the child's *muscular sense*, and it shows how exquisite the refinement of this sense may be as it develops in relation to the *muscular memory*, and side by side with the other forms of sensory memory.

Tests for Acuteness of Hearing

The only entirely successful experiments which we have made so far in the "Children's Houses" are those of the *clock*, and of the *lowered* or whispered *voice*. The trial is purely empirical, and does not lend itself to the measuring of the sensation, but it is, however, most useful in that it helps us to an approximate knowledge of the child's auditory acuteness.

The exercise consists in calling attention, when perfect silence has been established, to the ticking of the clock, and to all the little noises not commonly audible to the ear. Finally we call the little ones, one by one from an adjoining room, pronouncing each name in a low voice. In preparing for such an exercise it is necessary to *teach* the children the real meaning of *silence*.

Toward this end I have several *games* of *silence*, which help in a surprising way to strengthen the remarkable discipline of our children.

I call the children's attention to myself, telling them to see how silent I can be. I assume different positions; standing, sitting, and maintain each pose *silently, without movement*. A finger moving can produce a noise, even though it be imperceptible. We may breathe so that we may be heard. But I maintain *absolute* silence, which is not an easy thing to do. I call a child, and ask him to do as I am doing. He adjusts his feet to a better position, and this makes a noise! He moves an arm, stretching it out upon the arm of his chair; it is a noise. His breathing is not altogether silent, it is not tranquil, absolutely unheard as mine is.

During these maneuvers on the part of the child, and while my brief comments are followed by intervals of immobility and silence, the other children are watching and listening. Many of them are interested in the fact, which they have never noticed before; namely, that we make so many noises of which we are not conscious, and that there are *degrees* of *silence*. There is an absolute silence where nothing, *absolutely nothing* moves. They watch me in amazement when I stand in the middle of the room, so quietly that it is really as if "I were not." Then they strive to imitate me, and to do even better. I call attention here and there to a foot that moves, almost inadvertently. The attention of the child is called to every part of his body in an anxious eagerness to attain to immobility.

When the children are trying in this way, there is established a silence very different from that which we carelessly call by that name.

It seems as if life gradually vanishes, and that the room becomes, little, empty, as if there were no longer anyone in it. Then we begin to hear the tick-tock of the clock, and this sound seems to grow in intensity as the silence becomes absolute. From without, from the court which before seemed silent, there come varied noises, a bird chirps, a child passes. The children sit fascinated by that silence as if by some conquest of their own. "Here," says the directress, "here there is no longer anyone; the children have all gone away."

Having arrived at that point, we darken the windows, and tell the children to close their eyes, resting their heads upon their hands. They assume this position, and in the darkness the absolute silence returns.

"Now listen," we say. "A soft voice is going to call your name." Then going to a room behind the children, and standing within the open door, I call in a low voice, lingering over the syllables as if I were calling from across the mountains. This voice, almost occult, seems to reach the heart and to call to the soul of the child. Each one as he is called, lifts his head, opens his eyes as if altogether happy, then rises, silently seeking not to move the chair, and walks on the tips of his toes, so quietly that he is scarcely heard. Nevertheless his step resounds in the silence, and amid the immobility which persists.

Having reached the door, with a joyous face, he leaps into the room, choking back soft outbursts of laughter. Another child may come to hide his face against my dress, another, turning, will watch his companions sitting like statues silent and waiting. The one who is called feels that he is privileged, that he has received a gift, a prize. And yet they know that all will be called, "beginning with the most silent one in all the room." So each one tries to merit by his perfect silence the certain call. I once saw a little one of three years try to suffocate a sneeze, and succeed! She held her breath in her little breast, and resisted, coming out victorious. A most surprising effort![3] . . .

EDITOR'S NOTES

1. Montessori's discussion of a disk, designed by Pizzoli, to teach colors that she does not use on p. 203 is deleted.

2. Montessori's description on p. 204 of an apparatus, consisting of a series of bells, designed by Signorina Maccheroni, Directress of Children's House at the Franciscan Convent in Rome is deleted. Montessori decided the apparatus was impractical in children's education.

3. Montessori's additional comments on children's enjoyment of the silence game on pp. 211–14 are deleted.

14

General Notes on the Education of the Senses

I do not claim to have brought to perfection the method of sense training as applied to young children. I do believe, however, that it opens a new field for psychological research, promising rich and valuable results.

Experimental psychology has so far devoted its attention to *perfecting the instruments by which the sensations are measured*. No one has attempted the *methodical* preparation *of the individual for the sensations*. It is my belief that the development of psychometry will owe more to the attention given to the preparation of the *individual* than to the perfecting of the *instrument*.

But putting aside this purely scientific side of the question, the *education of the senses* must be of the greatest *pedagogical* interest.

Our aim in education in general is twofold, biological and social. From the biological side we wish to help the natural development of the individual, from the social standpoint it is our aim to prepare the individual for the environment. Under this last head technical education may be considered as having a place, since it teaches the individual to make use of his surroundings. The education of the senses is most important from both these points of view. The development of the senses indeed precedes that of superior intellectual activity and the child between three and seven years is in the period of formation.

We can, then, help the development of the senses while they are in this period. We may graduate and adapt the stimuli just as, for example, it is necessary to help the formation of language before it shall be completely developed.

All education of little children must be governed by this principle—to help the natural *psychic* and *physical development* of the child.

177

The other aim of education (that of adapting the individual to the environment) should be given more attention later on when the period of intense development is past.

These two phases of education are always interlaced, but one or the other has prevalence according to the age of the child. Now, the period of life between the ages of three and seven years covers a period of rapid physical development. It is the time for the formation of the sense activities as related to the intellect. The child in this age develops his senses. His attention is further attracted to the environment under the form of passive curiosity.

The stimuli, and not yet the reasons for things, attract his attention. This is, therefore, the time when we should methodically direct the sense stimuli, in such a way that the sensations which he receives shall develop in a rational way. This sense training will prepare the ordered foundation upon which he may build up a clear and strong mentality.

It is, besides all this, possible with the education of the senses to discover and eventually to correct defects which today pass unobserved in the school. Now the time comes when the defect manifests itself in an evident and irreparable inability to make use of the forces of life about him. (Such defects as deafness and nearsightedness.) This education, therefore, is physiological and prepares directly for intellectual education, perfecting the organs of sense, and the nerve paths of projection and association.

But the other part of education, the adaptation of the individual to his environment, is indirectly touched. We prepare with our method the infancy of the *humanity of our time*. The men of the present civilization are preeminently observers of their environment because they must utilize to the greatest possible extent all the riches of this environment.

The art of today bases itself, as in the days of the Greeks, upon observation of the truth.

The progress of positive science is based upon its observations and all its discoveries and their applications, which in the last century have so transformed our civic environment, were made by following the same line—that is, they have come through observation. We must therefore prepare the new generation for this attitude, which has become necessary in our modern civilized life. It is an indispensable means—man must be so armed if he is to continue efficaciously the work of our progress.[1] . . .

The education of the senses makes men observers, and not only accomplishes the general work of adaptation to the present epoch of civilization, but also prepares them directly for practical life. We have had up to the present time, I believe, a most imperfect idea of what is necessary in the practical living of life. We have always started from ideas, and have *proceeded thence to motor activities;* thus, for example, the method of education has always been to teach intellectually, and then to have the child follow the principles he has been taught. In general, when we are teaching, we talk about the object which interests us, and then we try to lead the scholar, when he has understood, to perform some kind of work with the object itself; but often the scholar who has understood the idea finds great difficulty in the execution of the work which we give him, because we have left out of his education a factor of the utmost importance, namely, the perfecting of the senses.[2] . . .

It is necessary to begin the education of the senses in the formative period, if we wish to perfect this sense development with the education which is to follow. The education of the senses should be begun methodically in infancy, and should continue during the entire period of instruction which is to prepare the individual for life in society.

Aesthetic and moral education are closely related to this sensory education. Multiply the sensations, and develop the capacity of appreciating fine differences in stimuli, and we *refine* the sensibility and multiply man's pleasures.

Beauty lies in harmony, not in contrast; and harmony is refinement; therefore, there must be a fineness of the senses if we are to appreciate harmony. The aesthetic harmony of nature is lost upon him who has coarse senses. The world to him is narrow and barren. In life about us, there exist inexhaustible fonts of aesthetic enjoyment, before which men pass as insensible as the brutes seeking their enjoyment in those sensations which are crude and showy, since they are the only ones accessible to them.

Now, from the enjoyment of gross pleasures, vicious habits very often spring. Strong stimuli, indeed, do not render acute, but blunt the senses, so that they require stimuli more and more accentuated and more and more gross.

Onanism, so often found among normal children of the lower classes, alcoholism, fondness for watching sensual acts of adults—these things represent the enjoyment of those unfortunate ones whose intellectual pleasures are few, and whose senses are blunted and dulled. Such pleasures kill the man within the individual, and call to life the beast.[3] . . .

EDITOR'S NOTES

1. Montessori's comments on Roentgen rays, Hertzian waves, and the Marconi telegraph as discoveries based on scientific observation on pp. 217–18 are deleted.

2. Montessori's examples on the relationship between the trained senses and the intellectual judgment as in cooking and diagnosing illnesses that reiterated earlier points on pp. 218–21 are deleted.

3. Montessori's diagram and detailed discussion of the physiological basis of sensation in relationship to stimuli on pp. 222–23 are deleted.

15

Intellectual Education

"... To lead the child from the education of the senses to ideas."

Edouard Seguin

The sense exercises constitute a species of auto-education, which, if these exercises be many times repeated, leads to a perfecting of the child's psycho-sensory processes. The directress must intervene to lead the child from sensations to ideas—from the concrete to the abstract, and to the association of ideas. For this, she should use a method tending to isolate the inner attention of the child and to fix it upon the perceptions—as in the first lessons his objective attention was fixed, through isolation, upon single stimuli.

The teacher, in other words, when she gives a lesson must seek to limit the field of the child's consciousness to the object of the lesson, as, for example, during sense education she isolated the sense which she wished the child to exercise.

For this, knowledge of a special technique is necessary. The educator must, *"to the greatest possible extent, limit his intervention; yet he must not allow the child to weary himself in an undue effort of auto-education."*

It is here, that the factor of individual limitation and differing degrees of perception are most keenly felt in the teacher. In other words, in the quality of this intervention lies the art which makes up the individuality of the teacher.

A definite and undoubted part of the teacher's work is that of teaching an exact nomenclature.

She should, in most cases, pronounce the necessary names and adjectives without adding anything further. These words she should pronounce distinctly, and in a clear strong voice, so that the *various sounds* composing the word may be distinctly and plainly perceived by the child.

So, for example, touching the smooth and rough cards in the first tactile exercise, she should say, "This is smooth. This is rough," repeating the words with varying modulations of the voice, always letting the tones be clear and the enunciation very distinct. "Smooth, smooth, smooth. Rough, rough, rough."

In the same way, when treating of the sensations of heat and cold, she must say, "This is cold." "This is hot." "This is ice-cold." "This is tepid." She may then begin to use the generic terms, "heat," "more heat," "less heat,"and so forth.

First. "The lessons in nomenclature must consist simply in provoking the association of the name with the object, or with the abstract idea which the name represents." Thus the *object* and the *name* must be united when they are received by the child's mind, and this makes it most necessary that no other word besides the name be spoken.

Second. The teacher must always *test* whether or not her lesson has attained the end she had in view, and her tests must be made to come within the restricted field of consciousness, provoked by the lesson on nomenclature.

The first test will be to find whether the name is still associated in the child's mind with the object. She must allow the necessary time to elapse, letting a short period of silence intervene between the lesson and the test. Then she may ask the child, pronouncing slowly and very clearly the name or the adjective she has taught: "Which is *smooth*? Which is *rough*?"

The child will point to the object with his finger, and the teacher will know that he has made the desired association. But if he has not done this, that is, if he makes a mistake, *she must not correct him,* but must suspend her lesson, to take it up again another day. Indeed, why correct him? If the child has not succeeded in associating the name with the object, the only way in which to succeed would be to *repeat* both the action of the sense stimuli and the *name;* in other words, to repeat the lesson. But when the child has failed, we should know that he was not at that instant ready for the psychic association which we wished to provoke in him, and we must therefore choose another moment.

If we should say, in correcting the child, "No, you have made a mistake," all these words, which, being in the form of a reproof, would strike him more forcibly than others (such as smooth or rough), would remain in the mind of the child, retarding the learning of the names. On the contrary, the *silence* which follows the error leaves the field of consciousness clear, and the next lesson may successfully follow the first. In fact, by revealing the error we may lead the child to make an undue *effort* to remember, or we may discourage him, and it is our duty to avoid as much as possible all unnatural effort and all depression.

Third. If the child has not committed any error, the teacher may provoke the *motor activity* corresponding to the idea of the object: that is, to the *pronunciation of the name*. She may ask him, "What is this?" and the child should respond, "Smooth." The teacher may then interrupt, teaching him how to pronounce the word correctly and distinctly, first, drawing a deep breath and, then, saying in a rather loud voice, "Smooth." When he does this the teacher may note his particular speech defect, or the special form of baby talk to which he may be addicted.

In regard to the *generalization* of the ideas received, and by that I mean the application of these ideas to his environment, I do not advise any lessons of this sort for a certain length of time, even for a number of months. There will be children who, after having touched a few times the stuffs, or merely the smooth and rough cards, *will quite spontaneously touch the various surfaces about them,* repeating "Smooth! Rough! It is velvet! etc." In dealing with normal children, we must *await* this spontaneous investigation of the surroundings, or, as I like to call it, this *voluntary explosion* of the exploring spirit. In such cases, the children experience a joy at each *fresh discovery*. They are conscious of a sense of dignity and satisfaction which encourages them to seek for new sensations from their environment and to make themselves spontaneous *observers*.

The teacher should *watch* with the most solicitous care to see when and how the child arrives at this generalisation of ideas. For example, one of our little four-year-olds while running about in the court one day suddenly stood still and cried out, "Oh! the sky is blue!" and stood for some time looking up into the blue expanse of the sky.

One day, when I entered one of the "Children's Houses," five or six little ones gathered quietly about me and began caressing, lightly, my hands, and my clothing, saying, "It is smooth." "It is velvet." "This is rough." A number of others came near and began with serious and intent faces to repeat the same words, touching me as they did so. The directress wished to interfere to release me, but I signed to her to be quiet, and I myself did not move, but remained silent, admiring this spontaneous intellectual activity of my little ones. The greatest triumph of our educational method should always be this: *to bring about the spontaneous progress of the child.*

One day, a little boy, following one of our exercises in design, had chosen to fill in with colored pencils the outline of a tree. To color the trunk he laid hold upon a red crayon. The teacher wished to interfere, saying, "Do you think trees have red trunks?" I held her back and allowed the child to color the tree red. This design was precious to us; it showed that the child was not yet an observer of his surroundings. *My way of treating this was to encourage the child to make use of the games for the chromatic sense.* He went daily into the garden with the other children, and could at any time see the tree trunks. When the sense exercises should have succeeded in attracting the child's spontaneous attention to colors about him, then, in some *happy moment* he would become aware that the tree trunks were not red, just as the other child during his play had become conscious of the fact that the sky was blue. In fact, the teacher continued to give the child outlines of trees to fill in. He one day chose a brown pencil with which to color the trunk, and made the branches and leaves green. Later, he made the branches brown, also, using green only for the leaves.

Thus we have *the test* of the child's intellectual progress. We can not create observers by saying, "*observe*," but by giving them the power and the means for this observation, and these means are procured through education of the senses. Once we have *aroused* such activity, auto-education is assured, for refined well-trained senses lead us to a closer observation of the environment, and this, with its infinite variety, attracts the attention and continues the psychosensory education.

If, on the other hand, in this matter of sense education we single out definite concepts of the quality of certain objects, these very objects become associated with, or a part of, the training, which is in this way limited to those concepts taken and recorded. So the sense training remains unfruitful. When, for example, a teacher has given in the old way a lesson on the names of the colors, she has imparted an idea concerning that particular *quality*, but she has not educated the chromatic sense. The child will know these colors in a superficial way, forgetting them from time to time; and at best his appreciation of them will lie within the limits prescribed by the teacher. When, therefore, the teacher of the old methods shall have provoked the generalization of the idea, saying, for example, "What is the color of this flower?" "of this ribbon?" the attention of the child will in all probability remain torpidly fixed upon the examples suggested by her.[1] . . .

Our educational aim with very young children must be to *aid the spontaneous development of the mental, spiritual, and physical personality,* and not to make of the child a cultured individual in the commonly accepted sense of the term. So, after we have offered to the child such didactic material as is adapted to provoke the development of his senses, we must wait until the activity known as observation develops. And herein lies the *art of the educator;* in knowing how to measure the action by which we help the young child's personality to develop. To one whose attitude is right, little children soon reveal *profound individual differences* which call for very different kinds of help from the teacher. Some of them require almost no intervention on her part, while others demand actual *teaching*. It is necessary, therefore, that the teaching shall be rigorously guided by the principle of limiting to the greatest possible point the active intervention of the educator.

Here are a number of games and problems which we have used effectively in trying to follow this principle.

GAMES OF THE BLIND

The Games of the Blind are used for the most part as exercises in general sensibility as follows:

The Stuffs. We have in our didactic material a pretty little chest composed of drawers within which are arranged rectangular pieces of stuff in great variety. There are velvet, satin, silk, cotton, linen, etc. We have the child touch each of these pieces, teaching the appropriate nomenclature and adding something regarding the quality, as coarse, fine, soft. Then, we call the child and seat him at one of the tables where he can be seen by his companions, blindfold him, and offer him the stuffs one by one. He touches them, smooths them, crushes them between his fingers and decides, "It is velvet—It is fine linen—It is rough cloth," etc. This exercise provokes general interest. When we offer the child some unexpected foreign object, as, for example, a sheet of paper, a veil, the little assembly trembles as it awaits his response.

Weight. We place the child in the same position, call his attention to the tablets used for the education of the sense of weight, have him notice again the already well-known differences of weight, and then tell him to put all the dark tablets, which are the heavier ones, at the right, and all the light ones, which are the lighter, to the left. We then blindfold him and he proceeds to the game, taking each time two tablets. Sometimes he takes two of the same color, sometimes two of different colors, but in a position opposite to that in which he must arrange them on his desk. These exercises are most exciting; when, for example, the child has in his hands two of the dark tablets and changes them from one hand to the other uncertain, and finally places them together on the right, the children watch in a state of intense eagerness, and a great sigh often expresses their final relief. The shouts of the audience when the entire game is followed without an error, gives the impression that their little friend *sees with his hands* the colors of the tablets.

Dimension and Form. We use games similar to the preceding one, having the child distinguish between different coins, the cubes and bricks of Froebel, and dry seeds, such as beans and peas. But such games never awaken the intense interest aroused by the preceding ones. They are, however, useful and serve to associate with the various objects those qualities peculiar to them, and also to fix the nomenclature.

APPLICATION OF THE EDUCATION OF THE VISUAL SENSE TO THE OBSERVATION OF THE ENVIRONMENT

Nomenclature. This is one of the most important phases of education. Indeed, nomenclature prepares for an *exactness* in the use of language which is not always met with in our schools. Many children, for example, use interchangeably the words thick and big, long and high. With the methods already described, the teacher may easily establish, by means of the didactic material, ideas which are very exact and clear, and may associate the proper word with these ideas.

Method of Using the Didactic Material

Dimensions. The directress, after the child has played for a long time with the three sets of solid insets and has acquired a security in the performance of the exercise, takes out all the cylinders of equal height and places them in a horizontal position on the table, one beside the other. Then she selects the two extremes, saying, "This is the *thickest*—This is the *thinnest*." She places them side by side so that the comparison may be more marked, and then taking them by the little button, she compares the bases, calling attention to the great difference. She then places them again beside each other in a vertical position in order to show that they are equal in height, and repeats several times, "thick—thin." Having done this, she should follow it with the test, asking, "Give me the thickest—Give me the thinnest," and finally she should proceed to the test of nomenclature, asking, "What is this?" In the lessons which follow this, the directress may take away the two extreme pieces and may repeat the lesson with the two pieces remaining at the extremities, and so on until she has used all the pieces. She may then take these up at random, saying, "Give me one a little thicker than this one," or "Give me one a little thinner than this one." With the second set of solid insets she proceeds in the same way. Here she stands the pieces upright, as each one has a base sufficiently broad to maintain it in this position, saying, "This is the highest" and "This is the lowest." Then placing the two extreme pieces side by side she may take them out of the line and compare the bases, showing that they are equal. From the extremes she may proceed as before, selecting each time the two remaining pieces most strongly contrasted.

With the third solid inset, the directress, when she has arranged the pieces in gradation, calls the child's attention to the first one, saying, "This is the largest," and to the last one, saying, "This is the smallest." Then she places them side by side and observes how they differ both in height and in base. She then proceeds in the same way as in the other two exercises.

Similar lessons may be given with the series of graduated prisms, of rods, and of cubes. The prisms are *thick* and *thin* and of equal *length*. The rods are *long* and *short* and of equal *thickness*. The cubes are *big* and *little* and differ in size and in height.

The application of these ideas to environment will come most easily when we measure the children with the anthropometer. They will begin among themselves to make comparisons, saying, "I am taller—you are thicker." These comparisons are also made when the children hold out their little hands to show that they are clean, and the directress stretches hers out also, to show that she, too, has clean hands. Often the contrast between the dimensions of the hands calls forth laughter. The children make a perfect game of measuring themselves. They stand side by side; they look at each other; they decide. Often they place themselves beside grown persons, and observe with curiosity and interest the great difference in height.

Form. When the child shows that he can with security distinguish between the forms of the plane geometric insets, the directress may begin the lessons in nomenclature. She should begin with two strongly contrasted forms, as the square and the circle, and should follow the usual method, using the three periods of Seguin. We do not teach all the names relative to the geometric figures, giving only those of the most familiar forms, such as square, circle, rectangle, triangle, oval. We now call attention to the fact that there are *rectangles which are narrow and long,* and others which are *broad and short,* while the *squares* are equal on all sides and can be only big and little. These things are most easily shown with the insets, for, though we turn the square about, it still enters its frame, while the rectangle, if placed across the opening, will not enter. The child is much interested in this exercise, for which we arrange in the frame a square and a series of rectangles, having the longest side equal to the side of the square, the other side gradually decreasing in the five pieces.

In the same way we proceed to show the difference between the oval, the ellipse, and the circle. The circle enters no matter how it is placed, or turned about; the ellipse does not enter when placed transversely, but if placed lengthwise will enter even if turned upside down. The oval, however, not only cannot enter the frame if placed transversely, but not even when turned upside down; it must be placed with the *large* curve toward the large part of the opening, and with the *narrow* curve toward the *narrow* portion of the opening.

The circles, *big* and *little,* enter their frames no matter how they are turned about. I do not reveal the difference between the oval and the ellipse until a very late stage of the child's education, and then not to all children, but only to those who show a special interest in the forms by choosing the game often, or by asking about the differences. I prefer that such differences should be recognized later by the child, spontaneously, perhaps in the elementary school.

It seems to many persons that in teaching these forms we are teaching *geometry,* and that this is premature in schools for such young children. Others feel that, if we wish to present geometric forms, we should use the *solids,* as being more concrete.

I feel that I should say a word here to combat such prejudices. To *observe* a geometric form is not to *analyze* it, and in the analysis geometry begins. When, for example, we speak to the child of sides and angles and explain these to him, even though with objective methods, as Froebel advocates (for example, the square has four sides and can be constructed with four sticks of equal length), then indeed we do enter the field of geometry, and I believe that little children are too immature for these steps. But the *observation of the form* cannot be too advanced for a child at this age. The plane of the table at which the child sits while eating his supper is probably a rectangle; the plate which contains his food is a circle, and we certainly do not consider that the child is too *immature* to be allowed to look at the table and the plate.

The insets which we present simply call the attention to a given *form.* As to the name, it is analogous to other names by which the child learns to call things. Why should we consider it premature to teach the child the words *circle, square, oval,* when in his home he repeatedly hears the word *round* used in connection with plates, etc.? He will hear his parents speak of the *square* table, the *oval* table, etc., and these words in common use will remain for a long time *confused* in his mind and in his speech, if we do not interpose such help as that we give in the teaching of forms.

We should reflect upon the fact that many times a child, left to himself, makes an undue effort to comprehend the language of the adults and the meaning of the things about him. Opportune and rational instruction *prevents* such an effort, and therefore does not *weary,* but *relieves,* the child and satisfies his desire for knowledge. Indeed, he shows his contentment by various expressions of pleasure. At the same time, his attention is called to the word which, if he is allowed to pronounce badly, develops in him an imperfect use of the language.

This often arises from an effort on his part to imitate the careless speech of persons about him, while the teacher, by pronouncing clearly the word referring to the object which arouses the child's curiosity, prevents such effort and such imperfections.

Here, also, we face a widespread prejudice; namely, the belief that the child left to himself gives absolute repose to his mind. If this were so he would re-

main a stranger to the world, and, instead, we see him, little by little, spontaneously conquer various ideas and words. He is a traveler through life, who
observes the new things among which he journeys, and who tries to understand the unknown tongue spoken by those about him. Indeed, he makes a
great and *voluntary effort* to understand and to imitate. The instruction given
to little children should be so directed as to *lessen this expenditure* of poorly
directed effort, converting it instead into the enjoyment of conquest made
easy and infinitely broadened. We are *the guides* of these travelers just entering the great world of human thought. We should see to it that we are intelligent and cultured guides, not losing ourselves in vain discourse, but illustrat-
ing briefly and concisely the work of art in which the traveler shows himself
interested, and we should then respectfully allow him to observe it as long as
he wishes to. It is our privilege to lead him to observe the most important and
the most beautiful things of life in such a way that he does not lose energy
and time in useless things, but shall find pleasure and satisfaction throughout
his pilgrimage.

I have already referred to the prejudice that it is more suitable to present
the geometric forms to the child in the *solid* rather than in the *plane,* giving
him, for example, the *cube,* the *sphere,* the *prism.* Let us put aside the physiological side of the question showing that the visual recognition of the solid
figure is more complex than that of the plane, and let us view the question
only from the more purely pedagogical standpoint of *practical life.*

The greater number of objects which we look upon every day present more
nearly the aspect of our plane geometric insets. In fact, doors, window
frames, framed pictures, the wooden or marble top of a table, are indeed *solid*
objects, but with one of the dimensions greatly reduced, and with the two dimensions determining the form of the plane surface made most evident.

When the plane form prevails, we say that the window is rectangular, the
picture frame oval, this table square, etc. *Solids having a determined form
prevailing in the plane surface* are almost the only ones which come to our
notice. And such solids are clearly represented by our *plane geometric insets.*

The child will *very often* recognize in his environment forms which he has
learned in this way, but he will rarely recognize the *solid geometric forms.*

That the table leg is a prism, or a truncated cone, or an elongated cylinder,
will come to his knowledge long after he has observed that the top of the table
upon which he places things is rectangular. We do not, therefore, speak of the
fact of recognizing that a house is a prism or a cube. Indeed, the pure solid
geometric forms *never exist* in the ordinary objects about us; these present, instead, a *combination of forms.* So, putting aside the difficulty of taking in at
a glance the complex form of a house, the child recognizes in it, not an *identity* of form, but an *analogy.*

He will, however, see the plane geometric forms perfectly represented in windows and doors, and in the faces of many solid objects in use at home. Thus the knowledge of the forms given him in the plane geometric insets will be for him a species of magic *key*, opening the external world, and making him feel that he knows its secrets.

I was walking one day upon the Pincian Hill with a boy from the elementary school. He had studied geometric design and understood the analysis of plane geometric figures. As we reached the highest terrace from which we could see the Piazza del Popolo with the city stretching away behind it, I stretched out my hand saying, "Look, all the works of man are a great mass of geometric figures"; and, indeed, rectangles, ovals, triangles, and semicircles, perforated, or ornamented, in a hundred different ways the grey rectangular façades of the various buildings. Such uniformity in such an expanse of buildings seemed to prove the *limitation* of human intelligence, while in an adjoining garden plot the shrubs and flowers spoke eloquently of the infinite variety of forms in nature.

The boy had never made these observations; he had studied the angles, the sides and the construction of outlined geometric figures, but without thinking beyond this, and feeling only annoyance at this arid work. At first he laughed at the idea of man's massing geometric figures together, then he became interested, looked long at the buildings before him, and an expression of lively and thoughtful interest came into his face. To the right of the Ponte Margherita was a factory building in the process of construction, and its steel framework delineated a series of rectangles. "What tedious work!" said the boy, alluding to the workmen. And, then, as we drew near the garden, and stood for a moment in silence admiring the grass and the flowers which sprang so freely from the earth, "It is beautiful!" he said. But that word "beautiful" referred to the inner awakening of his own soul.

This experience made me think that in the observation of the plane geometric forms, and in that of the plants which they saw growing in their own little gardens, there existed for the children precious sources of spiritual as well as intellectual education. For this reason, I have wished to make my work broad, leading the child, not only to observe the forms about him, but to distinguish the work of man from that of nature, and to appreciate the fruits of human labor.

(a) Free Design. I give the child a sheet of white paper and a pencil, telling him that he may draw whatever he wishes to. Such drawings have long been of interest to experimental psychologists. Their importance lies in the fact that they reveal the *capacity* of the child for observing, and also show his individual tendencies. Generally, the first drawings are unformed and confused, and the teacher should ask the child *what he wished to draw,* and should write

it underneath the design that it may be a record. Little by little, the drawings become more intelligible, and verily reveal the progress which the child makes in the observation of the forms about him. Often the most minute details of an object have been observed and recorded in the crude sketch. And, since the child draws what he wishes, he reveals to us which are the objects that most strongly attract his attention.

(*b*) *Design Consisting of the Filling in of Outlined Figures.* These designs are most important as they constitute "the preparation for writing." They do for the color sense what *free design* does for the sense of form. In other words, they reveal the capacity of the child *in the matter of observation of colors,* as the free design showed us the extent to which he was an observer of form in the objects surrounding him. I shall speak more fully of this work in the chapter on *writing.* The exercises consist in filling in with colored pencil, certain outlines drawn in black. These outlines present the simple geometric figures and various objects with which the child is familiar in the schoolroom, the home, and the garden. The child must *select* his color, and in doing so he shows us whether he has observed the colors of the things surrounding him.

Free Plastic Work

These exercises are analogous to those in free design and in the filling in of figures with colored pencils. Here the child makes whatever he wishes with *clay;* that is, he models those objects which he remembers most distinctly and which have impressed him most deeply. We give the child a wooden tray containing a piece of clay, and then we await his work. We possess some very remarkable pieces of clay work done by our little ones. Some of them reproduce, with surprising minuteness of detail, objects which they have seen. And what is most surprising, these models often record not only the form, but even the *dimensions* of the objects which the child handled in school.

Many little ones model the objects which they have seen at home, especially kitchen furniture, water jugs, pots, and pans. Sometimes, we are shown a simple cradle containing a baby brother or sister. At first it is necessary to place written descriptions upon these objects, as it is necessary to do with the free design. Later on, however, the models are easily recognizable, and the children learn to reproduce the geometric solids. These clay models are undoubtedly very valuable material for the teacher, and make clear many individual differences, thus helping her to understand her children more fully. In our method they are also valuable as psychological manifestations of development according to age. Such designs are precious guides also for the teacher in the matter of her intervention in the child's education. The children who, in this work reveal themselves as observers, will probably become spontaneous observers of all the world about them, and may be led toward such a goal by the indirect help of exercises tending to fix and to make more exact the various sensations and ideas.

These children will also be those who arrive most quickly at the act of *spontaneous writing*. Those whose clay work remains unformed and indefinite will probably need the direct revelation of the directress, who will need to call their attention in some material manner to the objects around them.

Geometric Analysis of Figures; Sides, Angles, Center, Base

The geometric analysis of figures is not adapted to very young children. I have tried a means for the *introduction* of such analysis, limiting this work to the *rectangle* and making use of a game which includes the analysis without fixing the attention of the child upon it. This game presents the concept most clearly.

The *rectangle* of which I make use is the plane of one of the children's tables, and the game consists in laying the table for a meal. I have in each of the "Children's Houses" a collection of toy table furnishings, such as may be found in any toy store. Among these are dinner plates, soup plates, soup tureen, saltcellars, glasses, decanters, little knives, forks, spoons, etc. I have them lay the table for six, putting *two places* on each of the longer sides, and one place on each of the shorter sides. One of the children takes the objects and places them as I indicate. I tell him to place the soup tureen in the *center* of the table; this napkin in a *corner*. "Place this plate in the center of the short *side*."

Then I have the child look at the table, and I say, "Something is lacking in this *corner*. We want another glass on this *side*. Now let us see if we have everything properly placed on the two longer sides. Is everything ready on the two shorter sides? Is there anything lacking in the four corners?"

I do not believe that we may proceed to any more complex analysis than this before the age of six years, for I believe that the child should one day take up one of the plane insets and *spontaneously* begin to count the sides and the angles. Certainly, if we taught them such ideas they would be able to learn them, but it would be a mere learning of formula, and not applied experience.

Exercises in the Chromatic Sense

I have already indicated what color exercises we follow. Here I wish to indicate more definitely the succession of these exercises and to describe them more fully.

Designs and Pictures. We have prepared a number of outline drawings which the children are to fill in with colored pencil, and, later on, with a brush, preparing for themselves the watercolor tints which they will use. The first designs are of flowers, butterflies, trees and animals, and we then pass to simple landscapes containing grass, sky, houses, and human figures.

These designs help us in our study of the natural development of the child as an observer of his surroundings; that is, in regard to color. The children *select the colors* and are left entirely free in their work. If, for example, they color a chicken red, or a cow green, this shows that they have not yet become observers. But I have already spoken of this in the general discussion of the method. These designs also reveal the effect of the education of the chromatic sense. As the child selects delicate and harmonious tints, or strong and contrasting ones, we can judge of the progress he has made in the refinement of his color sense.

The fact that the child must *remember* the color of the objects represented in the design encourages him to observe those things which are about him. And then, too, he wishes to be able to fill in more difficult designs. Only those children who know how to keep the color *within* the outline and to reproduce the *right colors* may proceed to the more ambitious work. These designs are very easy, and often very effective, sometimes displaying real artistic work. The directress of the school in Mexico, who studied for a long time with me, sent me two designs; one representing a cliff in which the stones were colored most harmoniously in light violet and shades of brown, trees in two shades of green, and the sky a soft blue. The other represented a horse with a chestnut coat and black mane and tail.

EDITOR'S NOTE

1. Montessori's metaphor of winding a clock to illustrate the spontaneous psychic development of the child on pp. 229–30 is deleted.

Methods for the Teaching of Reading and Writing

Spontaneous Development of Graphic Language. While I was directress of the Orthophrenic School at Rome, I had already begun to experiment with various didactic means for the teaching of reading and writing. These experiments were practically original with me.[1] . . .

Is it necessary to begin writing with the making of vertical strokes? A moment of clear and logical thinking is enough to enable us to answer, no. The child makes too painful an effort in following such an exercise. The first steps should be the easiest, and the up and down stroke, is, on the contrary, one of the most difficult of all the pen movements. Only a professional penman could fill a whole page and preserve the regularity of such strokes, but a person who writes only moderately well would be able to complete a page of presentable writing. Indeed, the straight line is unique, expressing the shortest distance between two points, while *any deviation* from that direction signifies a line which is not straight. These infinite deviations are therefore easier than that *one* trace which is perfection.

If we should give to a number of adults the order to draw a straight line upon the blackboard, each person would draw a long line proceeding in a different direction, some beginning from one side, some from another, and almost all would succeed in making the line straight. Should we then ask that the line be drawn in a *particular direction*, starting from a determined point, the ability shown at first would greatly diminish, and we would see many more irregularities, or errors. Almost all the lines would be long—for the individual *must needs gather impetus* in order to succeed in making his line straight.

Should we ask that the lines be made short, and included within precise limits, the errors would increase, for we would thus impede the impetus which helps to conserve the definite direction. In the methods ordinarily used in teaching writing, we add, to such limitations, the further restriction that the instrument of writing must be held in a certain way, not as instinct prompts each individual.

Thus we approach in the most conscious and restricted way the first act of writing, which should be voluntary. In this first writing we still demand that the single strokes be kept parallel, making the child's task a difficult and barren one, since it has no purpose for the child, who does not understand the meaning of all this detail.

I had noticed in the notebooks of the deficient children in France (and Voisin also mentions this phenomenon) that the pages of vertical strokes, although they began as such, ended in lines of C's. This goes to show that the deficient child, whose mind is less resistant than that of the normal child, exhausts, little by little, the initial effort of imitation, and the natural movement gradually comes to take the place of that which was forced or stimulated. So the straight lines are transformed into curves, more and more like the letter C. Such a phenomenon does not appear in the copybooks of normal children, for they resist, through effort, until the end of the page is reached, and, thus, as often happens, conceal the didactic error.

But let us observe the spontaneous drawings of normal children. When, for example, picking up a fallen twig, they trace figures in the sandy garden path, we never see short straight lines, but long and variously interlaced curves.

Seguin saw the same phenomenon when the horizontal lines he made his pupils draw became curves so quickly instead. And he attributed the phenomenon to the imitation of the horizon line!

That vertical strokes should prepare for alphabetical writing, seems incredibly illogical. The alphabet is made up of curves, therefore we must prepare for it by learning to make straight lines.

"But," says someone, "in many letters of the alphabet, the straight line does exist." True, but there is no reason why as a beginning of writing, we should select one of the details of a complete form. We may analyze the alphabetical signs in this way, discovering straight lines and curves, as by analyzing discourse, we find grammatical rules. But we all *speak* independently of such rules, why then should we not write independently of such analysis, and without the separate execution of the parts constituting the letter?

It would be sad indeed if we could *speak* only *after* we had studied grammar! It would be much the same as demanding that before we *looked* at the stars in the firmament, we must study infinitesimal calculus; it is much the same thing to feel that before teaching an idiot to write, we must make him understand the abstract derivation of lines and the problems of geometry!

No less are we to be pitied if, in order to write, we must follow analytically the parts constituting the alphabetical signs. In fact the *effort* which we believe to be a necessary accompaniment to learning to write is a purely artificial effort, allied, not to writing, but to the *methods* by which it is taught.

Let us for a moment cast aside every dogma in this connection. Let us take no note of culture, or custom. We are not, here, interested in knowing how humanity began to write, nor what may have been the origin of writing itself. Let us put away the conviction, that long usage has given us, of the necessity of beginning writing by making vertical strokes; and let us try to be as clear and unprejudiced in spirit as the truth which we are seeking.

"Let us observe an individual who is writing, and let us seek to analyze the acts he performs in writing," that is, the mechanical operations which enter into the execution of writing. This would be undertaking the *philosophical study of writing*, and it goes without saying that we should examine the individual who writes, not the *writing;* the *subject*, not the *object*. Many have begun with the object, examining the writing, and in this way many methods have been constructed.

But a method starting from the individual would be decidedly original—very different from other methods which preceded it. It would indeed signify a new era in writing, *based upon anthropology.*

In fact, when I undertook my experiments with normal children, if I had thought of giving a name to this new method of writing, I should have called it without knowing what the results would be, the *anthropological method.* Certainly, my studies in anthropology inspired the method, but experience has given me, as a surprise, another title which seems to me the natural one, "the method of *spontaneous* writing."

While teaching deficient children I happened to observe the following fact: An idiot girl of eleven years, who was possessed of normal strength and motor power in her hands, could not learn to sew, or even to take the first step, darning, which consists in passing the needle first over, then under the woof, now taking up, now leaving, a number of threads.

I set the child to weaving with the Froebel mats, in which a strip of paper is threaded transversely in and out among vertical strips of paper held fixed at top and bottom. I thus came to think of the analogy between the two exercises, and became much interested in my observation of the girl. When she had become skilled in the Froebel weaving, I led her back again to the sewing, and saw with pleasure that she was now able to follow the darning. From that time on, our sewing classes began with a regular course in the Froebel weaving.

I saw that the necessary movements of the hand in sewing *had been prepared without having the child sew*, and that we should really find the way to *teach* the child *how*, before *making him execute* a task. I saw especially that preparatory movements could be carried on, and reduced to a mechanism, by means of repeated exercises not in the work itself but in that which prepares for it. Pupils could then come to the real work, able to perform it without ever having directly set their hands to it before.

I thought that I might in this way prepare for writing, and the idea interested me tremendously. I marveled at its simplicity, and was annoyed that *I had not thought before* of the method which was suggested to me by my observation of the girl who could not sew.

In fact, seeing that I had already taught the children to touch the contours of the plane geometric insets, I had now only to teach them to touch with their fingers the *forms of the letters of the alphabet*.

I had a beautiful alphabet manufactured, the letters being in flowing script, the low letters 8 centimeters high, and the taller ones in proportion. These letters were in wood, ½ centimeter in thickness, and were painted, the consonants in blue enamel, the vowels in red. The under side of these letter forms, instead of being painted, were covered with bronze that they might be more durable. We had only one copy of this wooden alphabet; but there were a number of cards upon which the letters were painted in the same colors and dimensions as the wooden ones. These painted letters were arranged upon the cards in groups, according to contrast, or analogy of form.

Corresponding to each letter of the alphabet, we had a picture representing some object the name of which began with the letter. Above this, the letter was painted in large script, and near it, the same letter, much smaller and in its printed form. These pictures served to fix the memory of the sound of the letter, and the small printed letter united to the one in script, was to form the passage to the reading of books. These pictures do not, indeed, represent a new idea, but they completed an arrangement which did not exist before. Such an alphabet was undoubtedly most expensive and when made by hand the cost was fifty dollars.

The interesting part of my experiment was, that after I had shown the children how to place the movable wooden letters upon those painted in groups upon the cards, I had them *touch them repeatedly in the fashion of flowing writing*.

I multiplied these exercises in various ways, and the children thus learned to make *the movements necessary to reproduce the form of the graphic signs without writing*.

I was struck by an idea which had never before entered my mind—that in writing we make *two diverse* forms of movement, for, besides the movement by which the form is reproduced, there is also that of *manipulating the instrument of writing.* And, indeed, when the deficient children had become expert in touching all the letters according to form, *they did not yet know how to hold a pencil.* To hold and to manipulate a little stick securely, corresponds to the *acquisition of a special muscular mechanism which is independent of the writing movement;* it must in fact go along with the motions necessary to produce all of the various letter forms. It is, then, *a distinct mechanism,* which must exist together with the motor memory of the single graphic signs. When I provoked in the deficients the movements characteristic of writing by having them touch the letters with their fingers, I exercised mechanically the psycho-motor paths, and fixed the muscular memory of each letter. There remained the preparation of the muscular mechanism necessary in holding and managing the instrument of writing, and this I provoked by adding two periods to the one already described. In the second period, the child touched the letter, not only with the index finger of his right hand, but with two, the index and the middle finger. In the third period, he touched the letters with a little wooden stick, held as a pen in writing. In substance I was making him repeat the same movements, now with, and now without, holding the instrument.

I have said that the child was to follow the *visual* image of the outlined letter. It is true that his finger had already been trained through touching the contours of the geometric figures, but this was not always a sufficient preparation. Indeed, even we grown people, when we trace a design through glass or tissue paper, cannot follow perfectly the line which we see and along which we should draw our pencil. The design should furnish some sort of control, some mechanical guide, for the pencil, in order to follow with *exactness* the trace, *sensible in reality only to the eye.*

The deficients, therefore, did not always follow the design exactly with either the finger or the stick. The didactic material did not offer *any control* in the work, or rather it offered only the uncertain control of the child's glance, which could, to be sure, see if the finger continued upon the sign, or not. I now thought that in order to have the pupil follow the movements more exactly, and to guide the execution more directly, I should need to prepare letter forms so indented, as to represent a *furrow* within which the wooden stick might run. I made the designs for this material, but the work being too expensive I was not able to carry out my plan.

After having experimented largely with this method, I spoke of it very fully to the teachers in my classes in didactic methods at the State Orthophrenic School. These lectures were printed, and I give below the words which, though they were placed in the hands of more than two hundred elementary teachers, did not draw from them a single helpful idea.[2] . . .

"At this point we present the cards bearing the vowels painted in red. The child sees irregular figures painted in red. We give him the vowels in wood, painted red, and have him superimpose these upon the letters painted on the card. We have him touch the wooden vowels in the fashion of writing, and give him the name of each letter. The vowels are arranged on the cards according to analogy of form:

o e a
i   u

"We then say to the child, for example, 'Find o. Put it in its place.' Then, 'What letter is this?' We here discover that many children make mistakes in the letters if they only look at the letter.

"They could however tell the letter by touching it. Most interesting observations may be made, revealing various individual types: visual, motor.

"We have the child touch the letters drawn upon the cards—using first the index finger only, then the index with the middle finger—then with a small wooden stick held as a pen. The letter must be traced in the fashion of writing.

"The consonants are painted in blue, and are arranged upon the cards according to analogy of form. To these cards are annexed a movable alphabet in blue wood, the letters of which are to be placed upon the consonants as they were upon the vowels. In addition to these materials there is another series of cards, where, besides the consonant, are painted one or two figures the names of which begin with that particular letter. Near the script letter, is a smaller printed letter painted in the same color.

"The teacher, naming the consonant according to the phonetic method, indicates the letter, and then the card, pronouncing the names of the objects painted there, and emphasizing the first letter, as, for example, '*p-pear:* give me the consonant *p*—put it in its place, touch it,' etc. *In all this we study the linguistic defects of the child.*

"Tracing the letter, in the fashion of writing, begins the muscular education which prepares for writing. One of our little girls taught by this method has reproduced all the letters with the pen, though she does not as yet recognize them all. She has made them about eight centimeters high, and with surprising regularity. This child also does well in hand work. The child who looks, recognizes, and touches the letters in the manner of writing, prepares himself simultaneously for reading and writing.

"Touching the letters and looking at them at the same time, fixes the image more quickly through the cooperation of the senses. Later, the two facts separate; looking becomes reading; touching becomes writing. According to the type of the individual, some learn to read first, others to write."

I had thus, about the year 1899, initiated my method for reading and writing upon the fundamental lines it still follows. It was with great surprise that I noted the *facility* with which a deficient child, to whom I one day gave a piece of chalk, traced upon the blackboard, in a firm hand, the letters of the entire alphabet, writing for the first time.

This had arrived much more quickly than I had supposed. As I have said, some of the children wrote the letters *with a pen and yet could not recognize one of them*. I have noticed, also, in normal children, that the muscular sense is most easily developed in infancy, and this makes writing exceedingly easy for children. It is not so with reading, which requires a much longer course of instruction, and which calls for a superior intellectual development, since it treats of the *interpretation of signs*, and of the *modulation of accents of the voice*, in order that the word may be understood. And all this is a purely mental task, while in writing, the child, under dictation, *materially translates* sounds into signs, and *moves*, a thing which is always easy and pleasant for him. Writing develops in the little child with *facility* and *spontaneity*, analogous to the development of spoken language—which is a motor translation of audible sounds. Reading, on the contrary, makes part of an abstract intellectual culture, which is the interpretation of ideas from graphic symbols, and is only acquired later on.

My first experiments with normal children were begun in the first half of the month of November, 1907.

In the two "Children's Houses" in San Lorenzo, I had, from the date of their respective inaugurations (January 6 in one and March 7 in the other), used only the games of practical life, and of the education of the senses. I had not presented exercises for writing, because, like everybody else, I held the prejudice that it was necessary to begin as late as possible the teaching of reading and writing, and certainly to avoid it before the age of six.

But the children seemed to demand some *conclusion* of the exercises, which had already developed them intellectually in a most surprising way. They knew how to dress and undress, and to bathe, themselves; they knew how to sweep the floors, dust the furniture, put the room in order, to open and close boxes, to manage the keys in the various locks; they could replace the objects in the cupboards in perfect order, could care for the plants; they knew how to observe things, and how to see objects with their hands. A number of them came to us and frankly demanded to be taught to read and write. Even in the face of our refusal several children came to school and proudly showed us that they knew how to make an O on the blackboard.

Finally, many of the mothers came to beg us as a favor to teach the children to write, saying, "Here in the 'Children's Houses' the children are awakened, and learn so many things easily that if you only teach reading and writing they will soon learn, and will then be spared the great fatigue this always means in the elementary school." This faith of the mothers, that their little ones would, from us, be *able to learn to read and write without fatigue*, made a great impression upon me. Thinking upon the results I had obtained in the school for deficients, I decided during the August vacation to make a trial upon the reopening of the school in September. Upon second thought I decided that it would be better to take up the interrupted work in September, and not to approach reading and writing until October, when the elementary schools opened. This presented the added advantage of permitting us to compare the progress of the children of the first elementary with that made by ours, who would have begun the same branch of instruction at the same time.

In September, therefore, I began a search for someone who could manufacture didactic materials, but found no one willing to undertake it. I wished to have a splendid alphabet made, like the one used with the deficients. Giving this up, I was willing to content myself with the ordinary enameled letters used upon shop windows, but I could find them in script form nowhere. My disappointments were many.

So passed the whole month of October. The children in the first elementary had already filled pages of vertical strokes, and mine were still waiting. I then decided to cut out large paper letters, and to have one of my teachers color these roughly on one side with a blue tint. As for the touching of the letters, I thought of cutting the letters of the alphabet out of sandpaper, and of gluing them upon smooth cards, thus making objects much like those used in the primitive exercises for the tactile sense.

Only after I had made these simple things, did I become aware of the superiority of this alphabet to that magnificent one I had used for my deficients, and in the pursuit of which I had wasted two months! If I had been rich, I would have had that beautiful but barren alphabet of the past! We wish the old things because we cannot understand the new, and we are always seeking after that gorgeousness which belongs to things already on the decline, without recognizing in the humble simplicity of new ideas the germ which shall develop in the future.

I finally understood that a paper alphabet could easily be multiplied, and could be used by many children at one time, not only for the recognition of letters, but for the composition of words. I saw that in the sandpaper alphabet I had found the looked-for guide for the fingers which touched the letter. This was furnished in such a way that no longer the sight alone, but the touch, lent itself directly to teaching the movement of writing with exactness of control.

In the afternoon after school, the two teachers and I, with great enthusiasm, set about cutting out letters from writing paper, and others from sandpaper.

The first, we painted blue, the second, we mounted on cards, and, while we worked, there unfolded before my mind a clear vision of the method in all its completeness, so simple that it made me smile to think I had not seen it before.

The story of our first attempts is very interesting. One day one of the teachers was ill, and I sent as a substitute a pupil of mine, Signorina Anna Fedeli, a professor of pedagogy in a Normal school. When I went to see her at the close of the day, she showed me two modifications of the alphabet which she had made. One consisted in placing behind each letter, a transverse strip of white paper, so that the child might recognize the direction of the letter, which he often turned about and upside down. The other consisted in the making of a cardboard case where each letter might be put away in its own compartment, instead of being kept in a confused mass as at first. I still keep this rude case made from an old pasteboard box, which Signorina Fedeli had found in the court and roughly sewed with white thread.

She showed it to me laughing, and excusing herself for the miserable work, but I was most enthusiastic about it. I saw at once that the letters in the case were a precious aid to the teaching. Indeed, it offered to the eye of the child the possibility of comparing all of the letters, and of selecting those he needed. In this way the didactic material described below had its origin.

I need only add that at Christmas time, less than a month and a half later, while the children in the first elementary were laboriously working to forget their wearisome pothooks and to prepare for making the curves of O and the other vowels, two of my little ones of four years old, wrote, each one in the name of his companions, a letter of good wishes and thanks to Signor Edoardo Talamo. These were written upon note paper without blot or erasure and the writing was adjudged equal to that which is obtained in the third elementary grade.

EDITOR'S NOTES

1. Montessori's long series of quotes from Seguin's method of teaching reading to mentally impaired children on pp. 246–56 is deleted. Montessori rejects this part of Seguin's method. The influence of Seguin on the development of Montessori's method has been discussed earlier in the book.

2. Montessori's reference to an article on the teaching of writing on p. 264 is deleted.

17

Description of the Method and Didactic Material Used

FIRST PERIOD: EXERCISE TENDING TO DEVELOP THE MUSCULAR MECHANISM NECESSARY IN HOLDING AND USING THE INSTRUMENT IN WRITING

Design Preparatory to Writing—Didactic Material. Small wooden tables; metal insets, outline drawings, colored pencils. I have among my materials two little wooden tables, the tops of which form an inclined plane sloping toward a narrow cornice, which prevents objects placed upon the table from slipping off. The top of each table is just large enough to hold four of the square frames, into which the metal plane geometric insets are fitted, and is so painted as to represent three of these brown frames, each containing a square centre of the same dark blue as the centers of the metal insets.

The metal insets are in dimension and form a reproduction of the series of plane geometric insets in wood already described.

Exercises. Placed side by side upon the teacher's desk, or upon one of the little tables belonging to the children, these two little tables may have the appearance of being one long table containing eight figures. The child may select one or more figures, taking at the same time the frame of the inset. The analogy between these metal insets and the plane geometric insets of wood is complete. But in this case, the child can freely use the pieces, where before, he arranged them in the wooden frame. He first takes the metal frame, places it upon a sheet of white paper, and with a colored pencil *draws around the contour of the empty center.* Then, he takes away the frame, and upon the paper there remains a geometric figure.

This is the first time that the child has reproduced through design, a geometric figure. Until now, he has only placed the geometric insets above the figures delineated on the three series of cards. He now places upon the figure, which he himself has drawn, the metal inset, just as he placed the wooden inset upon the cards. His next act is to follow the contour of this inset with a pencil of a different color. Lifting the metal piece, he sees the figure reproduced upon the paper, in two colors.

Here, for the first time is born the abstract concept of the geometric figure, for, from two metal pieces so different in form as the frame and the inset, there has resulted the same design, which is a *line* expressing a determined figure. This fact strikes the attention of the child. He often marvels to find the same figure reproduced by means of two pieces so different, and looks for a long time with evident pleasure at the duplicate design—almost as if it were *actually produced* by the objects which serve to guide his hand.

Besides all this, the child learns *to trace lines* determining figures. There will come a day in which, with still greater surprise and pleasure, he will trace graphic signs determining words.

After this, he begins the work which directly prepares for the formation of the muscular mechanism relative to the holding and manipulation of the instrument of writing. With a colored pencil of his own selection, held as the pen is held in writing, he *fills* in the figure which he has outlined. We teach him not to pass outside the contour, and in doing so we attract his attention to this contour, and thus *fix* the idea that a line may determine a figure.

The exercise of filling in one figure alone, causes the child to perform repeatedly the movement of manipulation which would be necessary to fill ten copybook pages with vertical strokes. And yet, the child feels no weariness, because, although he makes exactly the muscular coordination which is necessary to the work, he does so freely and in any way that he wishes, while his eyes are fixed upon a large and brightly colored figure. At first, the children fill pages and pages of paper with these big squares, triangles, ovals, trapezoids; coloring them red, orange, green, blue, light blue, and pink.

Gradually they limit themselves to the use of the dark blue and brown, both in drawing the figure and in filling it in, thus reproducing the appearance of the metal piece itself. Many of the children, quite of their own accord, make a little orange-colored circle in the centre of the figure, in this way representing the little brass button by which the metal piece is to be held. They take great pleasure in feeling that they have reproduced exactly, like true artists, the objects which they see before them on the little shelf.

Observing the successive drawings of a child, there is revealed to us a duplicate form of progression:

First. Little by little, the lines tend less and less to go outside the enclosing line until, at last, they are perfectly contained within it, and both the center and the frame are filled in with close and uniform strokes.

Second. The strokes with which the child fills in the figures, from being at first short and confused, become gradually *longer, and more nearly parallel,* until in many cases the figures are filled in by means of perfectly regular up and down strokes, extending from one side of the figure to the other. In such a case, it is evident that the child is *master of the pencil.* The muscular mechanism, necessary to the management of the instrument of writing, *is established.* We may, therefore, by examining such designs, arrive at a clear idea of the maturity of the child in the matter of *holding the pencil or pen in hand.* To vary these exercises, we use the *outline drawings* already described. Through these designs, the manipulation of the pencil is perfected, for they oblige the child to make lines of various lengths, and make him more and more secure in his use of the pencil.[1] . . .

Even when the children *know how to write* they continue these exercises, which furnish an unlimited progression, since the designs may be varied and complicated. The children follow in each design essentially the same movements, and acquire a varied collection of pictures which grow more and more perfect, and of which they are very proud. For I not only *provoke,* but perfect, the writing through the exercises which we call preparatory. The control of the pen is rendered more and more secure, not by repeated exercises in the writing, but by means of these filled-in designs. In this way, my children *perfect themselves in writing, without actually writing.*

SECOND PERIOD: EXERCISES TENDING TO ESTABLISH THE VISUAL-MUSCULAR IMAGE OF THE ALPHABETICAL SIGNS, AND TO ESTABLISH THE MUSCULAR MEMORY OF THE MOVEMENTS NECESSARY TO WRITING

Didactic Material. Cards upon which the single letters of the alphabet are mounted in sandpaper; larger cards containing groups of the same letters.

The cards upon which the sandpaper letters are mounted are adapted in size and shape to each letter. The vowels are in light-colored sandpaper and are mounted upon dark cards, the consonants and the groups of letters are in black sandpaper mounted upon white cards. The grouping is so arranged as to call attention to contrasted, or analogous forms.

The letters are cut in clear script form, the shaded parts being made broader. We have chosen to reproduce the vertical script in use in the elementary schools.

Exercises. In teaching the letters of the alphabet, we begin with the *vowels* and proceed to the consonants, pronouncing the *sound,* not the name. In the case of the consonants, we immediately unite the sound with one of the vowel sounds, repeating the syllable according to the usual phonetic method.

The teaching proceeds according to the three periods already illustrated.

First. Association of the visual and muscular-tactile sensation with the letter sound.

The directress presents to the child two of the cards upon which vowels are mounted (or two of the consonants, as the case may be). Let us suppose that we present the letters i and o, saying, "This is i! This is o!" As soon as we have given the sound of a letter, we have the child trace it, taking care to show him *how* to trace it, and if necessary guiding the index finger of his right hand over the sandpaper letter *in the sense of writing.*

"Knowing how to trace" will consist in *knowing the direction* in which a given graphic sign must be followed.

The child learns quickly, and his finger, already expert in the tactile exercise, *is led,* by the slight roughness of the fine sandpaper, over the exact track of the letter. *He may then repeat indefinitely* the movements necessary to produce the letters of the alphabet, without the fear of the mistakes of which a child writing with a pencil for the first time is so conscious. If he deviates, the smoothness of the card immediately warns him of his error.

The children, as soon as they have become at all expert in this tracing of the letters, take great pleasure in repeating it *with closed eyes,* letting the sandpaper lead them in following the form which they do not see. Thus the perception will be established by the direct muscular-tactile sensation of the letter. In other words, it is no longer the visual image of the letter, but the *tactile sensation,* which guides the hand of the child in these movements, which thus become fixed in the muscular memory.

There develop, contemporaneously, three sensations when the directress *shows the letter* to the child and has him trace it; the visual sensation, the tactile sensation, and the muscular sensation. In this way the *image of the graphic sign* is fixed *in a much shorter space of time* than when it was, according to ordinary methods, acquired only through the visual image. It will be found that the *muscular memory* is in the young child the most tenacious and, at the same time, the most ready. Indeed, he sometimes recognizes the letters by touching them, when he cannot do so by looking at them. These images are, besides all this, contemporaneously associated with the alphabetical sound.

Second. Perception. *The child should know how to compare and to recognize the figures, when he hears the sounds corresponding to them.*

The directress asks the child, for example, "Give me o!—Give me i!" If the child does not recognize the letters by looking at them, she invites him to trace them, but if he still does not recognize them, the lesson is ended, and may be resumed another day. I have already spoken of the necessity of *not revealing* the error, and of not insisting in the teaching when the child does not respond readily.

Third. Language. *Allowing the letters to lie for some instants upon the table, the directress asks the child, "What is this?" and he should respond, o, i.*

In teaching the consonants, the directress pronounces only the *sound*, and as soon as she has done so unites with it a vowel, pronouncing the syllable thus formed and alternating this little exercise by the use of different vowels. She must always be careful to emphasize the sound of the consonant, repeating it by itself, as, for example, *m, m, m, ma, me, mi, m, m.* When the child *repeats* the sound he isolates it, and then accompanies it with the vowel.

It is not necessary to teach all the vowels before passing to the consonants, and as soon as the child knows one consonant he may begin to compose words. Questions of this sort, however, are left to the judgment of the educator.

I do not find it practical *to follow a special rule* in the teaching of the consonants. Often the curiosity of the child concerning a letter leads us to teach that desired consonant; a name pronounced may awaken in him a desire to know what consonants are necessary to compose it, and this *will*, or *willingness*, of the pupil is a much more *efficacious* means than any rule concerning the *progression* of the letters.

When the child pronounces *the sounds* of the consonants, he experiences an evident pleasure. It is a great novelty for him, this series of sounds, so varied and yet so distinct, *presenting* such enigmatic signs as the letters of the alphabet. There is mystery about all this, which provokes most decided interest. One day I was on the terrace while the children were having their free games; I had with me a little boy of two years and a half left with me, for a moment, by his mother. Scattered about upon a number of chairs, were the alphabets which we use in the school. These had become mixed, and I was putting the letters back into their respective compartments. Having finished my work, I placed the boxes upon two of the little chairs near me. The little boy watched me. Finally, he drew near to the box, and took one of the letters in his hand. It chanced to be an f. At that moment the children, who were running in single file, passed us, and, seeing the letter, called out in chorus the corresponding sound and passed on. The child paid no attention to them, but put back the f and took up an r. The children running by again, looked at him laughing, and then began to cry out "r, r, r! r, r, r!" Little by little the baby understood that, when he took a letter in hand, the children, who were passing, cried out a sound. This amused him so much that I wished to observe how long he would persist in this game without becoming tired. He kept it up for *three-quarters of an hour*! The children had become interested in the child, and grouped themselves about him, pronouncing the sounds in chorus, and laughing at his pleased surprise. At last, after he had several times held up f, and had received from his public the same sound, he took the letter again, showing it to me, and saying, "f, f, f!" He had learned this from out the great confusion of sounds which he had heard: the long letter which had first arrested the attention of the running children, had made a great impression upon him.

It is not necessary to show how the separate pronunciation of the alphabetical sounds *reveals* the condition of the child's speech. Defects, which are almost all related to the *incomplete* development of the language itself, manifest themselves, and the directress may take note of them one by one. In this way she will be possessed of a record of the child's progress, which will help her in her individual teaching, and will reveal much concerning the development of the language in this particular child.

In the matter of *correcting linguistic defects*, we will find it helpful to follow the physiological rules relating to the child's development, and to modify the difficulties in the presentation of our lesson. When, however, the child's speech is sufficiently developed, and when he *pronounces all the sounds*, it does not matter which of the letters we select in our lessons.

Many of the defects which have become permanent in adults are due to *functional errors in the development* of the language during the period of infancy. If, for the attention which we pay to the correction of linguistic defects in children in the upper grades, we would substitute *a direction of the development of the language* while the child is still young, our results would be much more practical and valuable. In fact, many of the defects in pronunciation arise from the use of *a dialect*, and these it is almost impossible to correct after the period of childhood. They may, however, be most easily removed through the use of educational methods especially adapted to the perfecting of the language in little children.[2] . . .

Turning directly to the method used in teaching writing, I may call attention to the fact that it is contained in the two periods already described. Such exercises have made it possible for the child to learn, and to fix, the muscular mechanism necessary to the proper holding of the pen, and to the making of the graphic signs. If he has exercised himself for a sufficiently long time in these exercises, he will be *potentially* ready to write all the letters of the alphabet and all of the simple syllables, without ever having taken chalk or pencil in his hand.

We have, in addition to this, begun the teaching of *reading* at the same time that we have been teaching *writing*. When we present a letter to the child and enunciate its sound, he fixes the image of this letter by means of the visual sense, and also by means of the muscular-tactile sense. He associates the sound with its relative sign; that is, he relates the sound to the graphic sign. But *when he sees and recognizes, he reads; and when he traces, he writes.* Thus his mind receives as one, two acts, which, later on, as he develops, will separate, coming to constitute the two diverse processes of *reading and writing.* By teaching these two acts contemporaneously, or, better, by their *fusion,* we place the child *before a new form of language* without determining which of the acts constituting it should be most prevalent.

We do not trouble ourselves as to whether the child in the development of this process, first learns to read or to write, or if the one or the other will be the easier. We must rid ourselves of all preconceptions, and must *await from experience* the answer to these questions. We may expect that individual differences will show themselves in the prevalence of one or the other act in the development of different children. This makes possible the most interesting psychological study of the individual, and should broaden the work of this method, which is based upon the free expansion of individuality.

THIRD PERIOD: EXERCISES FOR THE COMPOSITION OF WORDS

Didactic Material. This consists chiefly of alphabets. The letters of the alphabet used here are identical in form and dimension with the sandpaper ones already described, but these are cut out of cardboard and are not mounted. In this way each letter represents an object which can be easily handled by the child and placed wherever he wishes it. There are several examples of each letter, and I have designed cases in which the alphabets may be kept. These cases or boxes are very shallow, and are divided and subdivided into many compartments, in each one of which I have placed a group of four copies of the same letter. The compartments are not equal in size, but are measured according to the dimensions of the letters themselves. At the bottom of each compartment is glued a letter which is not to be taken out. This letter is made of black cardboard and relieves the child of the fatigue of hunting about for the right compartment when he is replacing the letters in the case after he has used them. The vowels are cut from blue cardboard, and the consonants from red.

In addition to these alphabets we have a set of the capital letters mounted in sandpaper upon cardboard, and another, in which they are cut from cardboard. The numbers are treated in the same way.

Exercises. As soon as the child knows some of the vowels and the consonants we place before him the big box containing all the vowels and the consonants which he knows. The directress pronounces *very* clearly a word; for example, "mama," brings out the sound of the m very distinctly, repeating the sounds a number of times. Almost always the little one with an impulsive movement seizes an m and places it upon the table. The directress repeats "ma—ma." The child selects the a and places it near the m. He then composes the other syllable very easily. But the reading of the word which he has composed is not so easy. Indeed, he generally succeeds in reading it only after a *certain effort.* In this case I help the child, urging him to read, and reading the word with him once or twice, always pronouncing very distinctly, *mama, mama*. But once he has understood the mechanism of the game, the child goes forward by himself, and becomes intensely interested. We may pronounce any word, taking care only that the child understands separately the letters of which it is composed. He composes the new word, placing, one after the other, the signs corresponding to the sounds.

It is most interesting indeed to watch the child at this work. Intensely attentive, he sits watching the box, moving his lips almost imperceptibly, and taking one by one the necessary letters, rarely committing an error in spelling. The movement of the lips reveals the fact that he *repeats to himself an infinite number of times* the words whose sounds he is translating into signs. Although the child is able to compose any word which is clearly pronounced, we generally dictate to him only those words which are well known, since we wish his composition to result in an idea. When these familiar words are used, he spontaneously rereads many times the word he has composed, repeating its sounds in a thoughtful, contemplative way.

The importance of these exercises is very complex. The child analyses, perfects, fixes his own spoken language—placing an object in correspondence to every sound which he utters. The composition of the word furnishes him with substantial proof of the necessity for clear and forceful enunciation.

The exercise, thus followed, associates the sound which is heard with the graphic sign which represents it, and lays a most solid foundation for accurate and perfect spelling.

In addition to this, the composition of the words is in itself an exercise of intelligence. The word which is pronounced presents to the child a problem which he must solve, and he will do so by remembering the signs, selecting them from among others, and arranging them in the proper order. He will have the *proof* of the exact solution of his problem when he *rereads* the word—this word which he has composed, and which represents for all those who know how to read it, *an idea*.[3] . . .

When the pupil has finished the composition and the reading of the word we have him, according to the habits of order which we try to establish in connection with all our work, "*put away*" all the letters, each one in its own compartment. In composition, pure and simple, therefore, the child unites the two exercises of comparison and of selection of the graphic signs; the first, when from the entire box of letters before him he takes those necessary; the second, when he seeks the compartment in which each letter must be replaced. There are, then, three exercises united in this one effort, all three uniting to *fix the image of the graphic sign* corresponding to the sounds of the word. The work of learning is in this case facilitated in three ways, and the ideas are acquired in a third of the time which would have been necessary with the old methods. We shall soon see that the child, on hearing the word, or on thinking of a word which he already knows, *will see*, with his mind's eye, all the letters, necessary to compose the word, arrange themselves. He will reproduce this vision with a facility most surprising to us.[4] . . .

These three periods contain the entire method for the acquisition of written language. The significance of such a method is clear. The psycho-physiological acts which unite to establish reading and writing are prepared separately and carefully. The muscular movements peculiar to the making of the signs or letters are prepared apart, and the same is true of the manipulation of the instrument of writing. The composition of the words, also, is reduced to a psychic mechanism of association between images heard and seen. There comes a moment in which the child, without thinking of it, fills in the geometric figures with an up and down stroke, which is free and regular; a moment in which he touches the letters with, closed eyes, and in which he reproduces their form, moving his finger through the air; a moment in which the composition of words has become a psychic impulse, which makes the child, even when alone, repeat to himself "To make Zaira I must have z-a-i-r-a."

Now this child, it is true, *has never written*, but he has mastered all the acts necessary to writing. The child who, when taking dictation, not only knows how to compose the word, but instantly embraces in his thought its composition as a whole, will be able to write, since he knows how to make, with his eyes closed, the movements necessary to produce these letters, and since he manages almost unconsciously the instrument of writing.

More than this, the freedom with which the child has acquired this mechanical dexterity makes it possible for the impulse or spirit to act at any time through the medium of his mechanical ability. He should, sooner or later, come into his full power by way of a spontaneous explosion into writing. This is, indeed, the marvelous reaction which has come from my experiment with normal children. In one of the "Children's Houses," directed by Signorina Bettini, I had been especially careful in the way in which writing was taught, and we have had from this school most beautiful specimens of writing, and for this reason, perhaps I cannot do better than to describe the development of the work in this school.

One beautiful December day when the sun shone and the air was like spring, I went up on the roof with the children. They were playing freely about, and a number of them were gathered about me. I was sitting near a chimney, and said to a little five-year-old boy who sat beside me, "Draw me a picture of this chimney," giving him as I spoke a piece of chalk. He got down obediently and made a rough sketch of the chimney on the tiles which formed the floor of this roof terrace. As is my custom with little children, I encouraged him, praising his work. The child looked at me, smiled, remained for a moment as if on the point of bursting into some joyous act, and then cried out, "I can write! I can write!" and kneeling down again he wrote on the pavement the word "hand." Then, full of enthusiasm, he wrote also "chimney," "roof." As he wrote, he continued to cry out, "I can write! I know how to write!" His cries of joy brought the other children, who formed a circle about him, looking down at his work in stupefied amazement. Two or three of them said to me, trembling with excitement, "Give me the chalk. I can write too." And indeed they began to write various words: *mama, hand, John, chimney, Ada.*

Not one of them had ever taken chalk or any other instrument in hand for the purpose of writing. It was the *first time* that they had ever written, and they traced an entire word, as a child, when speaking for the first time, speaks the entire word.[5] . . .

They believe that, as they grow bigger and stronger, there will come some beautiful day when they *shall know how to write*. And, indeed, this is what it is in reality. The child who speaks, first prepares himself unconsciously, perfecting the psycho-muscular mechanism which leads to the articulation of the word. In the case of writing, the child does almost the same thing, but the direct pedagogical help and the possibility of preparing the movements for writing in an almost material way, causes the ability to write to develop much more rapidly and more perfectly than the ability to speak correctly.

In spite of the ease with which this is accomplished, the preparation is not partial, but complete. The child possesses *all* the movements necessary for writing. And written language develops not gradually, but in an explosive way; that is, the child can write *any word*. Such was our first experience in the development of the written language in our children. Those first days we were a prey to deep emotions. It seemed as if we walked in a dream, and as if we assisted at some miraculous achievement.[6] . . .

After the first word, the children, with a species of frenzied joy, continued to write everywhere. I saw children crowding about one another at the blackboard, and behind the little ones who were standing on the floor another line would form consisting of children mounted upon chairs, so that they might write above the heads of the little ones. In a fury at being thwarted, other children, in order to find a little place where they might write, overturned the chairs upon which their companions were mounted. Others ran toward the window shutters or the door, covering them with writing. In these first days we walked upon a carpet of written signs. Daily accounts showed us that the same thing was going on at home, and some of the mothers, in order to save their pavements, and even the crust of their loaves upon which they found words written, made their children presents of *paper* and *pencil*. One of these children brought to me one day a little notebook entirely filled with writing, and the mother told me that the child had written all day long and all evening, and had gone to sleep in his bed with the paper and pencil in his hand.

This impulsive activity which we could not, in those first days control, made me think upon the wisdom of Nature, who develops the spoken language little by little, letting it go hand in hand with the gradual formation of ideas. Think of what the result would have been had Nature acted imprudently as I had done! Suppose Nature had first allowed the human being to gather, by means of the senses, a rich and varied material, and to acquire a store of ideas, and had then completely prepared in him the means for articulate language, saying finally to the child, mute until that hour, "Go—Speak!" The result would have been a species of sudden madness, under the influence of which the child, feeling no restraints, would have burst into an exhausting torrent of the most strange and difficult words.

I believe, however, that there exists between the two extremes a happy medium which is the true and practical way. We should lead the child more gradually to the conquest of written language, yet we should still have it come as a *spontaneous fact*, and his work should from the first be almost perfect.

Experience has shown us how to control this phenomenon, and how to lead the child more *calmly* to this new power. The fact that the children *see* their companions writing, leads them, through imitation, to write *as soon as* they can. In this way, when the child writes he does not have the entire alphabet at his disposal, and the number of words which he can write is limited. He is not even capable of making all of the words possible through a combination of the letters which he does know. He still has the great joy of the *first written word*, but this is no longer the source of *an overwhelming surprise*, since he sees just such wonderful things happening each day, and knows that sooner or later the same gift will come to all. This tends to create a calm and ordered environment, still full of beautiful and wonderful surprises.[7] . . .

The wisdom of the teacher shall decide when it is necessary to encourage a child to write. This can only be when he is already perfect in the three periods of the preparatory exercise, and yet does not write of his own accord. There is danger that in retarding the act of writing, the child may plunge finally into a tumultuous effort, due to the fact that he knows the entire alphabet and has no natural check.

The signs by which the teacher may almost precisely diagnose the child's maturity in this respect are: the *regularity* of the *parallel* lines which fill in the geometric figures; the recognition with closed eyes of the sandpaper letters; the security and readiness shown in the composition of words. Before intervening by means of a direct invitation to write, it is best to wait at least a week in the hope that the child may write spontaneously. When he has begun to write spontaneously the teacher may intervene to *guide* the progress of the writing. The first help which she may give is that of *ruling* the blackboard, so that the child may be led to maintain regularity and proper dimensions in his writing.

The second, is that of inducing the child, whose writing is not firm, to *repeat the tracing* of the sandpaper letters. She should do this instead of *directly* correcting his actual writing, for the child does not perfect himself by repeating the act of writing, but by repeating the acts preparatory to writing. I remember a little beginner who, wishing to make his blackboard writing perfect, brought all of the sandpaper letters with him, and before writing touched two or three times *all of the letters needed in the words he wished to write*. If a letter did not seem to him to be perfect he erased it and *retouched* the letter upon the card before rewriting.

Our children, even after they have been writing for a year, continue to repeat the three preparatory exercises. They thus learn both to write, and to perfect their writing, without really going through the actual act. With our children, actual writing is a test; it springs from an inner impulse, and from the pleasure of explaining a superior activity; it is not an exercise. As the soul of the mystic perfects itself through prayer, even so in our little ones, that highest expression of civilization, written language, is acquired and improved through exercises which are akin to, but which are not, writing.

There is educational value in this idea of preparing oneself before trying, and of perfecting oneself before going on. To go forward correcting his own mistakes, boldly attempting things which he does imperfectly, and of which he is as yet unworthy dulls the sensitiveness of the child's spirit toward his own errors. My method of writing contains an educative concept; teaching the child that prudence which makes him avoid errors, that dignity which makes him look ahead, and which guides him to perfection, and that humility which unites him closely to those sources of good through which alone he can make a spiritual conquest, putting far from him the illusion that the immediate success is ample justification for continuing in the way he has chosen.

The fact that all the children, those who are just beginning the three exercises and those who have been writing for months, daily repeat the same exercise, unites them and makes it easy for them to meet upon an apparently equal plane. Here there are no *distinctions* of beginners, and experts. All of the children fill in the figures with colored pencils, touch the sandpaper letters and compose words with the movable alphabets; the little ones beside the big ones who help them. He who prepares himself, and he who perfects himself, both follow the same path. It is the same way in life, for, deeper than any social distinction, there lies an equality, a common meeting point, where all men are brothers, or, as in the spiritual life, aspirants and saints again and again pass through the same experiences.

Writing is very quickly learned, because we begin to teach it only to those children who show a desire for it by spontaneous attention to the lesson given by the directress to other children, or by watching the exercises in which the others are occupied. Some individuals *learn* without ever having received any lessons, solely through listening to the lessons given to others.

In general, all children of four are intensely interested in writing, and some of our children have begun to write at the age of three and a half. We find the children particularly enthusiastic about tracing the sandpaper letters.[8] . . .

The average time that elapses between the first trial of the preparatory exercises and the first written word is, for children of four years, from a month to a month and a half. With children of five years, the period is much shorter, being about a month. But one of our pupils learned to use in writing all the letters of the alphabet in twenty days. Children of four years, after they have been in school for two months and a half, can write any word from dictation, and can pass to writing with ink in a notebook. Our little ones are generally experts after three months' time, and those who have written for six months may be compared to the children in the third elementary. Indeed, writing is one of the easiest and most delightful of all the conquests made by the child.

If adults learned as easily as children under six years of age, it would be an easy matter to do away with illiteracy. We would probably find two grave hindrances to the attainment of such a brilliant success: the torpor of the muscular sense, and those permanent defects of spoken language, which would be sure to translate themselves into the written language. I have not made experiments along this line, but I believe that one school year would be sufficient to lead an illiterate person, not only to write, but to express his thoughts in written language.

So much for the time necessary for learning. As to the execution, our children *write well* from the moment in which they begin. The *form* of the letters, beautifully rounded and flowing, is surprising in its similarity to the form of the sandpaper models. The beauty of our writing is rarely equaled by any scholars in the elementary schools, *who have not had special exercises in penmanship.* I have made a close study of penmanship, and I know how difficult it would be to teach pupils of twelve or thirteen years to write an entire word without lifting the pen, except for the few letters which require this. The up and down strokes with which they have filled their copybook make flowing writing almost impossible to them.

Our little pupils, on the other hand, spontaneously, and with a marvelous security, write entire words without lifting the pen, maintaining perfectly the slant of the letters, and making the distance between each letter equal. This has caused more than one visitor to exclaim, "If I had not seen it I should never have believed it." Indeed, penmanship is a superior form of teaching and is necessary to correct defects already acquired and fixed. It is a long work, for the child, *seeing* the model, must follow the *movements* necessary to reproduce it, while there is no direct correspondence between the visual sensation and the movements which he must make. Too often, penmanship is taught at an age when all the defects have become established, and when the physiological period in which the *muscular memory* is ready, has been passed.

We directly prepare the child, not only for writing, but also for *penmanship,* paying great attention to the *beauty of form* (having the children touch the letters in script form) and to the flowing quality of the letters. (The exercises in filling in prepare for this.)

READING

Didactic Material. The Didactic Material for the lessons in reading consists in slips of paper or cards upon which are written in clear, large script, words and phrases. In addition to these cards we have a great variety of toys.

Experience has taught me to distinguish clearly between *writing and reading* and has shown me that the two acts *are not absolutely contemporaneous.* Contrary to the usually accepted idea, writing *precedes reading.* I do not consider as *reading* the test which the child makes *when he verifies* the word that he has written. He is translating signs into sounds, as he first translated sounds into signs. In this verification he already knows the word and has repeated it to himself while writing it. What I understand by reading is the *interpretation* of an idea from the written signs. The child who has not heard the word pronounced, and who recognizes it when he sees it composed upon the table with the cardboard letters, and who can tell what it means; this child *reads.* The word which he reads has the same relation to written language that the word which he hears bears to articulate language. Both serve to *receive the language* transmitted to us *by others.* So, until the child reads a transmission of ideas from the written word, *he does not read.*

We may say, if we like, that writing as described is a fact in which the psycho-motor mechanism prevails, while in reading, there enters a work which is purely intellectual. But it is evident how our method for writing prepares for reading, making the difficulties almost imperceptible. Indeed, writing prepares the child to interpret mechanically the union of the letter sounds of which the written word is composed. When a child in our school knows how to write, *he knows how to read the sounds* of which the word is composed. It should be noticed, however, that when the child composes the words with the movable alphabet, or when he writes, he has *time to think* about the signs which he must select to form the word. The writing of a word requires a great deal more time than that necessary for reading the same word.

The child who *knows how to write,* when placed before a word which he must interpret by reading, is silent for a long time, and generally reads the component sounds with the same slowness with which he would have written them. But *the sense of the word* becomes evident only when it is pronounced clearly and with the phonetic accent. Now, in order to place the phonetic accent the child must recognize the word; that is, he must recognize the idea which the word represents. The intervention of a superior work of the intellect is necessary if he is to read. Because of all this, I proceed in the following way with the exercises in reading, and, as will be evident, I do away entirely with the old-time primer.

I prepare a number of little cards made from ordinary writing paper. On each of these I write in large clear script some well-known word, one which has already been pronounced many times by the children, and which represents an object actually present or well known to them. If the word refers to an object which is before them, I place this object under the eyes of the child, in order to facilitate his interpretation of the word. I will say, in this connection, the objects used in these writing games are for the most part toys of which we have a great many in the "Children's Houses." Among these toys, are the furnishings of a doll's house, balls, dolls, trees, flocks of sheep, or various animals, tin soldiers, railways, and an infinite variety of simple figures.

If writing serves to correct, or better, to direct and perfect the mechanism of the articulate language of the child, reading serves to help the development of ideas, and relates them to the development of the language. Indeed, writing aids the physiological language and reading aids the social language.

We begin, then, as I have indicated, with the nomenclature, that is, with the reading of names of objects which are well known or present.

There is no question of beginning with words that are *easy or difficult,* for the *child already knows how to read any word;* that is, he knows how to read *the sounds which compose it.* I allow the little one to translate the written word slowly into sounds, and if the interpretation is exact, I limit myself to saying, "Faster." The child reads more quickly the second time, but still often without understanding. I then repeat, "Faster, faster." He reads faster each time, repeating the same accumulation of sounds, and finally the word bursts upon his consciousness. Then he looks upon it as if he recognized a friend, and assumes that air of satisfaction which so often radiates our little ones. This completes the exercise for reading. It is a lesson which goes very rapidly, since it is only presented to a child who is already prepared through writing. Truly, we have buried the tedious and stupid A B C primer side by side with the useless copybooks!

When the child has read the word, he places the explanatory card under the object whose name it bears, and the exercise is finished.

One of our most interesting discoveries was made in the effort to devise a game through which the children might, without effort, learn to read words. We spread out upon one of the large tables a great variety of toys. Each one of them had a corresponding card upon which the name of the toy was written. We folded these little cards and mixed them up in a basket, and the children who knew how to read were allowed to take turns in drawing these cards from the basket. Each child had to carry his card back to his desk, unfold it quietly, and read it mentally, not showing it to those about him. He then had to fold it up again, so that the secret which it contained should remain unknown. Taking the folded card in his hand, he went to the table. He had then to pronounce clearly the name of a toy and present the card to the directress in order that she might verify the word he had spoken. The little card thus became current coin with which he might acquire the toy he had named. For, if he pronounced the word clearly and indicated the correct object, the directress allowed him to take the toy, and to play with it as long as he wished.

When each child had had a turn, the directress called the first child and let him draw a card from another basket. This card he read as soon as he had drawn it. It contained the name of one of his companions who did not yet know how to read, and for that reason could not have a toy. The child who had read the name then offered to his little friend the toy with which he had been playing. We taught the children to present these toys in a gracious and polite way, accompanying the act with a bow. In this way we did away with every idea of class distinction, and inspired the sentiment of kindness toward those who did not possess the same blessings as ourselves.

This reading game proceeded in a marvelous way. The contentment of these poor children in possessing even for a little while such beautiful toys can be easily imagined.

But what was my amazement, when the children, having learned to understand the written cards, *refused* to take the toys! They explained that they did not wish to waste time in playing, and, with a species of insatiable desire, preferred to draw out and read the cards one after another![9] . . .

Coming into the school one day, I found that the directress had allowed the children to take the tables and chairs out upon the terrace, and was having school in the open air. A number of little ones were playing in the sun, while others were seated in a circle about the tables containing the sandpaper letters and the movable alphabet.

A little apart sat the directress, holding upon her lap a long narrow box full of written slips, and all along the edge of her box were little hands, fishing for the beloved cards. "You may not believe me," said the directress, "but it is more than an hour since we began this, and they are not satisfied yet!" We tried the experiment of bringing balls, and dolls to the children, but without result; such futilities had no power beside the joys of *knowledge*.

Seeing these surprising results, I had already thought of testing the children with print, and had suggested that the directress *print* the word under the written word upon a number of slips. But the children forestalled us! There was in the hall a calendar upon which many of the words were printed in clear type, while others were done in Gothic characters. In their mania for reading the children began to look at this calendar, and, to my inexpressible amazement, read not only the print, but the Gothic script.

There therefore remained nothing but the presentation of a book, and I did not feel that any of those available were suited to our method.

The mothers soon had proofs of the progress of their children; finding in the pockets of some of them little slips of paper upon which were written rough notes of marketing done; bread, salt, etc. Our children were making lists of the marketing they did for their mothers! Other mothers told us that their children no longer ran through the streets, but stopped to read the signs over the shops.[10] . . .

As to the average time required for learning to read and write, experience would seem to show that, starting from the moment in which the child writes, the passage from such an inferior stage of the graphic language to the superior state of reading averages a fortnight. *Security* in reading is, however, arrived at much more slowly than perfection in writing. In the greater majority of cases the child who writes beautifully, still reads rather poorly.

Not all children of the same age are at the same point in this matter of reading and writing. We not only do not force a child, but we do not even *invite* him, or in any way attempt to coax him to do that which he does not wish to do. So it sometimes happens that certain children, *not having spontaneously presented themselves* for these lessons, are left in peace, and do not know how to read or write.

If the old-time method, which tyrannized over the will of the child and destroyed his spontaneity, does not believe in making a knowledge of written language *obligatory* before the age of six, much less do we!

I am not ready to decide, without a wider experience, whether the period when the spoken language is fully developed is, in every case, the proper time for beginning to develop the written language.

In any case, almost all of the normal children treated with our method begin to write at four years, and at five know how to read and write, at least as well as children who have finished the first elementary. They could enter the second elementary a year in advance of the time when they are admitted to first.

Games for the Reading of Phrases. As soon as my friends saw that the children could read print, they made me gifts of beautifully illustrated books. Looking through these books of simple fairy lore, I felt sure that the children would not be able to understand them. The teachers, feeling entirely satisfied as to the ability of their pupils, tried to show me I was wrong, having different children read to me, and saying that they read much more perfectly than the children who had finished the second elementary.

I did not, however, allow myself to be deceived, and made two trials. I first had the teacher tell one of the stories to the children while I observed to what extent they were spontaneously interested in it. The attention of the children wandered after a few words. I had *forbidden* the teacher to recall to order those who did not listen, and thus, little by little, a hum arose in the schoolroom, due to the fact that each child, not caring to listen had returned to his usual occupation.

It was evident that the children, who seemed to read these books with such pleasure, *did not take pleasure in the sense,* but enjoyed the mechanical ability they had acquired, which consisted in translating the graphic signs into the sounds of a word they recognized. And, indeed, the children did not display the same *constancy* in the reading of books which they showed toward the written slips, since in the books they met with so many unfamiliar words.

My second test, was to have one of the children read the book to me. I did not interrupt with any of those explanatory remarks by means of which a teacher tries to help the child follow the thread of the story he is reading, saying for example: "Stop a minute. Do you understand? What have you read? You told me how the little boy went to drive in a big carriage, didn't you? Pay attention to what the book says, etc."

I gave the book to a little boy, sat down beside him in a friendly fashion, and when he had read I asked him simply and seriously as one would speak to a friend, "Did you understand what you were reading?" He replied: "No." But the expression of his face seemed to ask an explanation of my demand. In fact, the idea that *through the reading of a series of words the complex thoughts of others might be communicated to us,* was to be for my children one of the beautiful conquests of the future, a new source of surprise and joy.

The *book* has recourse to *logical language,* not to the mechanism of the language. Before the child can understand and enjoy a book, the *logical language* must be established in him. Between knowing how to read the *words,* and how to read the *sense,* of a book there lies the same distance that exists between knowing how to pronounce a word and how to make a speech. I, therefore, stopped the reading from books and waited.

One day, during a free conversation period, *four* children arose at the same time and with expressions of joy on their faces ran to the blackboard and wrote phrases upon the order of the following:

"Oh, how glad we are that our garden has begun to bloom." It was a great surprise for me, and I was deeply moved. These children had arrived spontaneously at the art of *composition,* just as they had spontaneously written their first word.

The mechanical preparation was the same, and the phenomenon developed logically. Logical articulate language had, when the time was ripe, provoked the corresponding explosion in written language.

I understood that the time had come when we might proceed to *the reading of phrases*. I had recourse to the means used by the children; that is, I wrote upon the blackboard, "Do you love me?" The children read it slowly aloud, were silent for a moment as if thinking, then cried out, "Yes! Yes!" I continued to write; "Then make the silence, and watch me." They read this aloud, almost shouting, but had barely finished when a solemn silence began to establish itself, interrupted only by the sounds of the chairs as the children took positions in which they could sit quietly. Thus began between me and them a communication by means of written language, a thing which interested the children intensely. Little by little, they *discovered* the great quality of writing—that it transmits thought. Whenever I began to write, they fairly *trembled* in their eagerness to understand what was my meaning without hearing me speak a word.

Indeed, *graphic* language does not need spoken words. It can only be understood in all its greatness when it is completely isolated from spoken language.

This introduction to reading was followed by the following game, which is greatly enjoyed by the children. Upon a number of cards I wrote long sentences describing certain actions which the children were to carry out; for example, "Close the window blinds; open the front door; then wait a moment, and arrange things as they were at first." "Very politely ask eight of your companions to leave their chairs, and to form in double file in the center of the room, then have them march forward and back on tiptoe, making no noise." "Ask three of your oldest companions who sing nicely, if they will please come into the centre of the room. Arrange them in a nice row, and sing with them a song that you have selected," etc., etc. As soon as I finished writing, the children seized the cards, and taking them to their seats read them spontaneously with great intensity of attention, and all *amid the most complete silence.*

I asked then, "Do you understand?" "Yes! Yes!" "Then do what the card tells you," said I, and was delighted to see the children rapidly and accurately follow the chosen action. A great activity, a movement of a new sort, was born in the room. There were those who closed the blinds, and then reopened them; others who made their companions run on tiptoe, or sing; others wrote upon the blackboard, or took certain objects from the cupboards. Surprise and curiosity produced a general silence, and the lesson developed amid the most intense interest. It seemed as if some magic force had gone forth from me stimulating an activity hitherto unknown. This magic was graphic language, the greatest conquest of civilization.

And how deeply the children understood the importance of it! When I went out, they gathered about me with expressions of gratitude and affection, saying, "Thank you! Thank you! Thank you for the lesson!"

This has become one of the favorite games: We first establish *profound silence,* then present a basket containing folded slips, upon each one of which is written a long phrase describing an action. All those children who know how to read may draw a slip, and read it *mentally* once or twice until they are certain they understand it. They then give the slip back to the directress and set about carrying out the action. Since many of these actions call for the help of the other children who do not know how to read, and since many of them call for the handling and use of the materials, a general activity develops amid marvelous order, while the silence is only interrupted by the sound of little feet running lightly, and by the voices of the children who sing. This is an unexpected revelation of the perfection of spontaneous discipline.

Experience has shown us that *composition* must *precede logical* reading, as writing preceded the reading of the word. It has also shown that reading, if it is to teach the child to *receive an idea,* should be *mental* and not *vocal.*

Reading aloud implies the exercise of two mechanical forms of the language—articulate and graphic—and is, therefore, a complex task. Who does not know that a grown person who is to read a paper in public prepares for this by making himself master of the content? Reading aloud is one of the most difficult intellectual actions. The child, therefore, who *begins* to read by interpreting thought *should read mentally.* The written language must isolate itself from the articulate, when it rises to the interpretation of logical thought. Indeed, it represents the language which *transmits thought at a distance,* while the senses and the muscular mechanism are silent. It is a spiritualized language, which puts into communication all men who know how to read.

Education having reached such a point in the "Children's Houses," the entire elementary school must, as a logical consequence, be changed. How to reform the lower grades in the elementary schools, eventually carrying them on according to our methods, is a great question which cannot be discussed here. I can only say that the *first elementary* would be completely done away with by our infant education, which includes it.

The elementary classes in the future should begin with children such as ours who know how to read and write; children who know how to take care of themselves; how to dress and undress, and to wash themselves; children who are familiar with the rules of good conduct and courtesy, and who are thoroughly disciplined in the highest sense of the term, having developed, and become masters of themselves, through liberty; children who possess, besides a perfect mastery of the articulate language, the ability to read written language in an elementary way, and who begin to enter upon the conquest of logical language.

These children pronounce clearly, write in a firm hand, and are full of grace in their movements. They are the earnest of a humanity grown in the cult of beauty—the infancy of an all-conquering humanity, since they are intelligent and patient observers of their environment, and possess in the form of intellectual liberty the power of spontaneous reasoning.

For such children, we should found an elementary school worthy to receive them and to guide them further along the path of life and of civilization, a school loyal to the same educational principles of respect for the freedom of the child and for his spontaneous manifestations—principles which shall form the personality of these little men.

Vogliamo augurare la buona Pasqua all'ingegnere Edoardo, Talamo e alla principessa Maria? Diremo che conducano qui i loro bei bambini. Lasciate fare a me: Scriverò io per tutti 7 Aprile 1909.

Example of writing done with pen, by a child of five years. One-fourth reduction. Translation: We would like to wish a joyous Easter to the civil engineer Edoardo Talamo and the Princess Maria. We will ask them to bring their pretty children here. Leave it to me: I will write for all. April 7, 1909.

EDITOR'S NOTES

1. Montessori's comments on the security a child experiences in holding and using a pencil on p. 274 that reiterates points made earlier are deleted.

2. Montessori's announcement that she will defer comments on language deficiencies caused by physiological problems to a later time on p. 280 is deleted.

3. Montessori's comments on the joy children experience in mastering language on p. 284, which reiterates points already made, is deleted.

4. Montessori's discussion of how a child spelled a visitor's name on p. 285 is deleted.

5. Montessori's comments on the pleasure children experience as they learn to write on pp. 287–88 that reiterate points already made are deleted.

6. Montessori's examples of the joy a child experiences when learning to write on pp. 288–89, 291, and 293–94 which reiterate earlier comments are deleted.

7. Two short paragraphs in which Montessori describes children's joy in writing are deleted on p. 291 (in the original).

8. An example of children playing with letters is deleted on pp. 293–94.

9. A short paragraph in which Montessori expressed her amazement at her pupils' achievements on p. 300 is deleted.

10. Montessori's description of the pleasure a child experiences in learning to read on pp. 301–2, reiterating points made earlier, is deleted.

18

Language in Childhood

Graphic language, comprising dictation and reading, contains articulate language in its complete mechanism (auditory channels, central channels, motor channels), and, in the manner of development called forth by my method, is based essentially on articulate language.

Graphic language, therefore, may be considered from two points of view:

(*a*) That of the conquest of a new language of eminent social importance which adds itself to the articulate language of natural man; and this is the cultural significance which is commonly given to graphic language, which is therefore taught in the schools without any consideration of its relation to spoken language, but solely with the intention of offering to the social being a necessary instrument in his relations with his fellows.

(*b*) That of the relation between graphic and articulate language and, in this relation, of an eventual possibility of utilizing the written language to perfect the spoken: a new consideration upon which I wish to insist and which gives to graphic language *a physiological importance*.

Moreover, as spoken language is at the same time a *natural function* of man and an instrument which he utilizes for social ends, so written language may be considered in itself, in its *formation*, as an organic *ensemble* of new mechanisms which are established in the nervous system, and as an instrument which may be utilized for social ends.

In short, it is a question of giving to written language not only a physiological importance, but also a *period of development* independent of the high functions which it is destined to perform later.

It seems to me that graphic language bristles with difficulties in its beginning, not only because it has heretofore been taught by irrational methods, but because we have tried to make it perform, as soon as it has been acquired, the high function of teaching *the written language* which has been fixed by centuries of perfecting in a civilized people.

Think how irrational have been the methods we have used! We have analyzed the graphic signs rather than the physiological acts necessary to produce the alphabetical signs; and this without considering that *any graphic sign* is difficult to achieve, because the visual representation of the signs have no hereditary connection with the motor representations necessary for producing them; as, for example, the auditory representations of the word have with the motor mechanism of the articulate language. It is, therefore, always a difficult thing to provoke a stimulative motor action unless we have already established the movement before the visual representation of the sign is made. It is a difficult thing to arouse an activity that shall produce a motion unless that motion shall have been previously established by practice and by the power of habit.

Thus, for example, the analysis of writing into *little straight lines and curves* has brought us to present to the child a sign without significance, which therefore does not interest him, and whose representation is incapable of determining a spontaneous motor impulse. The artificial act constituted, therefore, an *effort* of the will which resulted for the child in rapid exhaustion exhibited in the form of boredom and suffering. To this effort was added the effort of constituting *synchronously* the muscular associations coordinating the movements necessary to the holding and manipulating the instrument of writing.

All sorts of *depressing* feelings accompanied such efforts and conduced to the production of imperfect and erroneous signs which the teachers had to correct, discouraging the child still more with the constant criticism of the error and of the imperfection of the signs traced. Thus, while the child was urged to make an effort, the teacher depressed rather than revived his psychical forces.

Although such a mistaken course was followed, the graphic language, so painfully learned, was nevertheless to be *immediately* utilized for social ends; and, still imperfect and immature, was made to do service in the *syntactical construction of the language*, and in the ideal expression of the superior psychic centers. One must remember that in nature the spoken language is formed gradually.[1] . . .

This is the first stage of spoken language, which has its own beginning and its own development, leading, through the perceptions, to the *perfecting* of the primordial mechanism of the language itself; and at this stage precisely is established what we call *articulate language*, which will later be the means which the adult will have at his disposal to express his own thoughts, and which the adult will have great difficulty in perfecting or correcting when it has once been established: in fact a high stage of culture sometimes accompanies an imperfect articulate language which prevents the æsthetic expression of one's thought.

The development of articulate language takes place in the period between the age of two and the age of seven: the age of *perceptions* in which the attention of the child is spontaneously turned toward external objects, and the memory is particularly tenacious. It is the age also of *motility* in which all the psycho-motor channels are becoming permeable and the muscular mechanisms establish themselves. In this period of life by the mysterious bond between the auditory channel and the motor channel of the spoken language it would seem that the auditory perceptions have the direct power of *provoking* the complicated movements of articulate speech which develop instinctively after such stimuli as if awaking from the slumber of heredity. It is well known that it is only at this age that it is possible to acquire all the characteristic modulations of a language which it would be vain to attempt to establish later. The mother tongue alone is well pronounced because it was established in the period of childhood; and the adult who learns to speak a new language must bring to it the imperfections characteristic of the foreigner's speech: only children who under the *upon which we can directly act*, rendering the motor channels permeable, and establishing psycho-muscular mechanisms.

This indeed is what is done by my method, which *prepares the movements directly;* so that the psycho-motor impulse of the heard speech *finds the motor channels already established*, and is manifested in the act of writing, like an explosion.

The real difficulty is in the *interpretation of the graphic signs;* but we must remember that we are in the *age of perceptions*, where the sensations and the memory as well as the primitive associations are involved precisely in the characteristic progress of natural development. Moreover our children are already prepared by various exercises of the senses, and by methodical construction of ideas and mental associations to perceive the graphic signs; something like a patrimony of perceptive ideas offers material to the language in the process of development. The child who recognizes a triangle and calls it a triangle can recognize a letter *s* and denominate it by the sound *s*. This is obvious.

Let us not talk of premature teaching; ridding ourselves of prejudices, let us appeal to experience which shows that in reality children proceed without effort, nay rather with evident manifestations of pleasure to the recognition of graphic signs presented as objects.

And with this premise let us consider the relations between the mechanisms of the two languages.

The child of three or four has already long begun his articulate language according to our scheme. But he finds himself in the period in which the *mechanism of articulate language is being perfected;* a period contemporary with that in which he is acquiring a content of language along with the patrimony of perception.

The child has perhaps not heard perfectly in all their component parts the words which he pronounces, and, if he has heard them perfectly, they may have been pronounced badly, and consequently have left an erroneous auditory perception. It would be well that the child, by exercising the motor channels of articulate language should establish exactly the movements necessary to a perfect articulation, *before* the age of easy motor adaptations is passed, and, by the fixation of erroneous mechanisms, the defects become incorrigible.

To this end the *analysis of speech* is necessary. As when we wish to perfect the language we first start children at composition and then pass to grammatical study; and when we wish to perfect the style we first teach to write grammatically and then come to the analysis of style—so when we wish to perfect the *speech* it is first necessary that the speech *exist*, and then it is proper to proceed to its analysis. When, therefore, the child *speaks*, but before the completion of the development of speech which renders it fixed in mechanisms already established, the speech should be analyzed with a view to perfecting it.

Now, as grammar and rhetoric are not possible with the spoken language but demand recourse to the written language which keeps ever before the eye the discourse to be analyzed, so it is with speech.

The analysis of the transient is impossible.

The language must be materialized and made stable. Hence the necessity of the written word or the word represented by graphic signs.[2] . . .

DEFECTS OF LANGUAGE DUE TO LACK OF EDUCATION

Defects and imperfections of language are in part due to organic causes, consisting in malformations or in pathological alterations of the nervous system; but in part they are connected with functional defects acquired in the period of the formation of language and consist in an erratic pronunciation of the component sounds of the spoken word. Such errors are acquired by the child who hears words imperfectly pronounced, or *hears bad speech*. The dialectic accent enters into this category; but there also enter vicious habits which make the natural defects of the articulate language of childhood persist in the child, or which provoke in him by imitation the defects of language peculiar to the persons who surrounded him in his childhood.

The normal defects of child language are due to the fact that the complicated muscular agencies of the organs of articulate language do not yet function well and are consequently incapable of reproducing the *sound* which was the sensory stimulus of a certain innate movement. The association of the movements necessary to the articulation of the spoken words is established little by little. The result is a language made of words with sounds which are imperfect and often lacking (whence incomplete words). Such defects are grouped under the name *blæsitas* and are especially due to the fact that the child is not yet capable of directing the movements of his tongue.[3] . . .

If one considers the charm of human speech one is bound to acknowledge the inferiority of one who does not possess a correct spoken language; and an æsthetic conception in education cannot be imagined unless special care be devoted to perfecting articulate language. Although the Greeks had transmitted to Rome the art of educating in language, this practice was not resumed by Humanism which cared more for the æsthetics of the environment and the revival of artistic works than for the perfecting of the man.

Today we are just beginning to introduce the practice of correcting by pedagogical methods the serious defects of language, such as stammering; but the idea of *linguistic gymnastics* tending to its perfection has not yet penetrated into our schools as a *universal method*, and as a detail of the great work of the æsthetic perfecting of man.[4] . . .

But in my methods are to be found all exercises for the corrections of language:

(a) *Exercises of Silence*, which prepare the nervous channels of language to receive new stimuli perfectly;

(b) *Lessons* which consist first of the distinct pronunciation by the teacher of *few words* (especially of *nouns* which must be associated with a concrete idea); by this means clear and perfect *auditory stimuli* of language are started, stimuli which are *repeated* by the teacher when the child has conceived the idea of the object represented by the word (recognition of the object); finally of the provocation of articulate language on the part of the child who must repeat *that word alone* aloud, pronouncing its separate sounds;

(c) *Exercises in Graphic Language*, which analyze the sounds of speech and cause them to be repeated separately in several ways: that is, when the child learns the separate letters of the alphabet and when he composes or writes words, repeating their sounds which he translates separately into composed or written speech;

(d) *Gymnastic Exercises*, which comprise, as we have seen, both *respiratory exercises* and those of *articulation*.

I believe that in the schools of the future the conception will disappear which is beginning today of *"correcting in the elementary schools"* the defects of language; and will be replaced by the more rational one of *avoiding them by caring for the development of language* in the "Children's Houses"; that is, in the very age in which language is being established in the child.

EDITOR'S NOTES

1. Diagrams and Montessori's discussion of Kussmaul's theory of the development of graphic language on pp. 312–14 are deleted.

2. Diagrams and Montessori's discussion of mechanism for writing and speech on pp. 320–22 are deleted.

3. Montessori's reference to specific speech defects, based the theory of Wilhelm Preyer, on pp. 322–23 is deleted.

4. Montessori's statement that this is not the place to comment on practices in elementary schools regarding speech on p. 324 is deleted.

19

Teaching of Numeration: Introduction to Arithmetic

Children of three years already know how to count as far as two or three when they enter our schools. They therefore *very easily* learn numeration, which consists *in counting objects*. A dozen different ways may serve toward this end, and daily life presents many opportunities; when the mother says, for instance, "There are two buttons missing from your apron," or "We need three more plates at the table."

One of the first means used by me, is that of counting with money. I obtain *new* money, and if it were possible I should have good reproductions made in cardboard. I have seen such money used in a school for deficients in London.

The *making of change* is a form of numeration so attractive as to hold the attention of the child. I present the one, two, and four centime pieces and the children, in this way learn to count to *ten*.

No form of instruction is more *practical* than that tending to make children familiar with the coins in common use, and no exercise is more useful than that of making change. It is so closely related to daily life that it interests all children intensely.

Having taught numeration in this empiric mode, I pass to more methodical exercises, having as didactic material one of the sets of blocks already used in the education of the senses; namely, the series of ten rods heretofore used for the teaching of length. The shortest of these rods corresponds to a decimeter, the longest to a meter, while the intervening rods are divided into sections a decimeter in length. The sections are painted alternately red and blue.

Some day, when a child has arranged the rods, placing them in order of length, we have him count the red and blue signs, beginning with the smallest piece; that is, *one*; one, two; one, two, three, and so forth, always going back to one in the counting of each rod, and starting from the side A. We then have him name the

233

single rods from the shortest to the longest, according to the total number of the sections which each contains, touching the rods at the sides B, on which side the stair ascends. This results in the same numeration as when we counted the longest rod—1, 2, 3, 4, 5, 6, 7, 8, 9, 10. Wishing to know the number of rods, we count them from the side A and the same numeration results; 1, 2, 3, 4, 5, 6, 7, 8, 9, 10. This correspondence of the three sides of the triangle causes the child to verify his knowledge and as the exercise interests him he repeats it many times.

We now unite to the exercises in *numeration* the earlier, sensory exercises in which the child recognized the long and short rods. Having mixed the rods upon a carpet, the directress selects one, and showing it to the child, has him count the sections; for example, 5. She then asks him to give her the one next in length. He selects it *by his eye*, and the directress has him *verify* his choice by *placing the two pieces side by side and by counting their sections.* Such exercises may be repeated in great variety and through them the child learns to assign a *particular name to each one of the pieces in the long stair.* We may now call them piece number one; piece number two, etc., and finally, for brevity, may speak of them in the lessons as one, two, three, etc.

THE NUMBERS AS REPRESENTED BY THE GRAPHIC SIGNS

At this point, if the child already knows how to write, we may present the figures cut in sandpaper and mounted upon cards. In presenting these, the method is the same used in teaching the letters. "This is one." "This is two." "Give me one." "Give me two." "What *number* is this?" The child traces the number with his finger as he did the letters.

Exercises with Numbers. Association of the graphic sign with the quantity.

I have designed two trays each divided into five little compartments. At the back of each compartment may be placed a card bearing a figure. The figures in the first tray should be 0, 1, 2, 3, 4, and in the second, 5, 6, 7, 8, 9.

The exercise is obvious; it consists in placing within the compartments a number of objects corresponding to the figure indicated upon the card at the back of the compartment. We give the children various objects in order to vary the lesson, but chiefly make use of large wooden pegs so shaped that they will not roll off the desk. We place a number of these before the child whose part is to arrange them in their places, one peg corresponding to the card marked one,and so forth. When he has finished he takes his tray to the directress that she may verify his work.

The Lesson on Zero. We wait until the child, pointing to the compartment containing the card marked zero, asks, "And what must I put in here?" We

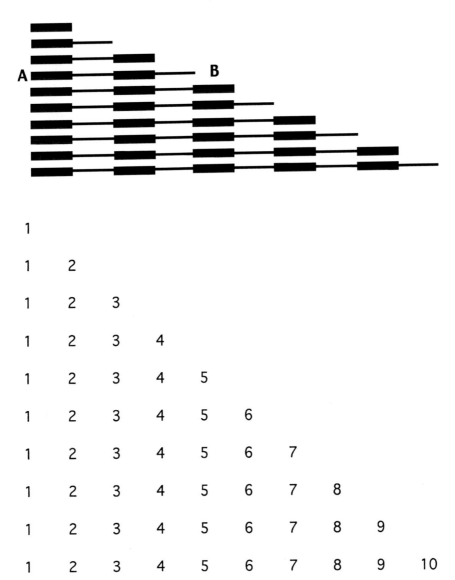

then reply, "Nothing; zero is nothing." But often this is not enough. It is necessary to make the child *feel* what we mean by *nothing*. To this end we make use of little games which vastly entertain the children. I stand among them, and turning to one of them who has already used this material, I say, "Come, dear, come to me *zero* times." The child almost always comes to me, and then runs back to his place. "But, my boy, you came *one* time, and I told you to come *zero* times." Then he begins to wonder. "But what must I do, then?" "Nothing; zero is nothing." "But how shall I do nothing?" "Don't do anything. You must sit still. You must not come at all, not any times. Zero times. No times at all." I repeat these exercises until the children understand, and they are then immensely amused at remaining quiet when I call to them to come to me zero times, or to throw me zero kisses. They themselves often cry out, "Zero is nothing! Zero is nothing!"

EXERCISES FOR THE MEMORY OF NUMBERS

When the children recognize the written figure, and when this figure signifies to them the numerical value, I give them the following exercise:

I cut the figures from old calendars and mount them upon slips of paper which are then folded and dropped into a box. The children draw out the slips, carry them still folded, to their seats, where they look at them and re-fold them, *conserving the secret*. Then, one by one, or in groups, these children (who are naturally the oldest ones in the class) go to the large table of the directress where groups of various small objects have been placed. Each one selects *the quantity* of objects corresponding to the number he has drawn. The number, meanwhile, has been left *at the child's place*, a slip of paper mysteriously folded. The child, therefore, must *remember* his number not only during the movements which he makes in coming and going, but while he collects his pieces, counting them one by one. The directress may here make interesting individual observations upon the number memory.

When the child has gathered up his objects he arranges them upon his own table, in columns of two, and if the number is uneven, he places the odd piece at the bottom and between the last two objects. The arrangement of the pieces is therefore as follows:

```
o    o    o    o    o    o    o    o    o    o
x    xx   xx   xx   xx   xx   xx   xx   xx   xx
          x    xx   xx   xx   xx   xx   xx   xx
                    x    xx   xx   xx   xx   xx
                              x    xx   xx   xx
                                        x    xx
```

The crosses represent the objects, while the circle stands for the folded slip containing the figure. Having arranged his objects, the child awaits the verification. The directress comes, opens the slip, reads the number, and counts the pieces.

When we first played this game it often happened that the children took *more objects* than were called for upon the card, and this was not always because they did not remember the number, but arose from a mania for the having the greatest number of objects. A little of that instinctive greediness, which is common to primitive and uncultured man. The directress seeks to explain to the children that it is useless to have all those things upon the desk, and that the point of the game lies in taking the exact number of objects called for.

Little by little they enter into this idea, but not so easily as one might suppose. It is a real effort of self-denial which holds the child within the set limit, and makes him take, for example, only two of the objects placed at his disposal, while he sees others taking more. I therefore consider this game more an exercise of will power than of numeration. The child who has the *zero*, should not move from his place when he sees all his companions rising and taking freely of the objects which are inaccessible to him. Many times zero falls to the lot of a child who knows how to count perfectly, and who would experience great pleasure in accumulating and arranging a fine group of objects in the proper order upon his table, and in awaiting with security the teacher's verification.

It is most interesting to study the expressions upon the faces of those who possess zero. The individual differences which result are almost a revelation of the "character" of each one. Some remain impassive, assuming a bold front in order to hide the pain of the disappointment; others show this disappointment by involuntary gestures. Still others cannot hide the smile which is called forth by the singular situation in which they find themselves, and which will make their friends curious. There are little ones who follow every movement of their companions with a look of desire, almost of envy, while others show instant acceptance of the situation. No less interesting are the expressions with which they confess to the holding of the zero, when asked during the verification, "and you, you haven't taken anything?" "I have zero." "It is zero." These are the usual words, but the expressive face, the tone of the voice, show widely varying sentiments. Rare, indeed, are those who seem to give with pleasure the explanation of an extraordinary fact. The greater number either look unhappy or merely resigned.

We therefore give lessons upon the meaning of the game, saying, "It is hard to keep the zero secret. Fold the paper tightly and don't let it slip away. It is the most difficult of all." Indeed, after awhile, the very difficulty of remaining quiet appeals to the children, and when they open the slip marked zero it can be seen that they are content to keep the secret.

ADDITION AND SUBTRACTION FROM ONE TO TWENTY:
MULTIPLICATION AND DIVISION

The didactic material which we use for the teaching of the first arithmetical operations is the same already used for numeration; that is, the rods graduated as to length which, arranged on the scale of the meter, contain the first idea of the decimal system.

The rods, as I have said, have come to be called by the numbers which they represent; one, two, three, etc. They are arranged in order of length, which is also in order of numeration.

The first exercise consists in trying to put the shorter pieces together in such a way as to form tens. The most simple way of doing this is to take successively the shortest rods, from one up, and place them at the end of the corresponding long rods from nine down. This may be accompanied by the commands. "Take one and add it to nine; take two and add it to eight; take three and add it to seven; take four and add it to six." In this way we make four rods equal to ten. There remains the five, but, turning this upon its head (in the long sense), it passes from one end of the ten to the other, and thus makes clear the fact that two times five makes ten.

These exercises are repeated and little by little the child is taught the more technical language; nine plus one equals ten, eight plus two equals ten, seven plus three equals ten, six plus four equals ten, and for the five, which remains, two times five equals ten. At last, if he can write, we teach the signs *plus* and *equals* and *times*. Then this is what we see in the neat notebooks of our little ones:

$$9 + 1 = 10$$
$$8 + 2 = 10$$
$$5 \times 2 = 10$$
$$7 + 3 = 10$$
$$6 + 4 = 10$$

When all this is well learned and has been put upon the paper with great pleasure by the children, we call their attention to the work which is done when the pieces grouped together to form tens are taken apart, and put back in their original positions. From the ten last formed we take away four and six remains; from the next we take away three and seven remains; from the next, two and eight remains; from the last, we take away one and nine remains. Speaking of this properly we say, ten less four equals six; ten less three equals seven; ten less two equals eight; ten less one equals nine.

In regard to the remaining five, it is the half of ten, and by cutting the long rod in two, that is dividing ten by two, we would have five; ten divided by two equals five. The written record of all this reads:

$$10 - 4 = 6$$
$$10 - 3 = 7$$
$$10 \div 2 = 5$$
$$10 - 2 = 8$$
$$10 - 1 = 9$$

Once the children have mastered this exercise they multiply it spontaneously. Can we make three in two ways? We place the one after the two and then write, in order that we may remember what we have done, $2 + 1 = 3$. Can we make two rods equal to number four? $3 + 1 = 4$, and $4 - 3 = 1$; $4 - 1 = 3$. Rod number two in its relation to rod number four is treated as was five in relation to ten; that is, we turn it over and show that it is contained in four exactly two times: $4 \div 2 = 2$; $2 \times 2 = 4$. Another problem: let us see with how many rods we can play this same game. We can do it with three and six; and with four and eight; that is,

$2 \times 2 = 4$	$3 \times 2 = 6$	$4 \times 2 = 8$	$5 \times 2 = 10$
$10 \div 2 = 5$	$8 \div 2 = 4$	$6 \div 2 = 3$	$4 \div 2 = 2$

At this point we find that the cubes with which we played the number memory games are of help:

From this arrangement, one sees at once which are the numbers which can be divided by two—all those which have not an odd cube at the bottom. These are the *even* numbers, because they can be arranged in pairs, two by two; and the division by two is easy, all that is necessary being to separate the two lines of twos that stand one under the other. Counting the cubes of each file we have the quotient. To recompose the primitive number we need only reassemble the two files thus $2 \times 3 = 6$. All this is not difficult for children of five years.

The repetition soon becomes monotonous, but the exercises may be most easily changed, taking again the set of long rods, and instead of placing rod number one after nine, place it after ten. In the same way, place two after nine, and three after eight. In this way we make rods of a greater length than ten; lengths which we must learn to name eleven, twelve, thirteen, etc., as far as twenty. The little cubes, too, may be used to fix these higher numbers.

Having learned the operations through ten, we proceed with no difficulty to twenty. The one difficulty lies in the *decimal numbers* which require certain lessons.

LESSONS ON DECIMALS:
ARITHMETICAL CALCULATIONS BEYOND TEN

The necessary didactic material consists of a number of square cards upon which the figure ten is printed in large type, and of other rectangular cards, half the size of the square, and containing the single numbers from one to nine. We place the numbers in a line; 1, 2, 3, 4, 5, 6, 7, 8, 9, 10. Then, having no more numbers, we must begin over again and take the 1 again. This 1 is like that section in the set of rods which, in rod number 10, extends beyond nine. Counting along *the stair* as far as nine, there remains this one section which, as there are no more numbers, we again designate as 1; but this is a higher 1 than the first, and to distinguish it from the first we put near it a zero, a sign which means nothing. Here then is 10. Covering the zero with the separate rectangular number cards in the order of their succession we see formed: 11, 12, 13, 14, 15, 16, 17, 18, 19. These numbers are composed by adding to rod number 10, first rod number 1, then 2, then 3, etc., until we finally add rod number 9 to rod number 10, thus obtaining a very long rod, which, when its alternating red and blue sections are counted, gives us nineteen.

The directress may then show to the child the cards, giving the number 16, and he may place rod 6 after rod 10. She then takes away the card bearing 6, and places over the zero the card bearing the figure 8, whereupon the child takes away rod 6 and replaces it with rod 8, thus making 18. Each of these acts may be recorded thus: $10 + 6 = 16$; $10 + 8 = 18$, etc. We proceed in the same way to subtraction.

When the number itself begins to have a clear meaning to the child, the combinations are made upon one long card, arranging the rectangular cards bearing the nine figures upon the two columns of numbers shown in the figures A and B.

10		10
10		20
10		30
10		40
10	A	50
10		60
10		70
10		80
10		90

Upon the card A we superimpose upon the zero of the second 10, the rectangular card bearing the 1: and under this the one bearing two, etc. Thus while the one of the ten remains the same the numbers to the right proceed from zero to nine, thus:

In card B the applications are more complex. The cards are superimposed in numerical progression by tens.

Almost all our children count to 100, a number which was given to them in response to the curiosity they showed in regard to learning it.

10
11
12
13
14
15
16
17
18
19
20

I do not believe that this phase of the teaching needs further illustrations. Each teacher may multiply the practical exercises in the arithmetical operations, using simple objects which the children can readily handle and divide.

20

Sequence of Exercises

In the practical application of the method it is helpful to know the sequence, or the various series, of exercises which must be presented to the child successively.

In the first edition of my book there was clearly indicated a progression for each exercise; but in the "Children's Houses" we began contemporaneously with the most varied exercises; and it develops that there exist *grades* in the presentation of the material in its entirety. These grades have, since the first publication of the book, become clearly defined through experience in the "Children's Houses."[1]

SEQUENCE AND GRADES IN THE
PRESENTATION OF MATERIAL AND IN THE EXERCISES

First Grade

As soon as the child comes to the school he may be given the following exercises:

Moving the seats, in silence (practical life).
Lacing, buttoning, hooking, and so forth.
The cylinders (sense exercises).

Among these the most useful exercise is that of the cylinders (solid insets). The child here begins to *fix his attention*. He makes his first comparison, his first selection, in which he exercises judgment. Therefore he exercises his intelligence.

Among these exercises with the solid insets, there exists the following progression from easy to difficult:

(*a*) The cylinders in which the pieces are of the same height and of decreasing diameter.

(*b*) The cylinders decreasing in all dimensions.

(*c*) Those decreasing only in height.

Second Grade

Exercises of Practical Life. To rise and be seated in silence. To walk on the line.

Sense Exercises. Material dealing with dimensions. The Long Stair. The prisms, or Big Stair. The cubes. Here the child makes exercises in the recognition of dimensions as he did in the cylinders but under a very different aspect. The objects are much larger. The differences much more evident than they were in the preceding exercises, but here, *only the eye of the child* recognizes the differences and controls the errors. In the preceding exercises, the errors were mechanically revealed to the child by the didactic material itself. The impossibility of placing the objects in order in the block in any other than their respective spaces gives this control. Finally, while in the preceding exercises the child makes much more simple movements (being seated he places little objects in order with his hands), in these new exercises he accomplishes movements which are decidedly more complex and difficult and makes small muscular efforts. He does this by moving from the table to the carpet, rises, kneels, carries heavy objects.

We notice that the child continues to be confused between the two last pieces in the growing scale, being for a long time unconscious of such an error after he has learned to put the other pieces in correct order. Indeed the difference between these pieces being throughout the varying dimensions the same for all, the relative difference diminishes with the increasing size of the pieces themselves. For example, the little cube which has a base of 2 centimeters is double the size, as to base, of the smallest cube which has a base of 1 centimeter, while the largest cube having a base of 10 centimeters, differs by barely from the base of the cube next it in the series (the one of 9 centimeters base).

Thus it would seem that, theoretically, in such exercises we should begin with the smallest piece. We can, indeed, do this with the material through which size and length are taught. But we cannot do so with the cubes, which must be arranged as a little "tower." This column of blocks must always have as its base the largest cube.

The children, attracted above all by the tower, begin very early to play with it. Thus we often see very little children playing with the tower, happy in believing that they have constructed it, when they have inadvertently used the next to the largest cube as the base. But when the child, repeating the exercise, *corrects himself of his own accord*, in a permanent fashion, we may be certain that *his eye* has become trained to perceive even the slightest differences between the pieces.

In the three systems of blocks through which dimensions are taught that of length has pieces differing from each other by 10 centimeters, while in the other two sets, the pieces differ only 1 centimeter. Theoretically it would seem that the long rods *should be the first to attract the attention* and to exclude errors. This, however, is not the case. The children are attracted by this set of blocks, but they commit the greatest number of errors in using it, and only after they have for a long time eliminated every error in constructing the other two sets, do they succeed in arranging the Long Stair perfectly. This may then be considered as the most difficult among the series through which dimensions are taught.

Arrived at this point in his education, the child is capable of fixing his attention, with interest, upon the thermic and tactile stimuli.[2] . . .

Together with the two series of sense exercises described above, we may begin what we call the "pairing of the colors," that is, the recognition of the identity of two colors. This is the first exercise of the chromatic sense.

Here, also, it is only the *eye* of the child that intervenes in the judgment, as it was with the exercises in dimension. This first color exercise is easy, but the child must already have acquired a certain grade of education of the attention through preceding exercises, if he is to repeat this one with interest.

Meanwhile, the child has heard music; has walked on the line, while the directress played a rhythmic march. Little by little he has learned to accompany the music spontaneously with certain movements. This of course necessitates the repetition of the same music. (To acquire the sense of rhythm *the repetition of the same exercise is necessary*, as in all forms of education dealing with spontaneous activity.)

The exercises in silence are also repeated.

Third Grade

Exercises of Practical Life. The children wash themselves, dress and undress themselves, dust the tables, learn to handle various objects, etc.

Sense Exercises. We now introduce the child to the recognition of gradations of stimuli (tactile gradations, chromatic, etc.), allowing him to exercise himself freely.

We begin to present the stimuli for the sense of hearing (sounds, noises), and also the baric stimuli (the little tablets differing in weight).

Contemporaneously with the gradations we may present the *plane geometric insets*. Here begins the education of the movement of the hand in following the contours of the insets, an exercise which, together with the other and contemporaneous one of the recognition of tactile stimuli in gradation, *prepares for writing*.

The series of cards bearing the geometric forms, we give after the child recognizes perfectly the same forms in the wooden insets. These cards serve to prepare for the *abstract signs* of which writing consists. The child learns to recognize a delineated form, and after all the preceding exercises have formed within him an ordered and intelligent personality, they may be considered the bridge by which he passes from the sense exercises to writing, from the *preparation*, to the actual *entrance into instruction*.

Fourth Grade

Exercises of Practical Life. The children set and clear the table for luncheon. They learn to put a room in order. They are now taught the most minute care of their persons in the making of the toilet. (How to brush their teeth, to clean their nails, etc.)

They have learned, through the rhythmic exercises on the line, to walk with perfect freedom and balance.

They know how to control and direct their own movements (how to make the silence—how to move various objects without dropping or breaking them and without making a noise).

Sense Exercises. In this stage we repeat all the sense exercises. In addition we introduce the recognition of musical notes by the help of the series of duplicate bells.

Exercises Related to Writing. Design. The child passes to the *plane geometric insets in metal*. He has already coordinated the movements necessary to follow the contours. Here he no longer *follows them with his finger*, but with a pencil, leaving the double sign upon a sheet of paper. Then he fills in the figures with colored pencils, holding the pencil as he will later hold the pen in writing.

Contemporaneously the child is taught to *recognize* and *touch* some of the letters of the alphabet made in sandpaper.

Exercises in Arithmetic. At this point, repeating the sense exercises, we present the Long Stair with a different aim from that with which it has been used up to the present time. We have the child *count* the different pieces, according to the blue and red sections, beginning with the rod consisting of one section and continuing through that composed of ten sections. We continue such exercises and give other more complicated ones.

In Design we pass from the outlines of the geometric insets to such outlined figures as the practice of four years has established and which will be published as models in design.

These have an educational importance, and represent in their content and in their gradations one of the most carefully studied details of the method.

They serve as a means for the continuation of the sense education and help the child to observe his surroundings. They thus add to his intellectual refinement, and, as regards writing, they prepare for the high and low strokes. After such practice it will be *easy for the child to make high or low letters*, and this will do away with the *ruled notebooks* such as are used in Italy in the various elementary classes.

In the *acquiring* of the use of *written language* we go as far as the knowledge of the letters of the alphabet, and of composition with the movable alphabet.

In Arithmetic, as far as a knowledge of the figures. The child places the corresponding figures beside the number of blue and red sections on each rod of the Long Stair.

The children now take the exercise with the wooden pegs.

Also the games which consist in placing under the figures, on the table, a corresponding number of colored counters. These are arranged in columns of twos, thus making the question of odd and even numbers clear. (This arrangement is taken from Seguin.)

Fifth Grade

We continue the preceding exercises. We begin more complicated rhythmic exercises.

In design we begin:

(*a*) The use of water colors.
(*b*) Free drawing from nature (flowers, etc.).

Composition of words and phrases with the movable alphabet.

(*a*) Spontaneous writing of words and phrases.
(*b*) Reading from slips prepared by the directress.

We continue the arithmetical operations which we began with the Long Stair.

The children at this stage present most interesting differences of development. They fairly *run* toward instruction, and order their *intellectual growth* in a way that is remarkable.

This joyous growth is what we so rejoice in, as we watch in these children, humanity, growing in the spirit according to its own deep laws. And only he who experiments can say how great may be the harvest from the sowing of such seed.

EDITOR'S NOTES

1. Montessori discussion of using appropriate didactic materials according to grades refers to levels in the Montessori school and should not be confused with grades in the American school system.

2. Montessori reiteration of points made in earlier chapters on sense development and training on p. 341 is deleted.

21

General Review of Discipline

The accumulated experience we have had since the publication of the Italian version has repeatedly proved to us that in our classes of little children, numbering forty and even fifty, the discipline is much better than in ordinary schools. For this reason I have thought that an analysis of the discipline obtained by our method—which is based upon liberty—would interest my American readers.

Whoever visits a well-kept school (such as, for instance, the one in Rome directed by my pupil Anna Maccheroni) is struck by the discipline of the children. There are forty little beings—from three to seven years old, each one intent on his own work; one is going through one of the exercises for the senses, one is doing an arithmetical exercise; one is handling the letters, one is drawing, one is fastening and unfastening the pieces of cloth on one of our little wooden frames, still another is dusting. Some are seated at the tables, some on rugs on the floor. There are muffled sounds of objects lightly moved about, of children tiptoeing. Once in a while comes a cry of joy only partly repressed, "Teacher! Teacher!" an eager call, "Look! see what I've done." But as a rule, there is entire absorption in the work in hand.

The teacher moves quietly about, goes to any child who calls her, supervising operations in such a way that anyone who needs her finds her at his elbow, and whoever does not need her is not reminded of her existence. Sometimes, hours go by without a word. They seem "little men," as they were called by some visitors to the "Children's House"; or, as another suggested, "judges in deliberation."

In the midst of such intense interest in work it never happens that quarrels arise over the possession of an object. If one accomplishes something especially fine, his achievement is a source of admiration and joy to others: no heart suffers from another's wealth, but the triumph of one is a delight to all. Very often he finds ready imitators. They all seem happy and satisfied to do what they can, without feeling jealous of the deeds of others. The little fellow of three works peaceably beside the boy of seven, just as he is satisfied with his own height and does not envy the older boy's stature. Everything is growing in the most profound peace.

If the teacher wishes the whole assembly to do something, for instance, leave the work which interests them so much, all she needs to do is to speak a word in a low tone, or make a gesture, and they are all attention, they look toward her with eagerness, anxious to know how to obey. Many visitors have seen the teacher write orders on the blackboard, which were obeyed joyously by the children. Not only the teachers, but anyone who asks the pupils to do something is astonished to see them obey in the minutest detail and with obliging cheerfulness. Often a visitor wishes to hear how a child, now painting, can sing. The child leaves his painting to be obliging, but the instant his courteous action is completed, he returns to his interrupted work. Sometimes the smaller children finish their work before they obey.

A very surprising result of this discipline came to our notice during the examinations of the teachers who had followed my course of lectures. These examinations were practical, and, accordingly, groups of children were put at the disposition of the teachers being examined, who, according to the subject drawn by lot, took the children through a given exercise. While the children were waiting their turn, they were allowed to do just as they pleased. *They worked incessantly*, and returned to their undertakings as soon as the interruption caused by the examination was over. Every once in a while, one of them came to show us a drawing made during the interval.[1] . . .

Anyone who has watched them setting the table must have passed from one surprise to another. Little four-year-old waiters take the knives and forks and spoons and distribute them to the different places; they carry trays holding as many as five water glasses, and finally they go from table to table, carrying big tureens full of hot soup. Not a mistake is made, not a glass is broken, not a drop of soup is spilled. All during the meal unobtrusive little waiters watch the table assiduously; not a child empties his soup plate without being offered more; if he is ready for the next course a waiter briskly carries off his soup plate. Not a child is forced to ask for more soup, or to announce that he has finished.

Remembering the usual condition of four-year-old children, who cry, who break whatever they touch, who need to be waited on, everyone is deeply moved by the sight I have just described, which evidently results from the development of energies latent in the depths of the human soul. I have often seen the spectators at this banquet of little ones, moved to tears.

But such discipline could never be obtained by commands, by sermonizings, in short, through any of the disciplinary devices universally known. Not only were the actions of those children set in an orderly condition, but their very lives were deepened and enlarged. In fact, such discipline is on the same plane with school exercises extraordinary for the age of the children; and it certainly does not depend upon the teacher but upon a sort of miracle, occurring in the inner life of each child.[2] . . .

The first dawning of real discipline comes through work. At a given moment it happens that a child becomes keenly interested in a piece of work, showing it by the expression of his face, by his intense attention, by his perseverance in the same exercise. That child has set foot upon the road leading to discipline. Whatever be his undertaking—an exercise for the senses, an exercise in buttoning up or lacing together, or washing dishes—it is all one and the same.

On our side, we can have some influence upon the permanence of this phenomenon, by means of repeated "Lessons of Silence." The perfect immobility, the attention alert to catch the sound of the names whispered from a distance, then the carefully coordinated movements executed so as not to strike against chair or table, so as barely to touch the floor with the feet—all this is a most efficacious preparation for the task of setting in order the whole personality, the motor forces and the psychical.

Once the habit of work is formed, we must supervise it with scrupulous accuracy, graduating the exercises as experience has taught us. In our effort to establish discipline, we must rigorously apply the principles of the method. It is not to be obtained by words; no man learns self-discipline "through hearing another man speak." The phenomenon of discipline needs as preparation a series of complete actions, such as are presupposed in the genuine application of a really educative method. Discipline is reached always by indirect means. The end is obtained, not by attacking the mistake and fighting it, but by developing activity in spontaneous work.

This work cannot be arbitrarily offered, and it is precisely here that our method enters; it must be work which the human being instinctively desires to do, work toward which the latent tendencies of life naturally turn, or toward which the individual step by step ascends.

Such is the work which sets the personality in order and opens wide before it infinite possibilities of growth. Take, for instance, the lack of control shown by a baby; it is fundamentally a lack of muscular discipline. The child is in a constant state of disorderly movement: he throws himself down, he makes queer gestures, he cries. What underlies all this is a latent tendency to seek that coordination of movement which will be established later. The baby is a man not yet sure of the movements of the various muscles of the body; not yet master of the organs of speech. He will eventually establish these various movements, but for the present he is abandoned to a period of experimentation full of mistakes, and of fatiguing efforts toward a desirable end latent in his instinct, but not clear in his consciousness. To say to the baby, "Stand still as I do," brings no light into his darkness; commands cannot aid in the process of bringing order into the complex psycho-muscular system of an individual in process of evolution. We are confused at this point by the example of the adult who through a wicked impulse *prefers* disorder, and who may (granted that he can) obey a sharp admonishment which turns his will in another direction, toward that order which he recognizes and which it is within his capacity to achieve. In the case of the little child it is a question of aiding the natural evolution of voluntary action. Hence it is necessary to teach all the coordinated movements, analysing them as much as possible and developing them bit by bit.

Thus, for instance, it is necessary to teach the child the various degrees of immobility leading to silence; the movements connected with rising from a chair and sitting down, with walking, with tiptoeing, with following a line drawn on the floor keeping an upright equilibrium. The child is taught to move objects about, to set them down more or less carefully, and finally the complex movements connected with dressing and undressing himself (analyzed on the lacing and buttoning frames at school), and for even each of these exercises, the different parts of the movement must be analyzed. Perfect immobility and the successive perfecting of action, is what takes the place of the customary command, "Be quiet! Be still!" It is not astonishing but very natural that the child by means of such exercises should acquire self-discipline, so far as regards the lack of muscular discipline natural to his age. In short, he responds to nature because he is in action; but these actions being directed toward an end, have no longer the appearance of disorder but of work. This is discipline which represents an end to be attained by means of a number of conquests. The child disciplined in this way, is no longer the child he was at first, who knows how to *be* good passively; but he is an individual who has made himself better, who has overcome the usual limits of his age, who has made a great step forward, who has conquered his future in his present.

He has therefore enlarged his dominion. He will not need to have someone always at hand, to tell him vainly (confusing two opposing conceptions), "Be quiet! Be good!" The goodness he has conquered cannot be summed up by inertia: his goodness is now all made up of action. As a matter of fact, good people are those who advance toward the good—that good which is made up of their own self-development and of external acts of order and usefulness.

In our efforts with the child, external acts are the means which stimulate internal development, and they again appear as its manifestation, the two elements being inextricably intertwined. Work develops the child spiritually; but the child with a fuller spiritual development works better, and his improved work delights him—hence he continues to develop spiritually. Discipline is, therefore, not a fact but a path, a path in following which the child grasps the abstract conception of goodness with an exactitude which is fairly scientific.

But beyond everything else he savors the supreme delights of that spiritual *order* which is attained indirectly through conquests directed toward determinate ends. In that long preparation, the child experiences joys, spiritual awakenings, and pleasures which form his inner treasure-house—the treasure-house in which he is steadily storing up the sweetness and strength which will be the sources of righteousness.

In short, the child has not only learned to move about and to perform useful acts; he has acquired a special grace of action which makes his gestures more correct and attractive, and which beautifies his hands and indeed his entire body now so balanced and so sure of itself; a grace which refines the expression of his face and of his serenely brilliant eyes, and which shows us that the flame of spiritual life has been lighted in another human being.

It is obviously true that coordinated actions, developed spontaneously little by little (that is, chosen and carried out in the exercises by the child himself), must call for less effort than the disorderly actions performed by the child who is left to his own devices. True rest for muscles, intended by nature for action, is in orderly action; just as true rest for the lungs is the normal rhythm of respiration taken in pure air. To take action away from the muscles is to force them away from their natural motor impulse, and hence, besides tiring them, means forcing them into a state of degeneration; just as the lungs forced into immobility, would die instantly and the whole organism with them.[3] . . .

A similar error is that which we repeat so frequently when we fancy that the desire of the student is to possess a piece of information. We aid him to grasp intellectually this detached piece of knowledge, and, preventing by this means his self-development, we make him wretched. It is generally believed in schools that the way to attain satisfaction is "to learn something." But by leaving the children in our schools in liberty we have been able with great clearness to follow them in their natural method of spontaneous self-development.

To have learned something is for the child only a point of departure. When he has learned the meaning of an exercise, then he begins to enjoy repeating it, and he does repeat it an infinite number of times, with the most evident satisfaction. He enjoys executing that act because by means of it he is developing his psychic activities.

There results from the observation of this fact a criticism of what is done today in many schools. Often, for instance when the pupils are questioned, the teacher says to someone who is eager to answer, "No, not you, because you know it" and puts her question specially to the pupils who she thinks are uncertain of the answer. Those who do not know are made to speak, those who do know to be silent. This happens because of the general habit of considering the act of knowing something as final.

And yet how many times it happens to us in ordinary life to *repeat* the very thing we know best, the thing we care most for, the thing to which some living force in us responds. We love to sing musical phrases very familiar, hence enjoyed and become a part of the fabric of our lives. We love to repeat stories of things which please us, which we know very well, even though we are quite aware that we are saying nothing new. No matter how many times we repeat the Lord's Prayer, it is always new. No two persons could be more convinced of mutual love than sweethearts and yet they are the very ones who repeat endlessly that they love each other.

But in order to repeat in this manner, there must first exist the idea to be repeated. A mental grasp of the idea is indispensable to the beginning of *repetition*. The exercise which develops life, consists *in the repetition, not in the mere grasp of the idea*. When a child has attained this stage, of repeating an exercise, he is on the way to self-development, and the external sign of this condition is his self-discipline.

This phenomenon does not always occur. The same exercises are not repeated by children of all ages. In fact, repetition corresponds to a *need*. Here steps in the experimental method of education. It is necessary to offer those exercises which correspond to the need of development felt by an organism, and if the child's age has carried him past a certain need, it is never possible to obtain, in its fullness, a development which missed its proper moment. Hence children grow up, often fatally and irrevocably, imperfectly developed.

Another very interesting observation is that which relates to the length of time needed for the execution of actions. Children, who are undertaking something for the first time are extremely slow. Their life is governed in this respect by laws especially different from ours. Little children accomplish slowly and perseveringly, various complicated operations agreeable to them, such as dressing, undressing, cleaning the room, washing themselves, setting the table, eating, etc. In all this they are extremely patient, overcoming all the difficulties presented by an organism still in process of formation. But we, on the other hand, noticing that they are "tiring themselves out" or "wasting time" in accomplishing something which we would do in a moment and without the least effort, put ourselves in the child's place and do it ourselves. Always with the same erroneous idea, that the end to be obtained is the completion of the action, we dress and wash the child, we snatch out of his hands objects which he loves to handle, we pour the soup into his bowl, we feed him, we set the table for him. And after such services, we consider him with that injustice always practiced by those who domineer over others even with benevolent intentions, to be incapable and inept. We often speak of him as "impatient" simply because we are not patient enough to allow his actions to follow laws of time differing from our own; we call him "tyrannical" exactly because we employ tyranny toward him. This stain, this false imputation, this calumny on childhood has become an integral part of the theories concerning childhood, in reality so patient and gentle.

The child, like every strong creature fighting for the right to live, rebels against whatever offends that occult impulse within him which is the voice of nature, and which he ought to obey; and he shows by violent actions, by screaming, and weeping that he has been overborne and forced away from his mission in life. He shows himself to be a rebel, a revolutionist, an iconoclast, against those who do not understand him and who, fancying that they are helping him, are really pushing him backward in the highway of life. Thus even the adult who loves him, rivets about his neck another calumny, confusing his defense of his molested life with a form of innate naughtiness characteristic of little children.[4] . . .

It is exactly in the repetition of the exercises that the education of the senses consists; their aim is not that the child shall *know* colors, forms, and the different qualities of objects, but that he refine his senses through an exercise of attention, of comparison, of judgment. These exercises are true intellectual gymnastics. Such gymnastics, reasonably directed by means of various devices, aid in the formation of the intellect, just as physical exercises fortify the general health and quicken the growth of the body. The child who trains his various senses separately, by means of external stimuli, concentrates his attention and develops, piece by piece, his mental activities, just as with separately prepared movements he trains his muscular activities. These mental gymnastics are not merely psycho-sensory, but they prepare the way for spontaneous association of ideas, for ratiocination developing out of definite knowledge, for a harmoniously balanced intellect. They are the powder trains that bring about those mental explosions which delight the child so intensely when he makes discoveries in the world about him, when he, at the same time, ponders over and glories in the new things which are revealed to him in the outside world, and in the exquisite emotions of his own growing consciousness; and finally when there spring up within him, almost by a process of spontaneous ripening, like the internal phenomena of growth, the external products of learning—writing and reading.[5] . . .

The majority of our children become calm as they go through such exercises, because their nervous system is at rest. Then we say that such children are quiet and good; external discipline, so eagerly sought after in ordinary schools is more than achieved.

However, as a calm man and a self-disciplined man are not one and the same, so here the fact which manifests itself externally by the calm of the children is in reality a phenomenon merely physical and partial compared to the real *self-discipline* which is being developed in them.

Often (and this is another misconception) we think all we need to do, to obtain a voluntary action from a child, is to order him to do it. We pretend that this phenomenon of a forced voluntary action exists, and we call this pretext, "the obedience of the child." We find little children specially disobedient, or rather their resistance, by the time they are four or five years old, has become so great that we are in despair and are almost tempted to give up trying to make them obey. We force ourselves to praise to little children "the virtue of obedience," a virtue which, according to our accepted prejudices, should belong specially to infancy, should be the "infantile virtue"; yet we fail to learn anything from the fact that we are led to emphasize it so strongly because we can only with the greatest difficulty make children practice it.

It is a very common mistake, this of trying to obtain by means of prayers, or orders, or violence, what is difficult, or impossible to get. Thus, for instance, we ask little children to be obedient, and little children in their turn ask for the moon.[6]

It is therefore entirely natural that, loving the child, we should point out to him that obedience is the law of life, and there is nothing surprising in the anxiety felt by nearly everyone who is confronted with the characteristic disobedience of little children. But obedience can only be reached through a complex formation of the psychic personality. To obey, it is necessary not only to wish to obey, but also to know how to. Since, when a command to do a certain thing is given, we presuppose a corresponding active or inhibitive power of the child, it is plain that obedience must follow the formation of the will and of the mind. To prepare, in detail, this formation by means of detached exercises is therefore indirectly, to urge the child toward obedience. The method which is the subject of this book contains in every part an exercise for the willpower, when the child completes coordinated actions directed toward a given end, when he achieves something he set out to do, when he repeats patiently his exercises, he is training his positive willpower. Similarly, in a very complicated series of exercises he is establishing through activity his powers of inhibition; for instance in the "lesson of silence," which calls for a long continued inhibition of many actions, while the child is waiting to be called and later for a rigorous self-control when he is called and would like to answer joyously and run to his teacher, but instead is perfectly silent, moves very carefully, taking the greatest pains not to knock against chair or table or to make a noise.

Other inhibitive exercises are the arithmetical ones, when the child having drawn a number by lot, must take from the great mass of objects before him, apparently entirely at his disposition, only the quantity corresponding to the number in his hand, whereas (as experience has proved) he would *like* to take the greatest number possible. Furthermore if he chances to draw the zero he sits patiently with empty hands. Still another training for the inhibitive will-power is in "the lesson of zero" when the child, called upon to come up zero times and give zero kisses, stands quiet, conquering with a visible effort the instinct which would lead him to "obey" the call. The child at our school dinners who carries the big tureen full of hot soup isolates himself from every external stimulant which might disturb him, resists his childish impulse to run and jump, does not yield to the temptation to brush away the fly on his face, and is entirely concentrated on the great responsibility of not dropping or tipping the tureen. A little thing of four and a half, every time he set the tureen down on a table so that the little guests might help themselves, gave a hop and a skip, then took up the tureen again to carry it to another table, repressing himself to a sober walk. In spite of his desire to play he never left his task before he had passed soup to the twenty tables, and he never forgot the vigilance necessary to control his actions.

Willpower, like all other activities, is invigorated and developed through methodical exercises, and all our exercises for willpower are also mental and practical. To the casual onlooker the child seems to be learning exactitude and grace of action, to be refining his senses, to be learning how to read and write; but much more profoundly he is learning how to become his own master, how to be a man of prompt and resolute will.

We often hear it said that a child's will should be "broken" that the best education for the will of the child is to learn to give it up to the will of adults. Leaving out of the question the injustice which is at the root of every act of tyranny, this idea is irrational because the child cannot give up what he does not possess. We prevent him in this way from forming his own willpower, and we commit the greatest and most blameworthy mistake. He never has time or opportunity to test himself, to estimate his own force and his own limitations because he is always interrupted and subjected to our tyranny, and languishes in injustice because he is always being bitterly reproached for not having what adults are perpetually destroying.

There springs up as a consequence of this, childish timidity, which is a moral malady acquired by a will which could not develop, and which with the usual calumny with which the tyrant consciously or not, covers up his own mistakes, we consider as an inherent trait of childhood. The children in our schools are never timid. One of their most fascinating qualities is the frankness with which they treat people, with which they go on working in the presence of others, and showing their work frankly, calling for sympathy. That moral monstrosity, a repressed and timid child, who is at his ease nowhere except alone with his playmates, or with street urchins, because his willpower was allowed to grow only in the shade, disappears in our schools. He presents an example of thoughtless barbarism, which resembles the artificial compression of the bodies of those children intended for "court dwarfs," museum monstrosities, or buffoons. Yet this is the treatment under which nearly all the children of our time are growing up spiritually.[7] . . .

Besides the exercises it offers for developing willpower, the other factor in obedience is the capacity to perform the act it becomes necessary to obey. One of the most interesting observations made by my pupil Anna Maccheroni (at first in the school in Milan and then in that in the Via Guisti in Rome), relates to the connection between obedience in a child and his "knowing how." Obedience appears in the child as a latent instinct as soon as his personality begins to take form. For instance, a child begins to try a certain exercise and suddenly some time he goes through it perfectly; he is delighted, stares at it, and wishes to do it over again, but for some time the exercise is not a success. Then comes a time when he can do it nearly every time he tries voluntarily but makes mistakes if someone else asks him to do it. The external command does not as yet produce the voluntary act. When, however, the exercise always succeeds, with absolute certainty, then an order from someone else brings about on the child's part, orderly adequate action; that is, the child *is able* each time to execute the command received. That these facts (with variations in individual cases) are laws of psychical development is apparent from everyone's experience with children in school or at home.

One often hears a child say, "I did do such and such a thing but now I can't!" and a teacher disappointed by the incompetence of a pupil will say, "Yet that child was doing it all right—and now he can't!"

Finally there is the period of complete development in which the capacity to perform some operation is permanently acquired. There are, therefore, three periods: a first, subconscious one, when in the confused mind of the child, order produces itself by a mysterious inner impulse from out the midst of disorder, producing as an external result a completed act, which, however, being outside the field of consciousness, cannot be reproduced at will; a second, conscious period, when there is some action on the part of the will which is present during the process of the development and establishing of the acts; and a third period when the will can direct and cause the acts, thus answering the command from someone else.

Now, obedience follows a similar sequence. When in the first period of spiritual disorder, the child does not obey it is exactly as if he were psychically deaf, and out of hearing of commands. In the second period he would like to obey, he looks as though he understood the command and would like to respond to it, but cannot—or at least does not always succeed in doing it, is not "quick to mind" and shows no pleasure when he does. In the third period he obeys at once, with enthusiasm, and as he becomes more and more perfect in the exercises he is proud that he knows how to obey. This is the period in which he runs joyously to obey, and leaves at the most imperceptible request whatever is interesting him so that he may quit the solitude of his own life and enter, with the act of obedience into the spiritual existence of another.[8] . . .

These are the first outlines of an experiment which shows a form of indirect discipline in which there is substituted for the critical and sermonizing teacher a rational organization of work and of liberty for the child. It involves a conception of life more usual in religious fields than in those of academic pedagogy, inasmuch as it has recourse to the spiritual energies of mankind, but it is founded on work and on liberty which are the two paths to all civic progress.

EDITOR'S NOTES

1. Montessori's comments on Anne George's observation of her method on p. 348 are deleted.

2. Montessori's comparison of children's sense of discipline to that of spiritual discipline of monks on p. 349 is deleted.

3. Montessori's comments on to the natural use of nervous energy in accomplishing a task and example of unwarranted adult interference in children's work on pp. 354–56, which cover points already made, are deleted.

4. Montessori's analogy about adults having their actions completed by jugglers to illustrate children's feelings about adult interference on p. 360 is deleted.

5. Montessori's story about a child who seeks to touch objects on his father's desk as an example of autoeducation on pp. 361–62, which repeated points made earlier, is deleted.

6. Montessori's comments on self-sacrifice in adult life on pp. 363–64 are deleted.

7. Montessori's brief criticism of educators who decry the lack of individual character in students on p. 367 is deleted.

8. Montessori's reference to the St. Paul's comments on the "fruits of the spirit" on p. 369 is deleted.

22

Conclusions and Impressions

In the "Children's Houses," the old-time teacher, who wore herself out maintaining discipline of immobility, and who wasted her breath in loud and continual discourse, has disappeared.

For this teacher we have substituted the *didactic material*, which contains within itself the control of errors and which makes auto-education possible to each child. The teacher has thus become a *director* of the spontaneous work of the children. She is not a *passive* force, a *silent* presence.

The children are occupied each one in a different way, and the directress, watching them, can make psychological observations which, if collected in an orderly way and according to scientific standards, should do much toward the reconstruction of child psychology and the development of experimental psychology. I believe that I have by my method established the conditions necessary to the development of scientific pedagogy; and whoever adopts this method opens, in doing so, a laboratory of experimental pedagogy.

From such work, we must await the positive solution of all those pedagogical problems of which we talk today. For through such work there has already come the solution of some of these very questions: that of the liberty of the pupils; auto-education; the establishment of harmony between the work and activities of home life and school tasks, making both work together for the education of the child.

The problem of religious education, the importance of which we do not fully realize, should also be solved by positive pedagogy. If religion is born with civilization, its roots must lie deep in human nature. We have had most beautiful proof of an instinctive love of knowledge in the child, who has too often been misjudged in that he has been considered addicted to meaningless play, and games void of thought. The child who left the game in his eagerness for knowledge, has revealed himself as a true son of that humanity which has been throughout centuries the creator of scientific and civil progress. We have belittled the son of man by giving him foolish and degrading toys, a world of idleness where he is suffocated by a badly conceived discipline. Now, in his liberty, the child should show us, as well, whether man is by nature a religious creature.

To deny, a priori, the religious sentiment in man, and to deprive humanity of the education of this sentiment, is to commit a pedagogical error similar to that of denying, a priori, to the child, the love of learning for learning's sake. This ignorant assumption led us to dominate the scholar, to subject him to a species of slavery, in order to render him apparently disciplined.

The fact that we assume that religious education is only adapted to the adult, may be akin to another profound error existing in education today, namely, that of overlooking the education of the senses at the very period when this education is possible. The life of the adult is practically an application of the senses to the gathering of sensations from the environment. A lack of preparation for this often results in inadequacy in practical life, in that lack of poise which causes so many individuals to waste their energies in purposeless effort. Not to form a parallel between the education of the senses as a guide to practical life, and religious education as a guide to the moral life, but for the sake of illustration, let me call attention to how often we find inefficiency, instability, among irreligious persons, and how much precious individual power is miserably wasted.[1] . . .

In America, the great positive scientist, William James, who expounds the physiological theory of emotions, is also the man who illustrates the psychological importance of religious "conscience."[2] We cannot know the future of the progress of thought: here, for example, in the "Children's Houses" the triumph of *discipline* through the conquest of liberty and independence marks the foundation of the progress which the future will see in the matter of pedagogical methods. To me it offers the greatest hope for human redemption through education.

Perhaps, in the same way, through the conquest of liberty of thought and of conscience, we are making our way toward a great religious triumph. Experience will show, and the psychological observations made along this line in the "Children's Houses" will undoubtedly be of the greatest interest.

This book of methods compiled by one person alone must be followed by many others. It is my hope that, starting from the *individual study of the child* educated with our method, other educators will set forth the results of their experiments. These are the pedagogical books which await us in the future.

From the practical side of the school, we have with our methods the advantage of being able to teach in one room, children of very different ages. In our "Children's Houses" we have little ones of two years and a half, who cannot as yet make use of the most simple of the sense exercises, and children of five and a half who because of their development might easily pass into the third elementary. Each one of them perfects himself through his own powers, and goes forward guided by that inner force which distinguishes him as an individual.

One great advantage of such a method is that it will make instruction in the rural schools easier, and will be of great advantage in the schools in the small provincial towns where there are few children, yet where all the various grades are represented. Such schools are not able to employ more than one teacher. Our experience shows that one directress may guide a group of children varying in development from little ones of three years old to the third elementary. Another great advantage lies in the extreme facility with which written language may be taught, making it possible to combat illiteracy and to cultivate the national tongue.

As to the teacher, she may remain for a whole day among children in the most varying stages of development, just as the mother remains in the house with children of all ages, without becoming tired.

The children work by themselves, and, in doing so, make a conquest of active discipline, and independence in all the acts of daily life, just as through daily conquests they progress in intellectual development. Directed by an intelligent teacher, who watches over their physical development as well as over their intellectual and moral progress, children are able with our methods to arrive at a splendid physical development, and, in addition to this, there unfolds within them, in all its perfection, the soul, which distinguishes the human being.

We have been mistaken in thinking that the natural education of children should be purely physical; the soul, too, has its nature, which it was intended to perfect in the spiritual life—the dominating power of human existence throughout all time. Our methods take into consideration the spontaneous psychic development of the child, and help this in ways that observation and experience have shown us to be wise.

If physical care leads the child to take pleasure in bodily health, intellectual and moral care make possible for him the highest spiritual joy, and send him forward into a world where continual surprises and discoveries await him; not only in the external environment, but in the intimate recesses of his own soul.

It is through such pleasures as these that the ideal man grows, and only such pleasures are worthy of a place in the education of the infancy of humanity.

Our children are noticeably different from those others who have grown up within the grey walls of the common schools. Our little pupils have the serene and happy aspect and the frank and open friendliness of the person who feels himself to be master of his own actions. When they run to gather about our visitors, speaking to them with sweet frankness, extending their little hands with gentle gravity and well-bred cordiality, when they thank these visitors for the courtesy they have paid us in coming, the bright eyes and the happy voices make us feel that they are, indeed, unusual little men. When they display their work and their ability, in a confidential and simple way, it is almost as if they called for a maternal approbation from all those who watch them. Often, a little one will seat himself on the floor beside some visitor silently writing his name, and adding a gentle word of thanks. It is as if they wished to make the visitor feel the affectionate gratitude which is in their hearts.

When we see all these things and when, above all, we pass with these children from the busy activity of the schoolroom at work, into the absolute and profound silence which they have learned to enjoy so deeply, we are moved in spite of ourselves and feel that we have come in touch with the very souls of these little pupils.

The "Children's House" seems to exert a spiritual influence upon everyone. I have seen here, men of affairs, great politicians preoccupied with problems of trade and of state, cast off like an uncomfortable garment the burden of the world, and fall into a simple forgetfulness of self. They are affected by this vision of the human soul growing in its true nature, and I believe that this is what they mean when they call our little ones, wonderful children, happy children—the infancy of humanity in a higher stage of evolution than our own. I understand how the great English poet Wordsworth, enamored as he was of nature, demanded the secret of all her peace and beauty. It was at last revealed to him—the secret of all nature lies in the soul of a little child. He holds there the true meaning of that life which exists throughout humanity. But this beauty which "lies about us in our infancy" becomes obscured; "shades of the prison house, begin to close about the growing boy . . . at last the man perceives it die away, and fade into the light of common day."

Truly our social life is too often only the darkening and the death of the natural life that is in us. These methods tend to guard that spiritual fire within man, to keep his real nature unspoiled and to set it free from the oppressive and degrading yoke of society. It is a pedagogical method informed by the high concept of Immanuel Kant: "Perfect art returns to nature."

EDITOR'S NOTES

1. Montessori's admonitions against religious fanaticism and lives deprived of spirituality on p. 373 are deleted.
2. Montessori's reference is to William James (1841–1910), American psychologist and pragmatist philosopher. Like Montessori, James studied anatomy and physiology and emphasized the important in applying the scientific method to psychology and education. His educational lectures were published as *Talks to Teachers on Psychology* in 1899; his major work, *Principles of Psychology*, was published in 1890.

II

RELATED DOCUMENTS

23

Interpretation of Montessori's Lecture

Translated by Anne E. George

It is an unusual pleasure for Dr. Montessori to speak in the City of Brooklyn because it is one of the cities that has sent the greatest number of students to study with her in her school at Rome.* She is glad to see some of them in the audience tonight. It is a great pleasure for her to know that some of them have started in "Children's Houses" to expound her principles and put forth her method.

That which is called her method is founded upon liberty—that liberty which is perhaps not yet very well understood throughout the world. We have within us, however, the power to feel instinctively the essence of liberty, the simple thing which liberty is. For instance, when we see the birds flying through the air, we feel that they are free and we express our admiration for their freedom and their liberty. And, when we are seated under the trees in their full life and blossom, we feel that they are growing freely and happily and we envy their spontaneous growth and happiness. If we can imagine false ideas so taking hold of society that this instinctive comprehension could be so distorted that we could imagine one saying, "This poor tree held fast in the ground by its roots, held firm in one spot, let us tear it up and set it at liberty; let us give it freedom." And, when we see the birds flying through the air in search of food let us imagine one saying, "Let us bring them into the house and put them in a cage; let us find their food for them; let us feed and care for them." We know it would mean death in the one case and imprisonment in the other.

These ideas, these things which we feel instinctively, in regard to the liberty of the things that grow naturally, we must feel and extent [*sic*] to all living creatures. We must understand by liberty the right and power to grow freely and we must understand that each creature must have its own kind of liberty. We must realize

---

*For a short biography on Anne E. George and a discussion of selection, see appendix.

that when we talk of the liberty that is finer and different from external liberty, that is finer than the liberty of physical nature, when we speak of the liberty of the spirit we are speaking of what is almost supernatural. We cannot discover the law of liberty which applies to this kind of life suddenly, it must take long, deep study and observation. In fact, we may call the history of civilization the history of the progressive strides and triumphs of partial liberty. Liberty always demands a finer, a freer bond of existence. So, when we talk of the liberty of the child we must understand that this liberty includes a kind of liberty which is still a problem to us.

If we could accept as our concept the simple idea that so many mothers have, the idea that we are giving the child liberty when we leave them alone to do what they want, it would mean that we were abandoning the child, and, a free child is never an abandoned child. The free child is the child to whom has been made possible the fullest and finest development of life, and, therefore, that child has need of a very fine, a very carefully determined guidance and care. For example, there was a mother of one of the children who attended Dr. Montessori's school who thought she understood Dr. Montessori's idea of liberty and thought she applied to her child this form of liberty. She allowed him to do anything he wanted to do spontaneously, whether these spontaneous acts were helpful or not. Ond [*sic*] day, Dr. Montessori was walking with this mother and child along a street in Milan. The bells in a nearby cloister began to ring and the child stopped to listen to them. Dr. Montessori watched with interest this sign of interior activity. But, the mother, who thought it was perfectly right for the child to do whatever he did spontaneously while at home, thought that when in the street the thing to do was to walk, so she said, "Come along! Come, hurry long [*sic*]!"

We can understand the end and aim of the child, we must understand its aspiration—the child must grow, it must attain maturity. To understand the aspiration of the child is not as difficult as to understand the aspiration of a mature adult. The child has one great aim—he must grow to his normal maturity. If we think of the life of the child we must think what a great creator he must be, he has to be, we have to think of the great work of the child. He has come into a new world, to move in this world, to organize his movements. He has to learn not a foreign language but a primitive one. When we think of the efforts of a man who has come to a strange land, the difficulty he has to learn the customs, the manners, the habits and the language of the people, we realize that the child's work is greater. He does not come from a country where he has been living with beings of the same kind, but he has to learn it all from the beginning. This great workman, this great creator, has need of great help, and yet, for the most part we do not help him to conquer the world and become master of himself. The child is one of the creatures least known, least understood by us. For instance, the child needs and wants to come to understand things throught [*sic*] the sense of touch. It is much easier for him to understand to distinguish things through the sense of touch than through the other senses. He needs to perfect this method of recognition in order to help him to understand and recognize them by the more complex senses. And yet, all we seem to learn from this desire to touch is that the child wants to touch everything and we have grown past this need, and as we have grown past the idea that we want to do this instinctively we say to the child, "Don't touch! Learn to let things alone! Learn not to touch things!"

Dr. Montessori once visited a physician, a friend of hers, who brought his little child to her to show her how well and strong and healthy he was. "But," said the physician, "he is not a good child. No matter how often we correct him he insists upon touching everything on my writing desk." Dr. Montessori watched the child as he handled the things on the writing desk, showing an intelligent interest in their various forms, the rectangle formed by the block of paper, the ink stand, the pen and pencil and the blotter upon which they lay.

Another need that the child has is to surmount and accomplish movements more and more complex which demand more delicate muscular organization. How many parents who allow their children to play in a corner with their own toys stop them when they do useful things? When the children of Dr. Montessori's school, who live in the tenements, go into the kitchen and try to imitate their mothers in the things they are doing, the mother generally says, "No, no, you do not belong here. Don't try to do this." We, instead of helping the children to master these movements which are more and more difficult hinder him by refusing to help him. We feel that we have done the best for him when we have put him in the corner with his toys. In spite of the lack of help, the desire is so great that he persists and does the things he needs to do, but he must do them with unnecessary fatigue and he must use engery that could be turned in other channels so as to be of greater benefit to him.

We speak of crossness, naughtiness, and irritability as the characteristics of infancy, but this crossness, this naughtiness is only a nervous condition brought about by the fact that the child has to combat the grown up people in order to get the necessary activities he needs. In fact, many of the physicians of Italy and Rome have come to consider Dr. Montessori's method which makes them work, or leaves them free to work, as a calming force which builds up the nervous child and helps the weak ones. Her method gives the greatest importance to the environment that is necessary for the full development, the full mental and physical development of the child. In fact her materials are constructed to supply the child with the simple sense training exercises, the simple activities which he must have and which are demanded from him by an internal force; which he will have no matter how he gets them, whether through waisting [*sic*] his energy or whether he has them given to him to help him to grow more strong where he is free to work.

In fact, he has different objects of various forms to touch, of different surfaces and finish and different textures to distinguish between. And, he is in a place where he is free to use them, in an environment where he is not hindered in his development. He has all the liberty and freedom and opportunity to accomplish and master the more difficult and complex activities. He needs to learn to button and unbutton, hook and unhook, tie and untie, in fact, to dress himself; to set the table; to move about as he will; to wash himself; to care for the room in which he is. He is also helped in the development of the language and helped so simply that he really does not know he is being helped in this wonderful step, yet, he is brought to a point where he can master written and spoken language.

One of the things which the children have shown when put in this environment and when given the right kind of help has been conspicuous in their work. They repeat over and over again the exercises which are giving them the help they need, repeating them a hundred or a hundred and fifty times. They give signs of joy and you can see that they are getting new force and new possibility for enjoyment of the outside world. This activity is the reponse to the instinctive need of the child. It is necessary to give but one small stimulus in order to see the child's activity open and to see the development of the individual set forth in many ways, and not only in the way you have intended with the one thing which you have given. It is the phenomenon of activity awakened by the presentation of a rational stimulus. This gives a new base to education. While we have held that to educate a child it is necessary to present a concept, an idea from the outside to make him absorb it and take it in, this shows that education can be gained in another way. It is only necessary to present a small stimulus, sufficiently strong to set activity in motion, to awaken activity in the individual. We find that the child wants the activity, and the activity he needs has been awakened by the presentation of the stimulus. And, he extends this activity to his general environment; he draws upon and enriches the experience he has had within and which has made him active, and extends it to the things about him. We may call this the second step in his education, where he makes a series of discoveries, after being well prepared and strongly equipped, in the environment where he is to move and live. In fact, this interest in the external world, this application, this enthusiasm, becomes so great that it surmounts the material enjoyment. For example, a guest at Dr. Montessori's school one day brought some sweet buscuits [*sic*] for the children, but before starting to eat them they showed him the various forms, calling them by name, "This is a rectangle. This a circle. See the triangle." It has been found that by leaving flowers of various colors in a room the children spontaneously bring the color spools to find the exact shade and color of the flowers.

We have, also, in these schools experiences which may be compared to explosions or outbursts of enthusiasm. For example, the act of writing takes place after the children have had and have mastered exercises which prepare them for writing and give them the ability to write spontaneously.

In this environment of liberty there have developed in the children also finer moral precepts, finer spiritual instincts and greater consideration for others. One of the greatest spiritual or moral surprises has been the conquest of the children of discipline. If we wish to understand this phenomenon of the conquest of discipline which takes place in these schools, we come to see that it is due to the well-ordered and related work with which the children are furnished; that the work they have been given is the work they need. Freedom is necessary to every individual, to every living thing, which must grow freely to its finest attainment.

To give this kind of orderly instruction and freedom to the child it is necessary that the teacher shall have a new attitude, that she shall be different from the teacher who has conceived as her mission to force into the child's mind right concepts. She must learn to watch for activity once it has been stimulated. This teacher must come to have an attitude of humility. She must become at the same time an observer of the freely developing child and a wise director of the spiritual growth of the children about her. She must perfect herself to the point where she will not intervene; she must learn to abolish her own personality, her own ego. She must at the same time learn from her observations to distinguish which are the acts she must encourage and leave free, and which are those rare acts which lead to debasement, and, therefore, which she must check. She must develop a certain fine sensibility which will enable her to discern almost unconsciously those acts which are useless or harmful. She must be like a mother who guards her child when he is in danger of falling, but she leaves the child free to play when he is in a beautiful garden, leaves him free in the enjoyment in which he is safe! She must learn to intervene, to check the harmful things, but to vanish when the child shows that activities which are helpful have been awakened and to allow the child to have the illusion that he has accomplished it all himself.

In one school a visitor came in and after watching the children at working he notice [*sic*] the teacher standing at one side, apparently doing nothing. He said to her, "You have not a very responsible position, you do nothing but stand watching after you have given the children the necessary materials when the [*sic*] arrive at the school." The teacher said to him "I don't even do that for when the children come into the school they get their own material."

One teacher quoted proudly the experience she had with a little child who had just learned to write, who came to her full of enthusiasm, eager to share this newly found joy, and showed her his work, and then looked up and said in all sincerity, "Do you know how to write?"

This method of liberty allowed the child not only to develop and grow freely but allows him to develop with the peculiar color and form which is his own personality. He does not give himself over to the force of some outside, mature personality which may force and mold him from the outside as a stronger force which is guiding him. He is safe from that danger.

One of the most common objections made to this method of education is that while indeed the child grow [*sic*] and develops so that he may have the desire and strength to do things by himself, yet, this work is the work he wants to do, the work that is pleasing to him as an individual. What will become of him when he must force himself to respect some command which the necessity of life has forced upon him as something he must do? They ask what will happen when it is demanded of him that he makes a sacrifice? What will become of him when he goes out into the ugliness, the coldness, and the courseness [*sic*] of the worl [*sic*] around him? How will he develop in this ugliness and courseness [*sic*] when he has been accustomed to do only those things which are pleasing to him? The children themselves have already begun to make answer to this objection because they have shown that they were not only capable to make a sacrifice, to do willingly a work that was demanded of them from the outside, but ready to leave work in which they were passionately interested.

We need not marvel at this because the children have been grwoing [*sic*] in moral strength, they have been forming beautiful characters and strong ones, which thus enable them to give this free sacrifice, this self-denial.

You might compare this objection with one which might be drawn in the physical world. Suppose some on [*sic*] were to say, "Why do you give this great care to the new-born infant? You are too careful about its milk being pure, of the right temperature, and giving it its food only a [*sic*] certain times. You are too careful about the tempertur [*sic*] of its bath, about the time when it shall sleep, and the temperature of the room in which it shall sleep, the air of that room being pure. Yet, you know that the world in which the child must live is full of microbes full of diseases. Why do you keep the child away from these, why do you not start him in these conditions at the beginning and so strengthen him that he may be able to live in these conditions?" We, however, know through investigation of science, that in following these lines we are preparing a strong race, a race which will be better able to fight in any circumstances, a race that will be able to conquer disease, to lesson [*sic*] evil. We are preparing stronger men, and the strongest men are those that have had the best health in youth and have laid the best foundation for their manhood. And, so in the school we now wish to establish by the same method of science a sort of people who will be stronger morally and spiritually, who can better fight the evils existing in the world about them, who will be better able to combat the difficulties which may come to them.

We shall have need in the future of a race not only stronger physically, but stronger mentally and spiritually, because the body is stronger and more perfect will cry out for a corresponding growth of the spirit and the intellect. The body is but of secondary importance. The important fact is that man carries in this body a mind and a soul that can attain to the progress of civilization.

NOTE

The original source for this chapter is as follows: "The interpretation of Dr. Montessori's Lecture, delivered at the Academy of Music, Brooklyn, December 11, 1913, as rendered by Miss Anne E. George of Washington, D.C. in McClure Mass. Manuscript Collections, Lilly Library, Indiana University, Bloomington, Indiana.

24

Excerpts from *The Montessori System Examined*

William H. Kilpatrick

It must be said, however, that while Madam Montessori's interest in the scientific attitude is entirely praiseworthy, her actual science cannot be so highly commended.* Her biology is not always above reproach, as, for example, the alleged disinfecting influence of garlic upon the intestines and lungs. She generalizes unscientifically as to the condition of contemporary educational thought and practice from observation limited, it would seem, to the Italian schools. If she had known more of what was being thought and done elsewhere, her discussions would have been saved some blemishes and her system some serious omissions. Her psychology in particular would have been improved, had she known better what Wundt was doing in Germany, to mention no other names. . . .

Some, on the contrary, have taken the position, previously suggested, that in the child's nature as given at birth there is contained—in some unique sense— all that the child is to become, and this in such fashion that we should tend the child as the gardener does the plant, assured that the natural endowment would properly guide its own process of unfolding. Such is Madam Montessori's view. "The child is a body which grows and a soul which develops . . . we must neither mar nor stifle the mysterious powers which lie within these two forms of growth, but must *await from them* the manifestations which we know will succeed one another." "The educational conception of this age must be solely that of aiding the psycho-physical development of the individual." "If any educational act is to be efficacious, it will be only that which tends to *help* toward the complete unfolding" of the child's individuality.

Such a doctrine of education has borne good fruit; but there is danger in it. It has led in the past to unwise emphasis and to wrong practice. We have already

---

*For a short biography on William H. Kilpatrick and a discussion of selection, see appendix.

seen that it carries with it a depreciation of the value rightly belonging to the solutions that man has devised for his ever-recurring problems. In fact, such a theory leads easily, if not inevitably, to Rousseau's opposition to man's whole institutional life. It further fails to provide adequately for the most useful of modern conceptions, that of intelligent, self-directing adaptation to a novel environment. If development be but the unfolding of what was from the first enfolded, then the adaptation is made in advance of the situation, and consequently without reference to its novel aspects. Such a form of predetermined adaptation proves successful in the case of certain insects, as the wasp; for there the environment is relatively fixed. With man, however, each generation finds—and makes—a new situation. If education is to prepare for such a changing environment, its fundamental concept must take essential cognizance of that fact. Still further, this erroneous notion of education gives to the doctrine of child liberty a wrong and misleading foundation. If the child already uniquely contains that which he is properly destined to manifest, then the duty of the educator is to allow the fullest expression of what is implicitly given. But such a doctrine of liberty is notoriously disastrous. The result has, therefore, been that many have opposed every scheme of liberty in the schoolroom. By putting the demand for liberty on a false basis, its friends have too often proved its worst foes. It would not be fair to Madam Montessori to say that she herself draws all of these objectionable conclusions from her doctrine of the nature of education. She does not. She has not thought consecutively enough. But the conclusions are there to be drawn. They have been drawn from logically similar doctrines at other times. We must, therefore, reject Madam Montessori's interpretation of the doctrine of development as inadequate and misleading. The useful elements of this doctrine are covered up in error whenever development is identified with the mere unfolding of latency. . . .

If cooperation be forced from without, is it not largely a sham and a counterfeit? The desirable group work is that joint activity which springs from the felt necessity of joint action. We are here but repeating the discussion of the preceding paragraph. What we wish, then, is to put the children into such a socially conditioned environment that they will of themselves spontaneously unite into larger or smaller groups to work out their life impulses as these exist on the childish plane. From these considerations we criticize both Montessori and Froebel, the one that she does not provide situations for more adequate social cooperation, the other that the cooperation comes too largely from outside suggestion and from adult considerations. . . .

Freedom apart from self-expression is a contradiction of terms. The discussion of Madam Montessori's doctrine of freedom given in the preceding chapter is, therefore, incomplete without a consideration of the adequacy of self-expression allowed by her system. The didactic apparatus which forms the principal means of activity in the Montessori school affords singularly little variety. Without discussing here the grounds for this restriction, it suffices to say that this apparatus by its very theory presents a limited series of exactly distinct and very precise activities, formal in character and very remote from social interests and connections. So narrow and limited a range of activity cannot go far in satisfying the normal child. . . .

In the same way, we must not hastily conclude that no child could enjoy the relatively formal exercises of the didactic apparatus. Mechanical manipulation has strong attractions for childhood. But after all is said, the Montessori school apparatus affords but meager diet for normally active children. Further, while happy childhood knows no stronger or more fruitful impulse than imaginative and constructive play, still, in these schools *playing* with the didactic apparatus is strictly forbidden, and usually no other play material is furnished. Madam Montessori has, in fact, been publicly quoted as saying, "If I were persuaded that children needed to play, I would provide the proper apparatus; but I am not so persuaded." The best current thought and practice in America would make constructive and imitative play, socially conditioned, the foundation and principal constituent of the program for children of the kindergarten age, but Madam Montessori rejects it. Closely allied with play is the use of games. One finds more attention paid to this, but the games seen in the Montessori schools of Rome are far inferior in every respect to those found in the better American kindergartens. Madam Montessori herself seems, from her use of the very word "game," to have a most narrow and restricted conception of what games are, and of what they can do. Those more advanced forms of self-expression, drawing and modeling, are, on the whole, inferior to what we have in this country. Modeling is, in fact, hardly at all in evidence. Drawing and painting are occasionally good, but frequently amount to nothing but the coloring of conventionalized drawings furnished by the teacher. Stories have little or no place—a most serious oversight. There is very little of dramatization. On the whole, the imagination, whether of constructive play or of the more æsthetic sort, is but little utilized. It is thus a long list of most serious omissions that we have to note. . . .

The general idea of including among the school exercises such occupations as are mainly valuable from demands of immediate utility is one that proves attractive. It is well recognized that cooking as a school subject, for example, does not arouse the same serious interest among our pupils that it formerly aroused in the home, when the girl who took it up did so to meet the immediate need in the household. The motivation, as we say, is largely lacking in the artificial situation of the schoolroom. If, now, the school can bring into its service something of the gripping interest that attaches to actual and immediate social demand, we shall have the real effort that counts. It must be admitted, however, that this will not hold of all the "practical life" activities, because some of the most insistent of these have never aroused in young children any great internal motivation even in the best homes: washing the face and hands, for example. In such cases, the social approval or disapproval of the school-room may prove distinctly helpful in fixing a habit that might never be learned in inferior home surroundings.

While no one could suppose that a curriculum devised for a particular class in Rome would serve, unmodified, in America, we have no hesitation in concluding that we can find suggestion for thought in the long school day, in the practical effort to adapt the school exercises to the needs of the community, and in the possible increase of motivation by the introduction of activities the demand for which is immediate and actual. The whole conception is but part of the worldwide demand that the school shall function more definitely as a social institution, adapting itself to its own environment and utilizing more fully actual life situations. . . .

The formal and mechanical aspect of the training is, however, practically valueless. Any play in which the consideration of a size-experience, for example, enters, will do just as well as does the broad stair of the didactic apparatus. All must approve Madam Montessori's wish to provide more fruitful sense-experiences. Most children need more activity of this kind. The natural fondness of the young child for manipulation and the like is sufficient proof of the fact. Care, too, is necessary that the opportunities offered be sufficiently varied and sufficiently ordered to bring the desired richness of experience. But these considerations—all important though they be—afford no support for the dogma of general transfer, nor do they call for an apparatus so formal and mechanical in character as the system under review offers.

We must, then, take exactly the opposite view from Madam Montessori as to the nature of sense-training. She says that the "aim is not that the child shall *know* colors, forms, and the different qualities of objects." We say that the aim is exactly that he may know such things, and we don't care about his getting any sense training outside of this. We conclude, accordingly, that Madam Montessori's doctrine of sense-training is based on an outworn and cast off psychological theory; that the didactic apparatus devised to carry this theory into effect is in so far worthless; that what little value remains to the apparatus could be better got from the sense-experiences incidental to properly directed play with wisely chosen, but less expensive and more childlike, playthings. . . .

If we compare the work of Madam Montessori with that of such a writer and thinker as Professor Dewey, we are able to get an estimate of her worth from still a different point of view. The two have many things in common. Both have organized experimental schools; both have emphasized the freedom, self-activity, and self-education of the child; both have made large use of "practical life" activities. (In a word, the two are cooperative tendencies in opposing entrenched traditionalism.) There are, however, wide differences. For the earliest education, Madam Montessori provides a set of mechanically simple devices. These in large measure do the teaching. A simple procedure embodied in definite, tangible apparatus is a powerful incentive to popular interest. Professor Dewey could not secure the education which he sought in so simple a fashion. Madam Montessori was able to do so only because she had a much narrower conception of education, and because she could hold to an untenable theory as to the value of formal and systematic sense-training. Madam Montessori centered much of her effort upon devising more satisfactory methods of teaching reading and writing, utilizing thereto in masterly fashion the phonetic character of the Italian language. Professor Dewey, while recognizing the duty of the school to teach these arts, feels that early emphasis should rather be placed upon activities more vital to child-life which should at the same time lead toward the mastery of our complex social environment. Madam Montessori, in a measure following Pestalozzi, constantly uses logically simple units as if they were also the units of psychological experience. In reading and writing, it is the letter and the single sound, not the word or thought connection, that receive attention. Sense-qualities are taught preferably in isolation, apart from life situations. She speaks also of leading the child "from sensations to ideas . . . and to the association of ideas." Professor Dewey insists that the experience is the unit, and that the logically simple units emerge for consciousness by differentiation from the experience. Things, as a rule, are best taught, then, in connection with what is for the child a real experience, when they enter as significant parts into such an experience; and this because learning is essentially the differentiation and organization of meanings. It is, of course, to be borne in mind that a child experience is vastly different from the adult experience. What to a child is a whole satisfying experience, to us may be very fragmentary and disconnected.

But there are even more comprehensive contrasts. Madam Montessori hoped to remake pedagogy; but her idea of pedagogy is much narrower than is Professor Dewey's idea of education. . . .

NOTE

The original source for this chapter is as follows: Kilpatrick, William H. *The Montessori Method Examined*. Boston: Houghton Mifflin Co., 1914, pp. 4–5, 8–11, 20, 27, 28–29, 40–41, 51–52, 63–64.

Appendix

Anne E. George, an elementary teacher at the Chicago Latin School, visited the Casa dei Bambini in San Lorenzo in 1909 and had an interview with Maria Montessori. At the time, George did not know Italian and conversed with Montessori in French. When she returned to the United States, George brought with her a copy of Montessori's *Il Metodo della Pedagogica Scientifica applicato all'educazione infantile nelle Case dei Bambine* and some of Montessori's didactic materials. Committed to researching Montessori's method, George learned Italian so that she could read Montessori's book. She decided to go back to Rome and was the first American to enroll and complete the eight months' training course that Montessori directed.

After completing the training course, George returned to the United States and established the first American Montessori school at Tarrytown, New York, in 1911. Leaving her assistant in charge of the Tarrytown school, George next established a Montessori school in Washington, D.C., in 1912 with the support of Alexander Graham Bell. Montessori held George in high esteem and regarded her as the only person qualified to implement her method in the United States. George was asked to translate Montessori's *Il Methodo* into an English version that was published by Frederick A. Stokes as The Montessori Method.[1] The book quickly became a best-selling nonfiction work.

George became a member of the Montessori American Committee in 1912 that grew into the Montessori Educational Association. George, along with McClure, accompanied Montessori on her American speaking tour that the Association sponsored in 1913. George was acted as Montessori's translator

---

[1]Rita Kramer, *Maria Montessori: A Biography* (Reading, Mass.: Perseus Books, 1988), pp. 162–67.

for the lectures and press conferences that took place during the tour. George's translation of the lectures emphasized the following Montessori themes: (1) The liberty of children to develop, without unnecessary adult interference, through self-active learning activities in a structured environment; (2) the use of didactic apparatus and materials in children's auto-education; (3) examples of children's interactions and discoveries in the prepared environment; (4) the difference between the Montessori directress and traditional teacher.

William Heard Kilpatrick (1871–1965) was a leading Pragmatist and Progressive educator. As a public school teacher in Georgia, he developed a highly child-centered and activity method of instruction. Rejecting competition and grades, he emphasized children's whole cooperation in learning through group activities.

In 1912, Kilpatrick became a professor of education at Columbia University's Teachers College; he became a proponent of John Dewey's Instrumentalist or Experimentalist Pragmatism. He identified with and was regarded as the leader of the progressive education wing of the Teachers College Faculty and associated with George S. Counts, John Childs, and Harold Rugg. Seeking to implement Dewey's learning by the "Complete Act of Thought" into methods of instruction, Kilpatrick developed the project method, an activity-based approach in which pupils worked in groups to solve problems or pursue projects. Kilpatrick asserted that group-based education not only provided children with experience in implementing the scientific method but that it had concomitant learning consequences such as learning to share, to listen to others, and to practice democratic procedures. Kilpatrick, a popular and influential professor at Teachers College, was highly successful in promoting his Project Method. Project-based learning was a highly popular teaching method in the United States in the 1920s and 1930s.

Early in his professional career, Kilpatrick wrote two books in which he analyzed and criticized the educational ideas and methods of leading figures; *The Montessori System Examined* (1914) and *Froebel's Kindergarten Principles Critically Examined* (1916). His critique of Montessori was based on an interview with her, visits to Montessori schools in Italy, and a detailed analysis of *The Montessori Method*, which had been published in English in 1912. The timing of Kilpatrick's critique came at a key period for the first introduction of Montessori to the United States. Montessori's philosophy and method of education had attracted an enthusiastic following in the United States. Her lecture tour in 1913 had generated a favorable and well-publicized response from American audiences and journalists. Kilpatrick's book had the effect of blunting the enthusiasm for Montessori, especially among professional educators, and of seriously weakening the Montessori movement.

In the excerpts from *The Montessori System Examined*, Kilpatrick claims that Montessori's educational generalizations are unscientific and her knowledge of education limited. He criticizes her concept of development, lack of group work, overreliance on mechanical didactic apparatus, and use of formal mental discipline in transfer of training. He finds Montessori's claims about children's success in mastering practical life activities to be exaggerated. Kilpatrick concluded that Montessori's educational theory was a mid-nineteenth-century piece that was fifty years behind the times and much inferior to John Dewey's philosophy of education.

Bibliography

Montessori, Maria. *The Absorbent Mind*. New York: Henry Holt, 1995.

Montessori, Maria. *The Advanced Montessori Method; Scientific Pedagogy as Applied to the Education of Children from Seven to Eleven Years, Volume I, Spontaneous Activity in Education*. Oxford: Clio Press, 1991.

Montessori, Maria. *The Advanced Montessori Method; Volume 2, Materials for Educating Elementary School Children*. New York: Schocken Books, 1973.

Montessori, Maria, Paul Oswald, and Gunter Schulz-Benesch. *Basic Ideas of Montessori's Educational Theory: Extracts from Maria Montessori's Writings and Teachings*. Oxford: Clio Press, 1997.

Montessori, Maria, and Robert G. Buckenmeyer. *The California Lectures of Maria Montessori: Collected Speeches and Writings*. Oxford: Clio Press, 1997.

Montessori, Maria. *The Child*. Adyar, India: Theosophical Publish House, 1965.

Montessori, Maria, and E. M. Standing. *The Child in the Church*. St. Paul, Catechetical Guild, 1965.

Montessori, Maria. *The Child in the Family*. Oxford: Clio Press, 1989.

Montessori, Maria. *The Child, Society and the World*. Oxford: Clio Press, 1989.

Montessori, Maria. *Child Training: Twelve Talks Broadcast from the Madras Station of All India Radio, June 1–12, 1948*. Delphi: Publications Division, Ministry of Information and Broadcasting, 1948.

Montessori, Maria. *Disciplining Children*. Philadelphia: American Institute of Child Life, 1913.

Montessori, Maria. *The Discovery of the Child*. Oxford: Clio Press, 1988.

Montessori, Maria. *Dr. Montessori's Own Handbook*. New York: Schocken Books, 1965.

Montessori, Maria. *Education and Peace*. Oxford: Clio Press, 1992.

Montessori, Maria. *Education for a Better World*. U.S. American Institute for Psychological Research, 1990.

Montessori, Maria. *Education for a New World*. Oxford: Clio Press, 1989.

Montessori, Maria. *Education in Relation to the Imagination of the Little Child.* New York: The House of Childhood, Inc., 1915.

Montessori, Maria. *The Formation of Man.* Oxford: Clio Press, 1989.

Montessori, Maria. *From Childhood to Adolescence: Including Erdkinder and the Function of the University.* Oxford: Clio Press, 1994.

Montessori, Maria, and Aline D. Wolf. *Look at the Child: An Expression of Maria Montessori's Insights.* Altoona, Pa.: Montessori Learning Center, 1978.

Montessori, Maria, and A. M. Joosten. *Maria Montessori's Contribution to Educational Thought and Practice: Souvenir in Honour of Dr. Maria Montessori's Birth Centenary, 31 August, 1970.* New Delhi: Association of Delhi Montessorians, 1971.

Montessori, Maria, and Ellamay Horan. *The Mass Explained to Boys and Girls.* London, New York, Chicago: Sheed and Ward; W. H. Sadlier, 1934.

Montessori, Maria. *The Montessori Elementary Material.* Cambridge, Mass: R. Bentley, 1971.

Montessori, Maria, Anne Everett George, and Henry Wyman Holmes. *The Montessori Method; Scientific Pedagogy as Applied to Child Education in "The Children's Houses" with Additions and Revisions by the Author.* New York: Frederick A. Stokes Company, 1912.

Montessori, Maria. *The Mother and the Child.* New York: The National Montessori Promotion Fund, 1915.

Montessori, Maria. *My System of Education.* New York: The House of Childhood, Inc., 1915.

Montessori, Maria. *On Discipline.* Washington, D.C.: H. Fagan Print Co., 1966.

Montessori, Maria. *The Organization of Intellectual Work in School.* New York: The House of Childhood, Inc., 1915.

Montessori, Maria. *Peace and Education.* Adyar, Madras, India: Theosophical Publishing House, 1962.

Montessori, Maria, and Aline D. Wolf. *Peaceful Children, Peaceful World: the Challenge of Maria Montessori.* Altoona, Pa.: Parent Child Press, 1989.

Montessori, Maria. *Pedagogical Anthropology.* New York: Stokes, 1913.

Montessori, Maria. *Reconstruction in Education.* Adyar, Madras, Wheaton, Ill., London: Theosophical Pub. House, 1968.

Montessori, Maria. *The Secret of Childhood.* New York: Ballatine Books, 1981.

Montessori, Maria. *Spontaneous Activity in Education.* New York: Schocken Books, 1974.

Montessori, Maria. *To Educate the Human Potential.* Oxford: Clio Press, 1989.

Montessori, Maria. *The Unconscious in History.* Adyar, Madras, India: Theosophical Pub. House, 1949.

Montessori, Maria. *The Voice of Dr. Maria Montessori: Lectures, Madras, India, 1941–1942.* Silver Spring, Md.: International Montessori Society, 1990.

Montessori, Maria, and A. Gnana Prakasam. *What You Should Know About Your Child: Based on Lectures Delivered.* Adyar, Madras, India: Kalakshetra Publications, 1961.

Index

absorbent mind stage of development: characteristics of, 49–51; curriculum for, 52–54
active discipline, 113
Addams, Jane, 14, 15, 26, 38, 42
addition, 238–40
The Advanced Montessori Method (Montessori), 21
aesthetic sense, 179
age-appropriate activities, Itard's theory of, 7
alphabet, 19, 198, 202–3, 206–8, 211, 216, 246
American Montessori Association, 26
American Montessori Society, 40
AMI. *See* Association Montessori Internationale
animal care, 139, 145–46
anthropology, 13, 43–44, 69–71
anthropometry, 13, 43–44, 70, 71, 73, 80n4, 108, 187
L'Antropologia Pedagogica (Montessori), 13, 71
arithmetic: achievement levels in, 247; didactic materials for, 166, 238–41; and discipline, 256–57; instruction in, 238–41; readiness for, 19
articulate language, 227–31

Association for Good Building. *See* Istituto Romano di Beni Stabili (Good Building Association)
Association Montessori Internationale (AMI), 10, 35, 37, 39, 40
auto-education: didactic materials and, 154–55, 157; differential perception through, 159; Fascism and, 36; freedom in classroom and, 20; language readiness and, 19; through plant/animal care, 145; through sensory training, 184
Avanguardisti, 37

Baccelli, Guido, 83, 91n2
Bagnell, Miss (Montessori educator), 24
Baldwin, J. M., 107, 111n1
Balilla, 37
banking analogy in education, 3
baric sense, 162, 185
beauty, 179, 190, 217–18
Bell, Mrs. Alexander Graham, 23, 34
bells, instruction with, 172–73
blindfolds, sensory training using, 159–60, 162–64, 185
books, reading of, 221–22
Briesen and Knauth (law firm), 27

About the Editor

Gerald Lee Gutek is professor emeritus at Loyola University. In 1989, he was the Loyola University of Chicago Outstanding Faculty Member. Among his books are *A History of the Western Educational Experience* (1995), *Philosophical and Ideological Perspectives in Education* (1997), *American Education 1945–2000: A History and Commentary* (2000), and *Historical and Philosophical Foundations of Education: A Biographical Introduction* (2000).